ARTHURIAN STUDIES XXIX

THE LIFE AND TIMES OF SIR THOMAS MALORY

Malory's stories of King Arthur and the Round Table have been widely read for centuries, but their author's own life has been as variously reported as that of any Arthurian knight. The first serious attempts to identify him were made in the 1890s, but the man who then seemed most likely to have written the book was later found to have been accused of attempted murder, rape, extortion, and sacrilegious robbery, and, although he seems never to have been brought to trial, to have spent ten years or more in prison. Some found this difficult to reconcile with authorship of the most famous chivalric romance in English, and a number of other candidates for authorship were proposed.

This book gives the most comprehensive consideration of the competing arguments yet undertaken, followed by a full account of the life of the man identified, which sets him in his historical context. Close consideration of individual documents, many of which were entirely unknown in 1966, when the last book on Malory's life appeared, makes possible a fuller and more convincing story than has been possible before.

P.J.C. FIELD is Reader in the Department of English at the University of Wales, Bangor, where he has taught since 1964.

ARTHURIAN STUDIES

ISSN 0261–9814

Previously published volumes in the series
are listed at the back of this book

THE LIFE AND TIMES OF
SIR THOMAS MALORY

P. J. C. Field

D. S. BREWER

First published 1993 by D. S. Brewer, Cambridge

D. S. Brewer is an imprint of Boydell & Brewer Ltd
PO Box 9, Woodbridge, Suffolk IP12 3DF, UK
and of Boydell & Brewer Inc.
PO Box 41026, Rochester, NY 14604, USA

ISBN 0 85991 385 6

British Library Cataloguing-in-Publication Data
Field, P. J. C.
   Life and Times of Sir Thomas Malory. –
(Arthurian Studies Series, ISSN 0261–9814;
Vol. 29)
I. Title II. Series
823.2
ISBN 0–85991–385–6

   Library of Congress Cataloging-in-Publication Data
Field, P. J. C.
   The life and times of Sir Thomas Malory / P.J.C. Field.
       p.   cm. – (Arthurian studies, ISSN 0261–9814 ; 29)
   Includes bibliographical references (p.) and index.
   ISBN 0–85991–385–6 (alk. paper)
   1. Malory, Thomas, Sir, 15th cent. – Biography. 2. Great Britain –
History – Lancaster and York, 1399–1485 – Biography. 3. Malory,
Thomas, Sir, 15th cent. – Contemporary England. 4. Authors,
English – Middle English, 1100–1500 – Biography. 5. Knights and
knighthood – England – Biography. 6. Arthurian romances –
Authorship. I. Title. II. Series.
PR2045.F54   1993
823'.2–dc20
[B]   93–20187

The paper used in this publication meets the minimum requirements
of American National Standard for Information Sciences –
Permanence of Paper for Printed Library Materials, ANSI Z39.48–1984

Printed in Great Britain by
St Edmundsbury Press Ltd, Bury St Edmunds, Suffolk

Contents

To Vanessa

Preface

In this attempt at as full a description of Sir Thomas Malory's life as present knowledge allows, I have accumulated a debt of gratitude to many archivists and librarians who care for the documentary evidence on which such an attempt must be based, in county record offices from Exeter to Lincoln and from Chelmsford to Shrewsbury, and other institutions from the Borthwick Institute in York to the Public Record Office in London.

First versions of Chapters I and II appeared in *Medium Aevum*, of Chapter IV in *Midland History*, of Chapter V in *The Journal of Ecclesiastical History*, of Chapters VI and VII in *The Bulletin of the Institute of Historical Research*, and of Chapter VIII in the *The Bulletin of the John Rylands Library*. I am obliged to the editors of those journals for the permission to reproduce whatever first appeared in their pages. I am also grateful to the University of Wales at Bangor for two terms of study leave, and to Commander C.G. Vyner for permission to use the Vyner family papers, once at Studley Royal and now in the Leeds City Archives Department.

I have also benefited from the advice and assistance of many individuals. Some particular obligations are acknowledged in my notes, but I must name here Dr Rowena Archer, Dr Richard Barber, Mr Robert Bearman, Dr Lionel Butler, Mr J.M. Collinson, Professor W.H. Dunham, Mrs Eileen Gooder, Professor Richard R. Griffith, Dr M.A. Hicks, Mr A. Giles Jones, Miss M.A.L. Locherbie-Cameron, Dr Caterina Maddalena, Miss Helen Miller, Rev. Fr. Joseph Mizzi, Dr Carole Rawcliffe, Mr Tomos Roberts, Mrs Janette Shepherd, Mr G.A. Usher, Dr Roger Virgoe, and Miss Pamela Willis. All other debts, however, are dwarfed by those to my wife Vanessa, without whose encouragement, forbearance, and help this book would never have been completed.

P.J.C. Field
Bangor, North Wales
November 1992

Abbreviations

A.J.	*Antiquaries Journal.*
Ancient Deeds	*A Descriptive Calendar of Ancient Deeds.* 6 vols. London 1890–1915.
Baker, *Northants.*	George Baker. *The History and Antiquities of the County of Northampton.* 2 vols. London 1822–41.
Baugh	A.C. Baugh. 'Documenting Sir Thomas Malory'. *Speculum* 8 (1933) 3–29.
B.I.H.R.	*Bulletin of the Institute of Historical Research.*
B.J.R.L.	*Bulletin of the John Rylands University Library of Manchester.*
B.L.	London, British Library.
Bodl.	Oxford, Bodleian Library.
Bridges and Whalley	J. Bridges and P. Whalley. *The History of Northamptonshire.* 2 vols. Oxford 1791.
'Brief Notes'	'Brief Notes of Occurrences under Henry VI and Edward IV, from MS. Lambreth 448', in *Three Fifteenth-Century Chronicles*, ed. J. Gairdner. Camden Soc., n.s. 28 (1880) pp. 148–63.
Cal. Ch. Rolls	*Calendar of Charter Rolls.* 6 vols. London 1903–27.
Cal. Inq. Misc.	*Calendar of Inquisitions Miscellaneous (Chancery).* 7 vols. London 1916–68.
Cal. I.P.M.	*Calendar of Inquisitions Post Mortem* [Henry III – Richard II]. In progress. London 1904– .
Cal. I.P.M., Hen. VII	*Calendar of Inquisitions Post Mortem, Henry VII.* 3 vols. London 1898–1955.
Cal. Lib. Rolls	*Calendar of Liberate Rolls.* In progress. London 1916– .
Cal. Pap. Reg.	*Calendar of Entries in the Papal Registers relating to Great Britain and Ireland.* In progress. London 1893– .
Carpenter, 'Warwickshire'	Mary Christine Carpenter. 'Political Society in Warwickshire, c.1401–72'. Ph.D. thesis. Cambridge 1976.
Carpenter, *Locality*	[Mary] Christine Carpenter. *Locality and Polity: a Study of Warwickshire Landed Society 1401–99.* Cambridge 1992.
Catalogue des rolles gascons	*Catalogue des rolles gascons, normands, et françois*, ed. T. Carte. 2 vols. London 1743.
C.C.R.	*Calendar of Close Rolls* [Henry III – Henry VII]. 59 vols. London 1902–63.

C.D.I.	*Calendar of Documents relating to Ireland.* 5 vols. London 1875–86.
C.F.R.	*Calendar of Fine Rolls* [Edward I – Henry VII]. 22 vols. London 1911–62.
C.I.P.M.	*Calendarium Inquisitionum Post Mortem.* London 1806–38.
C.P.R.	*Calendar of Patent Rolls* [Henry III – Henry VII]. 54 vols. London 1901–16.
Complete Peerage	*The Complete Peerage,* ed. G.E. C[ockayne]. 14 vols. London 1910–40.
C.R.O.	County Record Office.
C.S.P.	*Calendar of State Papers.*
D.N.B.	*The Dictionary of National Biography.* 71 vols. London 1885–1903.
Dugdale, *Warwickshire*	Sir William Dugdale. *The History and Antiquities of Warwickshire.* 2 vols. London 1730.
E.E.T.S.	Early English Text Society.
E.L.N.	*English Language Notes.*
E.H.R.	*English Historical Review.*
Farnham, *Notes*	George Farnham. *Leicestershire Medieval Village Notes.* 6 vols. Leicester 1929–33.
Feudal Aids	*Inquisitions and Assessments relating to Feudal Aids.* 6 vols. London 1899–1920.
H.M.C.	Historical Manuscripts Commission.
J.E.G.P.	*Journal of English and Germanic Philology.*
J.L.	*Journal of Librarianship.*
J.S.A.	*Journal of the Society of Archivists.*
Martin	A.T. Martin, 'The Identity of the Author of the "Morte d'Arthur", with Notes on the Will of Thomas Malory and the Genealogy of the Malory Family'. *Archaeologia* 56 (1898) 165–82.
Matthews	William Matthews. *The Ill-Framed Knight.* Berkeley, Calif., 1966.
M.H.	*Midland History.*
M.S.	*Medieval Studies.*
Nichols, *Leicestershire*	John Nichols, *The History and Antiquities of the County of Leicester.* 4 vols. London 1795–1807.
N.M.	*Neuphilologische Mitteilungen.*
P.B.A.	*Proceedings of the British Academy.*
P.C.C. Wills	*Index to Wills proved in the Prerogative Court of Canterbury 1383–1558,* ed. J.C.C. Smith. Index Library. London 1893.
P.Q.	*Philological Quarterly.*
P.R.O.	London, The Public Record Office.
Proc. & Ord. P.C.	*Proceeding and Ordinances of the Privy Council of England,* ed. Sir [Nicholas] Harris Nicolas. 7 vols. 1834–37.

R.E.S.	*Review of English Studies.*
Return of Members	*Return of the Name of Every Member of the Lower House of Parliament of England, Scotland, and Ireland [1213–1874],* House of Commons Parliamentary Papers for 1878, vol 72. London 1878–9.
Rot. Parl.	*Rotuli Parliamentorum.* 7 vols. London 1832.
R.S.	Rolls Series.
Scofield	Cora L. Scofield. *The Life and Reign of Edward IV.* 2 vols. London 1923.
S.Litt.I.	*Studies in the Literary Imagination.*
s.p.	*sine prole,* 'without (surviving) children'.
S.R.	*Statutes of the Realm.* 12 vols. London 1810–28.
Treaty Rolls	*Treaty Rolls preserved in the Public Record Office.* In progress. London 1955– .
v.m.	*vite matris,* 'in the lifetime of his/her mother'.
U.T.L.J.	*University of Toronto Law Journal.*
v.p.	*vite patris,* 'in the lifetime of his/her father'.
Wedgwood, Biographies	Josiah Wedgwood and Anne Holt, *History of Parliament: Biographies of Members of the Commons House 1439–1509.* London 1936.
Works	Sir Thomas Malory. *The Works,* ed. Eugène Vinaver, revised P.J.C. Field. 3 vols. Oxford 1990.
V.C.H.	The Victoria History of the Counties of England.
Y.A.T.A.R.S.	Yorkshire Archaeological and Topographical Association, Record Series.
Y.A.T.J.	*Yorkshire Archaeological and Topographical Journal.*
Y.E.S.	*Yearbook of English Studies.*

References are by page number unless otherwise indicated. Dates in the form 1460/71 mean 'at some time in the period 1460 to 1471 inclusive'.

I

Alternatives

Writing the life of a mediaeval Englishman is notoriously like making bricks without straw, especially if the subject is neither a peer nor a cleric. In literature, the available evidence is not uncommonly so limited as to prevent us even naming authors of major works.[1] In the case of *Le Morte Darthur*, however, those who do not mind living dangerously can hope for more than that: an identification, some kind of outline of a life, perhaps an insight or two into personality. The importance of the book has encouraged scholars to do what can be done, and so has generated two books and a good many shorter essays about the author.[2]

All that is known for certain about him comes from his book. Its closing words say its author was called Thomas Malory, that he was a knight and a prisoner, that he wanted his readers to pray for him, and that he finished his book between 3 March 1469 and 4 March 1470. He calls himself a knight-prisoner earlier in the book as well.[3] The book cannot have taken much less than two years to write, but neither the writing nor the author's imprisonment need have been continuous.[4] The story is taken mainly from the best-known French Arthurian romances, but also draws on a number of English ones, some of them probably even then difficult to find. It shows

---

1 On the identity, for example, of the author of *Sir Gawain and the Green Knight* see Edward Wilson, '*Sir Gawain and the Green Knight* and the Stanley Family of Stanley', *R.E.S* 30 (1979) 308–16, and Erik Kooper, 'The Case of the Encoded Author', *N.M.* 83 (1982) 158–68.

2 Edward Hicks, *Sir Thomas Malory: His Turbulent Career* (Cambridge, Mass., 1928); William Matthews, *The Ill-Framed Knight* (Berkeley, Calif., 1966); and for other items to 1976 see Page West Life, *Sir Thomas Malory and the Morte Darthur: A Survey of Scholarship and Annotated Bibliography* (Charlottesville, Va., 1980). Since that time see particularly [Mary] Christine Carpenter, 'Sir Thomas Malory and Fifteenth-Century Local Politics', *B.I.H.R.* 53 (1980) 31–43, and R.R. Griffith, 'The Authorship Question Reconsidered: A Case for Thomas Malory of Papworth St Agnes, Cambridgeshire' in *Aspects of Malory*, ed. T. Takamiya and D. Brewer (Cambridge 1981) pp. 159–77.

3 Sir Thomas Malory, *The Works*, ed. Eugène Vinaver, revised P.J.C. Field (Oxford 1990) p. 180.22, and cf. pp. 363.19, 845.29, 1037.12, and 1154.19.

4 *Works*, p. 180.18 ff. may imply that Malory expected to write no more.

very few traces of non-Arthurian reading.[5] It also shows that its author had the use of some very expensive manuscripts, knew French and was proud of it,[6] and loved hunting, tournaments, and chivalry. One passage has been taken to reflect an illness while in prison.[7] Others may reflect historical events of his time, of which some have thought to reflect a Lancastrian view of politics. One passage, for instance, which is near the end of the book and so must have been written under the Yorkist king Edward IV, reproaches the English for ingratitude to good kings; in another, one of Malory's favourite knights is attacked by a 'traytoure' from a castle that belonged to a Yorkist peer; and in a third, the traitor Mordred raises troops in what some have identified as Yorkist counties.[8] Not all readers, however, have been persuaded by this. Some have even argued that Malory was a Yorkist partisan, but the most plausible reading of the text may be that he felt a sympathy for chivalrous actions by individuals on both sides in the civil war, and the war in France too.[9]

Malory may well have written a second book, an Arthurian poem some 850 lines long called *The Wedding of Sir Gawain and Dame Ragnell*, which has some surprising resemblances to the *Morte Darthur*, including an ending in which the author says that he is in prison and asks God's help in gaining his freedom.[10] Since *The Wedding* is less well written than the *Morte*, it is natural to assume that if Malory wrote it, it came first and the *Morte* second. However, even if both authorship and order of composition could be proved, *The Wedding* would tell us little or nothing about Malory that is not already evident from the *Morte Darthur*.

The *Morte Darthur* might give a clue to its author's identity through its language. In the fifteenth century, the English language was not uniform across England, and a third of a million words might be expected to reveal the geographical origins of the man who wrote them. Unfortunately, however, we do not have those words as Malory wrote them: we have only the Winchester manuscript and the edition William Caxton printed in 1485. Both are several stages removed from Malory's original manuscript, and Caxton's edition indeed appears to have been 'translated' into Caxton's

---

5 On sources, see particularly *Works*, pp. 1263–1663, and P.J.C. Field, 'Malory and Chrétien de Troyes', *Reading Medieval Studies* 17 (1991) 19–30, and references given there.

6 P.J.C. Field and M.A. Muir, 'French Words and Phrases in Sir Thomas Malory's *Le Morte Darthur*', *N.M.* 72 (1971) 483–500.

7 *Works*, p. 540.28.

8 *Works*, pp. 1229.6, 677.20 (cf. 635.24), 1233.6–7.

9 Cf. Matthews, p. 130; R.R. Griffith, 'The Political Bias of Malory's *Morte Darthur*', *Viator* 5 (1974) 365–86; and P.J.C. Field, 'Fifteenth-Century History in Malory's "Morte Darthur" ' in *Cultural Intermediaries in Medieval Britain*, ed. Françoise Le Saux (forthcoming).

10 See P.J.C. Field, 'Malory and *The Wedding of Sir Gawain and Dame Ragnell*', *Archiv für das Studium der neueren Sprachen* 219 (1982) 374–381.

own Kentish dialect.[11] The same could have happened to the surviving manuscript: both its scribes seem to have come from west Northamptonshire, but that does not mean that Malory did too.

Unless a scribe who translates his copy into his own dialect is exceptionally careful, traces of the author's dialect will probably survive into the new copy. Professor Angus McIntosh, the leading authority on Middle English dialectology, thought that the archetype of the two extant texts contained some forms too northerly for west Northamptonshire, forms that would normally suggest an origin in Lincolnshire.[12] He himself, however, thought that those forms did not represent the author's native dialect, but were more likely to be elements of the language of Malory's English sources that he had adopted because he felt them appropriate to a composition in the same mode. One could base a further argument on that: if the northerly forms are a dialectically alien element supplied by the author for a special literary purpose and the scribes of the manuscript did not normalise them, then it is unlikely that they normalised any other dialectically alien elements either. If so, we can assume that the author's dialect must have been similar to theirs. However, even if the logic of this is impeccable, it will be difficult to assert the conclusion confidently on the strength of a short review, however authoritative. The dialect of the *Morte Darthur* needs a competent and complete examination from both texts, with published results.

The fact that both scribes of the surviving manuscript came from west Northamptonshire might itself be evidence of the author's origins if only it could be established that he commissioned the manuscript, whether for himself or for someone else. Unfortunately, it cannot. As it stands, the manuscript has characteristics that suggest a presentation copy.[13] The scribes were not as careful with the wording as they should have been, but they produced handsome professional-looking pages in harmonious scripts, on which the limited amount of conventional decoration is compensated for by copying the proper names in red – an attractive feature, but one that would have taken longer and presumably cost more than writing uniformly in black ink. However, if the manuscript was a presentation copy, we have no way of knowing who presented it to whom: the first and last gatherings, which might have contained a dedication or other solid evidence, are lost.

---

[11] Jeremy J. Smith, 'Some Spellings in Caxton's Malory', *Poetica* 24 (1986) 58–63; and cf. idem, 'Studies in the Language of Some Manuscripts of Gower's "Confessio Amantis" ', Ph.D. diss. (Glasgow 1985), and Tom Shippey, review of the *Linguistic Atlas of Late Medieval English* in *T.L.S.* 30 Oct. 1987, p. 1200.

[12] Angus McIntosh, review of William Matthews, *The Ill-Framed Knight* (Berkeley, Calif., 1966) in *Medium Aevum* 37 (1968) 346–8.

[13] See *The Winchester Malory: A Facsimile*, ed. N.R. Ker, E.E.T.S. s.s. 4 (1976).

One theory, however, is worth keeping in mind. The surviving Malory manuscript, although it was not the one Caxton used to print from, was apparently in Caxton's printing shop in 1482/83, 1489, and 1498 (presumably continuously), but by the second quarter of the sixteenth century seems to have been in Northamptonshire,[14] where one Richard Folwell wrote his name in it several times. Partly for this reason, it has been suggested that the manuscript was commissioned by Anthony Wydeville, Earl Rivers, who was Caxton's most important patron and had strong Northamptonshire connections. The theory suggests that Rivers lent the manuscript to Caxton as the basis for an edition, and that it found its way back from Caxton's establishment to Northamptonshire, to the Folwells, and so to a neighbouring family that early in the next century had several sons educated at Winchester College, where it was rediscovered in 1934. The manuscript could have come back to Northamptonshire to people its author knew rather than to Rivers's family because the latter had died out in the direct line in 1491, when the manuscript was still probably in Caxton's printing house. It is, however, a complicated theory, and the most that can be claimed for it is that it is the most economical explanation yet offered of the facts known at present.

There were several men called Thomas Malory alive in 1469/70, and no direct evidence has yet been put forward to link any of them with the *Morte Darthur*. The first question that arises therefore is whether any of them can be identified as the author. However, even if matching the internal evidence provided by the book against the evidence of their lives eliminated all but one of them, it would still be possible that the book was written by a Sir Thomas Malory so far unknown. The Fair Unknown has been a recurrent theme in Arthurian literature, and there would be a kind of poetic justice in the reappearance of that theme in the biography of an Arthurian author. The would-be biographer might have to console himself with the

---

14 For Caxton's use of a different MS., see *Works*, pp. c–cvi; and for the Caxton connection to 1489, Lotte Hellinga, 'The Malory Manuscript and Caxton' in *Aspects of Malory*, ed. Takamiya and Brewer, pp. 127–41. By 1498 Wynkyn de Worde had taken over Caxton's printing house, and Tsuyoshi Mukai has reported a significant agreement between de Worde's 1498 edition and the MS. against the Caxton edition: review of *Caxton's Malory*, ed. J.W. Spisak (Berkeley, Calif., 1983) in *Studies in English Literature* (Japan), English Number for 1986, pp. 88–9. This agreement is most easily explained if the MS. remained in Caxton's printing house until 1498. For the rest of this sentence and the next, see Hilton Kelliher, 'The Early History of the Malory Manuscript' in *Aspects of Malory*, pp. 143–58. For a different theory, see R.R. Griffith, 'Caxton's Copy-Text for *Le Morte Darthur*: Tracing the Provenance' in *Traditions and Innovations: Essays on British Literature of the Middle Ages and Renaissance*, ed. David G. Allen and Robert A. White (Newark, N.J., 1990) pp. 75–87.

reflection that such an event was highly improbable: the internal evidence at least shows that the *Morte Darthur* was written by a member of the best-recorded class of fifteenth-century English secular society.

At first sight, these preliminaries seem largely formal. For identification purposes, the most important part of the evidence that the *Morte* provides is that of its closing words, whose patent sincerity, confirmed by their request for prayers, makes it unthinkable that the man who wrote them should not be what he there said he was, and of nine men who bore the right name and were or might have been alive at the right time, only Sir Thomas Malory of Newbold Revel in Warwickshire is known to have fulfilled either of the other two criteria the closing words supply, of being a knight or a prisoner. His name was first mentioned as author in 1890, and for most of the time since then he has seemed so much the strongest candidate as to be unchallenged.[15] As it happens, he held the manor of Winwick in west Northamptonshire, which had been his family's home before they acquired Newbold Revel, and both he and his father may at times have lived there. It is true that his recorded imprisonments ended in 1460, but there are grounds, as we shall see, for supposing that the authorities would have wanted him in prison at the end of the 1460s as well. The accepted picture of his life suggested he was rather old to have written a substantial book in 1469–70, but, as we shall also see, that picture puts his date of birth much too early. However, he also stands accused of rape, church-robbery, extortion, and attempted murder – activities surprising in the author of the most famous chivalric romance in English. Some have tried to explain the discrepancy, others have relaxed and relished it, and others again have proposed different Thomas Malorys – men unknown or almost unknown and so possibly fairer – as author. Any satisfactory account of the author's life must also give some account of all possible competitors, because the very existence of namesakes makes it possible that the book may not be the only thing to have been attributed to the wrong man.

The Fair Unknown aside, Sir Thomas of Newbold Revel has eight competitors for the authorship of the *Morte Darthur*. Those competitors fall into three groups. In the first come a trio who can be shown to have had no independent existence: Sir Thomas Malory of Fenny Newbold in

---

[15] His name was first put forward when Oskar Sommer reported from Burton's *Description of Leicester Shire* the existence of a Sir Thomas Malory who lived at the right time to have been the author: *Le Morte Darthur*, ed. H.O. Sommer, 3 vols (London 1889–91) ii 1. Four years later, George Lyman Kittredge, in a remarkably thorough survey of the record evidence, showed that the Newbold Revel knight was the only man of the right name and rank known to have been alive between 1469 and 1470: Johnson's *Universal Cyclopedia* v (1894) 498, revised as *Who Was Sir Thomas Malory?* (Boston, Mass., 1897).

Warwickshire, Thomas Malory M.P. for Bedwin and Wareham, and Sir Thomas Malory of Maelor in Flintshire (now part of the county of Clwyd).

The first of them is certainly Sir Thomas of Newbold Revel under a different appellation. Dr Gweneth Whitteridge noticed that the mid-fifteenth-century records that specified a domicile for a Warwickshire Sir Thomas fell into two groups: the criminal charges spoke of Sir Thomas Malory of Fenny Newbold and the others of Sir Thomas Malory of Newbold Revel. She therefore suggested that the criminal and the author were different men, disposing at a stroke of the incompatibility between the numerous and well-attested criminal charges on the one hand, and a number of more respectable documents and the *Morte Darthur* itself on the other.[16] However, Fenny Newbold and Newbold Revel are simply different names for the same place, and the former, derived from geography, was during the fifteenth century being displaced by the latter, derived from the name of a family that had held the manor in the previous century.[17] When Elizabeth Lady Malory died in possession of the manor in 1479, her *inquisitio post mortem* described it as 'Newbold Fenne alias Newbold Ryvell', and when her great-granddaughters, to whom her estates had descended, took legal action over it in 1516 and 1527, it was in each case called 'Newbold Revel alias Fenny Newbold'.[18] It is unlikely that two men would have been called by different names for the same place when there must have been many less confusing ways of distinguishing them. It seems more probable that whoever made out the first set of charges was old-fashioned in his choice of place-name, and that later scribes just followed him, as scribes do. That is the more likely in that the charges against Sir Thomas of Fenny Newbold also describe all the other men from the estate who were accused with him as being 'of Fenny Newbold': Newbold Revel is never mentioned. Moreover, in October 1452, during a decade in which Sir Thomas of Fenny Newbold was being shuttled from one London prison to another, we find a Sir Thomas Malory explicitly 'of Newbold Revel' on the threshold of a London prison as well. He entered into a bond with the Keeper of the Fleet Prison guaranteeing the Keeper against the consequences of various kinds of misbehaviour by himself and his servants, a bond that was part of the process whereby prisoners could get themselves confined to the relatively mild regime of the Fleet instead of viler durance elsewhere.[19] Finally, although Sir Thomas of Fenny Newbold would

---

16 Gweneth Whitteridge, 'The Identity of Sir Thomas Malory, Knight-prisoner', *R.E.S.* n.s. 24 (1973) 257–65.

17 *The Place-Names of Warwickshire*, ed. J.E.B. Gover et al., English Place-Name Soc. 13 (Cambridge 1936) 120.

18 P.R.O. C140/75/46, translated in Hicks, p. 109. For the great-granddaughters, see Dugdale's transcript, Bodl. MS. Dugdale 2, pp. 424, 429.

19 C.C.R. (1447–54) p. 396; cf. Margery Bassett, 'The Fleet Prison in the Middle Ages', *U.T.L.J.* 5 (1943–44) 383–402.

presumably have been a close kinsman of his namesake of Newbold Revel, none of the surviving genealogies of the family gives two Sir Thomases in the right generation.[20] That two Sir Thomases should have alternated in Warwickshire and then in London, and one of them have been utterly forgotten by his descendants is not impossible – few things in history are – but believing it seems too high a price for establishing that the author of the *Morte Darthur* did not have a criminal record.

The second man in this group is the M.P. It is universally assumed that the same man was M.P. for both Bedwin and Wareham, and that he too was a kind of *doppelgänger*. Small boroughs like Bedwin and Wareham were much given to choosing outsiders to represent them in parliament, and there is no trace of a Malory family living in the neighbourhood of either at the time of the elections or for centuries before. There is therefore no reason to suppose that the man had an independent existence. Although that is all we need establish for our present purposes, in due course we shall have to return to the question of which Thomas Malory the two boroughs chose as their representative.

The third candidate, Sir Thomas Malory of Maelor, is an exceptionally tenacious ghost created by John Bale, the sixteenth-century Protestant bishop and bibliophile, who took two unrelated observations by the antiquary John Leland to imply that the name Malory was derived from the place-name Maelor, and that Malory therefore came from that place.[21] Bale and Leland's contribution to Chaucer studies has caused them to be described as the men who defiled the well of English literary biography at its source,[22] but they achieved even more with Malory. For three hundred and fifty years, the man they accidentally invented was the only one proposed to enquirers as author, and although their error was was refuted in 1894, the ghost they conjured up is not entirely exorcised even now.[23] It need not, however, detain us here.

There remain five candidates who really existed: Thomas Malory who

[20] See Eugène Vinaver, *Malory* (Oxford 1970) pp. 116–19.

[21] Leland, *Assertio inclytissimi Arturii regis Britanniae* (London 1544), unnumbered page facing fol. 1^r; and 'Syllabus et interpretatio antiquarum dictionum' in *Genethliacon illustrissimi Eäduerdi principis Cambriae* (London 1543) fols e ii^r–g v^v; Bale, *Illustrium Maioris Britanniae scriptorum summarium* (Ipswich 1548) fols 208^v–209^r, followed by e.g. Sir Richard Baker, *A Chronicle of the Kings of England* (London 1679) 252; [W. Oldys], *Biographia Britannica* (London 1747–66) ii 1243; Robert Watt, *Bibliotheca Britannica* (Edinburgh 1824) *s.v.* Malory; Sir John Rhys, introduction to *Le Morte Darthur* (London 1893–4) vol. i, pp. xi–xii; and to *Le Morte Darthur* (London 1906) vol. i, pp. v–vi. This last edition was recently in print and copies may still be on sale.

[22] Richard D. Altick, *Lives and Letters: A History of Literary Biography in England and America* (New York 1965) pp. 4–5, and cf. P.O. Kristeller, *Medieval Aspects of Renaissance Learning* (Durham, N.C., 1974) p. 128.

[23] An alternative was first hinted at in Sommer's report in 1890 and established in Kittredge's demonstration in 1894. See note 15 supra.

became rector of Holcot in Northamptonshire at some time between 1450 and 1460,[24] Thomas Malory esquire of Papworth St Agnes in Cambridgeshire,[25] Thomas Malory of Tachbrook Mallory in Warwickshire, allegedly a labourer,[26] Thomas Malory of Long Whatton in Leicestershire,[27] and Thomas Malory of Hutton Conyers in Yorkshire.[28] The first two of these five form a group that can be discounted on grounds of rank. In the case of the rector of Holcot, it was not impossible for a knight to become a priest – Sir Thomas of Newbold Revel had a neighbour, Sir Baldwin Mountford, who did so – but it happened so rarely that it should only be postulated when there is evidence to suggest it. In fact, the evidence, although negative and indirect, all points the other way. In the valediction at the end of the Morte Darthur, for instance, the author gives himself only one social rank, that of knight: if he had had two, one would have expected that him to have given both and called himself, as Sir Baldwin Mountford does in a legal deed of comparable formality,[29] 'knight and priest'.

Thomas Malory of Papworth St Agnes is a more promising case, sufficiently so for a number of scholars to have suggested that he was the author.[30] He was the son and heir of Sir William Malory of Papworth, who died in June 1445 with estates at Papworth, Shelton in Bedfordshire, and Sudborough in Northamptonshire.[31] Earlier in his life, Sir William had held land at Shawbury in Shropshire and (until May 1443) the manor of Careby and other lands in Lincolnshire.[32] Thomas was born on 6 Dec. 1425, at Morton Corbet in Shropshire.[33] He was therefore not of age when his father died. Because Sir William held land of the king in chief, Thomas's ward-

---

24 The bishop who instituted him was elected c.February 1451, and his own successor was instituted in March 1459: Bridges and Whalley, ii 145.
25 A.T. Martin, 'The Identity of the Author of the Morte Darthur', Archaeologia 56 (1898) 165–82; J.P. Gilson, The Athenaeum 3931 (28 February 1903) 275; Matthews, pp. 5–7, 158–9; Griffith, 'The Authorship Question'.
26 Witness on 15 April 1459, paid a small rent 20 December 1465 and 10 March 1466, feoffee in Tachbrook 1467, allegedly a labourer 1467: Warwick C.R.O. MS. CR 1908/82; Ministers' Accounts of the Church of St Mary, Warwick, Dugdale Soc. 26 (1969) p. 91; P.R.O. E326/4928, which has his seal attached; Matthews, pp. 72–3 and 150, citing 'a legal roll of 1467.' Judgement must be reserved on the last item until it has been verified from a conventional reference.
27 Witness on 29 September 1463: G. Farnham, Medieval Leicestershire Village Notes (Leicester 1929–33) iv 297.
28 Matthews, passim.
29 See Dugdale, Warwickshire, ii 1011.
30 He was first proposed by Martin in 'The Identity of the Author of the Morte Darthur', and endorsed by Griffith, 'The Authorship Question' and elsewhere. Cf. also R.M. Lumiansky, 'Sir Thomas Malory's "Le Morte Darthur" 1947–1987: Author, Title, Text', Speculum 62 (1987) 878–97, esp. 883.
31 P.R.O. C139/144/41, C139/125/4, C139/117/10, E149/80/3.
32 Feudal Aids, iv 248, 252; Martin, p. 169; Lincs. C.R.O. H71/15a.
33 P.R.O. C139/144/45.

ship and marriage fell to the king, who three days after Sir William's death granted them to one Leo Louthe.[34] Thomas did not get full control of his estates until he was twenty-five.[35] Despite this initial handicap, he himself dealt in wardships,[36] held one or two minor offices in local government,[37] made connections with the mercers' company in London,[38] married,[39] and begot ten children.[40] He was also said to have achieved one or two less praiseworthy exploits. Sir William, when one of his cousins died, occupied an estate in Northamptonshire held by the widow, whose family only regained it after Sir William's death.[41] Thomas seized it again and held it until he died, after which his cousins regained it once more. On another occasion, he was accused of having armed himself with a variety of weapons, kidnapped his parish priest, and carried him round the countryside threatening his life until he agreed to resign his church to his persecutor.[42] His wife died on an unknown date very shortly before him, so that when he made his will, shortly before he died, no nurse had yet been found for their youngest child.[43] Thomas himself died in late September or early October 1469.[44]

Unlike the rector of Holcot, Thomas of Papworth plainly has things to commend him as the author of the *Morte Darthur*. Those who have made a case for him have drawn attention to his relatively clean record (at least compared with the accusations against Sir Thomas of Newbold Revel) and his connections with both Lincolnshire and Northamptonshire. Those

---

34 *C.F.R.* (1437–45) pp. 334–5.

35 *C.C.R.* (1447–54) p. 225.

36 *C.F.R.* (1445–52) pp. 101–2, 149, 197–8.

37 *C.P.R.* (1452–61) pp. 556, 612 (commissioner for fishtraps on the River Ouse); *C.F.R.* (1461–71) p. 103 (tax assessor for Huntingdonshire).

38 His will (P.R.O. Prob. 11/5, fol. 221) asks that his son William should be apprenticed *ad artem pannariorum* in London.

39 The preliminaries to the marriage are probably signalled by a bond dated 17 May 1451 by Thomas Malorye of Papworth Agnes esq. in £300 for unspecified good behaviour until Pentecost next to Elizabeth Palmer of Carleton widow Simon Kinsman and Thomas Palmer esqs: B.L. Add. Ch. 41416. Malory's will speaks of his 'brothers' (i.e. brothers-in-law) Palmer, and according to his Cambs. I.P.M. his son and heir was born 7 Oct. 1451/6 Oct. 1452. His Northants. I.P.M. tells a different story, but the Cambs. I.P.M. is compatible with the ultimate records of his heir's heirs, and the Northants. one is not. For Elizabeth widow of John Palmer of Carlton, Northants., Thomas Palmer of Holt, Leics., her late husband's brother, and Simon Kinsman, a regular associate of both, cf. *C.C.R.* (1441–47) passim.

40 Named in his will, ut supra.

41 P.R.O. C139/125/4, C140/31/16, *V.C.H., Northants.,* iii 245–7.

42 P.R.O. C1/26/619, Matthews, pp. 7, 243.

43 Her death is implied in his will by the provision for prayers for her soul as well as in the arrangement for a respectable wet nurse to be found for the baby if he lived.

44 Both his I.P.M.s say he died 1 Sept. (C140/31/16), but his will dates itself 16 Sept. and is more likely to be right. A *terminus ad quem* for his death is provided by the first writ of *diem clausit extremum,* on 6 Oct.: *C.F.R.* (1461–71) pp. 246–7.

factors, however, cannot be decisive on their own. On the two most important criteria, there is no record that he was ever in prison, and, although he was clearly of the knightly class – his ancestors for at least six generations had been knights – there is solid evidence that he himself was not one. On every occasion when he is given a rank he calls himself or is called esquire, both during his life (including in his will) and after his death.[45] The last two records are a Chancery petition by his second daughter Alice and her husband Christopher Carlisle, and Alice's epitaph, presumably composed by or for her husband. As one of the country's senior heralds – he was Norroy King of Arms – Carlisle earned his living partly by distinguishing social ranks from one another.[46] He must have known his late father-in-law's rank, and it is difficult to think of any motive he could have had for pretending it to have been lower than it was. And if Thomas of Papworth was not a knight, he was not the author of the *Morte Darthur*.[47]

Of the original nine possibles, three remain. All of them have left indubitable contemporary traces in a mere handful of terse and unrevealing records: four for the Tachbrook man, one for the Whatton man, and two for the man from Hutton. The poverty of these records, in contrast to those left by the knight from Newbold Revel, even excluding his richly scandalous career of crime, is a testimony to their lack of social consequence, and so to the improbability of their having been knighted. Yet the Hutton man's claims to the authorship of the *Morte* were championed in a subtle and wide-ranging book by Professor William Matthews,[48] and during the decades since its publication Matthews's case has been widely accepted.[49]

The acceptance of that case among historians and literary critics has been a tribute to the range of linguistic, literary, and historical arguments it deploys for the Yorkshire Malory and against the claims of the other contenders who were then known.[50] This range of argument has made Matthews's case seem stronger than it is. If his linguistic arguments that the *Morte* was written in Yorkshire English had been valid, they alone would have made his case almost irresistible. As we have seen, however,

---

45 For the latter, *C.F.R.* (1461–71) pp. 247, 258, 261; P.R.O. C1/129/19; *Collectanea topographica et genealogica* v (1838) 282. He was also frequently called esquire during his lifetime: *C.F.R.* (1445–52) pp. 101–2, 149, 197; Gilson, ut supra, n. 25.

46 See Antony R. Wagner, *Heralds of England* (London 1967) pp. 132, 160.

47 Matthews said (p. 151) that Thomas of Papworth was also excluded by having died too soon, but the dates on which his will was made and proved, given by Matthews himself (p. 158), show that he did not.

48 Matthews was anticipated by F. Ragg, 'Appendix to "Feoffees of the Cliffords" ', *Cumberland and Westmorland Archaeological Society Transactions* n.s. 22 (1922) 340–1.

49 E.g. Charles Ross, *Edward IV* (London 1974) p. 411n, and Larry D. Benson, *Malory's 'Morte Darthur'* (Cambridge, Mass., 1976) p. ix.

50 Matthews did not know of the Whatton or Holcot Malorys, and thought the M.P. might be a separate person.

the leading authority decisively rejected his linguistic arguments,[51] and since his literary arguments were never offered as more than supporting evidence, his case was left resting on the historical ones. Historians seem to have assumed that the linguistic arguments still stood, and no-one else realised the weaknesses of the historical ones. Those weaknesses are worth rehearsing at some length because, if scrutinised sufficiently closely, the documents Professor Matthews used will yield more information than he realised. The remainder of this chapter will attempt to show that that information fatally undermines the case for Thomas Malory of Hutton having written the *Morte*. The next chapter will argue that that information also excludes all other Thomas Malorys, known or as yet unknown, except one, and so shows who did write the *Morte Darthur*.

The life of Thomas Malory of Hutton has to be built up almost entirely from eight contemporary documents and a set of later genealogies. Four of the contemporary documents may not (and I shall argue, do not) concern him, and two of the others are important because they might be expected to name him but do not. The two remaining documents and the genealogies fall into a sufficiently tight geographical, social, and chronological cluster to make it appear they all refer to the same person. This is made the more likely by a factor they all have in common. Medieval documents of record – as they all, in different ways, are – find appellations of rank, domicile, and so on to distinguish contemporaries of the same name who might be confused with one another. Most appellations could be used as part of a man's name in formal and elaborate documents, so their presence does not always prove that there was known to be more than one man of that name in the vicinity, but their absence proves that no other man of the same name was so known, and none of these documents gives its Thomas any appellation. The cluster made up by the two documents and the genealogies is not quite tight enough to turn probability into proof, but if more than one person were referred to, each would become proportionately more obscure, and thus proportionately less likely to be a knight and the author of the *Morte Darthur*. In what follows I shall assume that the same man was being referred to in each case.

The first genealogies of the late-fifteenth-century Malorys of Hutton have more authority than many of their kind, since, as Matthews pointed out, they are based on early – in some cases contemporary – information given by the family itself. All the genealogies agree that there was a Thomas among the dozen children of William Malory of Hutton Conyers who died in 1475 and Denise his wife.[52] They disagree on the order in

---

[51] McIntosh, ut supra, and cf. M. Benskin, 'Local Archives and Middle English Dialects', *J.S.A.* v (1977) 500–14.

[52] Matthews, pp. 125–6, 161, 165, 248–9.

which the children were born, and put Thomas variously sixth among the sons (1480/1500), fourth (1563/64), first (1584/85), and third (seventeenth century). The discrepancies themselves make first place unlikely, since it is improbable that the family would forget the son and heir in a recent generation. The genealogies also suggest that Thomas was not a knight, since none of them calls him one, even though all of them take the trouble to describe his brother John as a knight. Genealogies, however, are uncertain things, and record evidence proper can give more reliable information.

To discover what the record evidence can reveal about Thomas Malory of Hutton Conyers, it is necessary to know something of his family. All the evidence suggests that William and Denise and their descendants were the only Malorys in the Ripon area in the mid and late fifteenth century.[53] William was a minor but already married to Denise in 1422, when her father sued another man on William's behalf for the manor of Hutton Conyers.[54] The arbitrators' ruling seems to imply that they thought that William's minority had sixteen years to run, but that they were not absolutely sure: they made alternative provisions in case he should come of age sooner. He may have attained his majority in 1434, when the defendant's widow sued him for dowry; but 1438, the year the arbiters expected, is more probable, since the suit was finally settled that year.[55] If that was so, William was born in 1417, and was married by the time he was five. Denise would have been slightly older: she was born in 1414/15.[56] They both lived fifty years after their marriage, since he made her one of his executors of his will on 1 May 1472; but both of them died within the following three years, he presumably shortly before his will was proved on 25 April 1475, she at an unknown time before that date.[57]

Of the eight sons attributed to them, John was certainly the eldest. All but one of the genealogies say so, and all the contemporary evidence supports them. He must have been the son of both William and Denise since, although there is no known contemporary statement that he was Denise's son, John's son inherited Denise's lands as well as William's in

53 There was a Malour family in Ripon at the time: J.R. Walbran, *Memorials of the Abbey of St Mary of Fountains* iii, Surtees Soc. 130 (1918) pp. 14, 96; *Acts of Chapter of the Collegiate Church of SS. Peter and Wilfrid, Ripon*, Surtees Soc. 64 (1874) pp. 104–5. *Malour*, however, has two syllables, and it was shown long ago that *Malory* always has three: G.L. Kittredge, 'Who Was Sir Thomas Malory?' [Harvard] *Studies and Notes in Philology and Literature* v (1896) 85–106, esp. p. 97 ff.

54 Leeds City Archives MS. V.R. 1672 (olim 53/2). I give references first to the Leeds Archives, where the Vyner MSS. all now are, then the Studley Estate Office references used by Matthews.

55 *V.C.H., Yorks. N.R.*, i 403–4.

56 Walbran, ii, Surtees Soc. 67 (1876) p. 314.

57 York, Borthwick Institute MS. Prob. Reg. 4A fol. 125ᵛ. For the text of the will see Walbran p. 316; the probation clause, not given there, calls her *nuper defuncta*, but the *nuper* may not mean much.

1475, at a time when several of her other sons were still alive.[58] John's son, who inherited from her, was born by 1454, since he was not a minor when he succeeded to the estate; and, since Denise was born 1414/15, John himself was probably born in or very near to 1435. His siblings would all presumably have been born by 1455, when Denise was forty. John would have come of age about 1456; and a John Malory appears in legal documents in the Hutton area in 1456–57: as John Malory senior making a payment to Fountains Abbey in 1456/57, and as John Malory (with no addition) in agreement with his father in June 1456 and with both his parents in June 1457.[59] The 'senior' presumably implies the birth of his second son John; as often in the Middle Ages, he appears to have called his first son after his father and his second son after himself. This interpretation of 'senior' requires that his marriage to Isobel, daughter of Sir Lawrence Hamerton of Hamerton-in-Craven,[60] should have taken place before he came of age, not later than 1455 – a date that accords reasonably with that deduced above for the birth of his eldest son. At an unknown date, he founded a chantry in Ripon Minster.[61] Also at an unknown date he was knighted, since his son succeeded in 1475 as grandson of William and son of *Sir* John. Sir John is not named in the important settlement of Denise's lands made in 1462.[62] His death is not to be inferred from his not being a beneficiary, since Studley, the largest component of Denise's estate, is not named either, and primogeniture would bring it to him after his parents died, unless the reversion had already been settled on him (say) when he was married. What makes it almost certain that he was dead is that he does not witness the settlement to protect his younger brothers. He was certainly dead in 1465, when his widow was dispensed to remarry.[63]

William is clearly the second son. He is called son of William and Denise in the 1462 land settlement. The earliest genealogies make him the second son, as his having his father's Christian name would suggest; and the contemporary evidence strongly supports this. In 1457 a quitclaim calls his father William Malory esquire senior, which implies that the younger

58 *Acts of Chapter*, 246–7.
59 Walbran, iii 33; MSS. V.R. 4410 (olim 304/22), 4413 (olim 51/37). Matthews (p. 166) changes Walbran's *Malore* to *Malour*, thus changing the man's family, and adds a second William Malory to MS. V.R. 4413.
60 Walbran, ii 316. Matthews notes (loc. cit.) that the 1563/64 visitation says Isobel may have been the daughter of Christopher Curwen of Cumberland. This is unlikely: cf. *Acts of Chapter*, p. 320.
61 Walbran, ii 317; *Memorials of the Church of SS. Peter and Wilfrid* iii, Surtees Soc. 81 (1886) p. 6.
62 MS. V.R. 4414 (olim 51/27).
63 *Cal. Pap. Reg.*, xii 493; *Register of the Guild of Corpus Christi, York*, Surtees Soc. 57 (1871) p. 75.

William has now come of age and is William Malory esquire junior.[64] In the 1462 settlement, it also looks as though he is the second son. In that settlement, his parents provided for five named sons of both of them by setting up an ingenious hierarchy of properties for the sons to inherit when both parents had died. Only William had his share specified in the deed. If he was alive when his parents died, he was to have the Malorys' half of the manor of Hilton Floghen in Westmoreland, the most distant of the properties involved, and one apparently smaller than Sir John's share of Denise's lands but larger than the share that any of his four named brothers could expect.[65] The other four were to have a variety of bits and pieces of land divided equally among them by their parents' feoffees when their parents were dead. It is reasonable to suppose that one reason why lands were not allocated to them was that they were still minors: it would be surprising, given Denise's date of birth, if most of her children had not still been minors in 1462. All the five sons named in the settlement were to have their properties for life only. When one of them died, his share would go to the next eldest remaining, not to be redivided among all the others; and when the last one died, the whole was to go to 'the heyre of the body lawfully begeten' of Denise. There was no provision at all for children of the younger sons, unless of course one of them became 'the heyre lawfully begeten' by the failure of older lines. In case their children failed to produce a single lawful heir between them, William and Denise listed further remainder-men: Denise's sister's son and his lawful heirs, then her sister's daughter and hers, and finally her father's and mother's ultimate heirs. At some cost to their younger sons and still more to those sons' offspring if any, this arrangement provided as far as human ingenuity could that one person would always have sufficient landed property to continue the Malorys – and if they died out, their cousins – as a family of consequence among the gentry.

The 1457 quitclaim had carefully distinguished the younger William and his father as 'esquire senior' and 'esquire junior', presumably because the estate clerks had been keeping in mind the possibility that a second son or his descendants might some day inherit the whole estate. Other records do not always aim at the same precision. In 1464 and 1469, the Abbot of Fountains referred to what must be the elder William simply as William

---

64 MS. V.R. 1676 (olim 51/58). Matthews (p. 164) follows the catalogue of the Vyner MSS., which reads 'William Malory *knight* senior'.
65 William was to inherit 'if he happen that he beeth on lyffe' when his parents died. Matthews (pp. 124, 136, 164) misread the phrase as referring to the time when the deed was drawn up, and suggested that William's parents feared he might be dead because he was then engaged in Lancastrian rebellion. Matthews also says that deed describes the other four sons named in it as 'all our sons of me the said Dyonesse lawfully begotten', a significant phrase but one that does not occur in the deed.

Malory esquire.[66] It is natural to assume that the younger William had already moved to Hilton Floghen, and that the Abbot felt that this made further appellations superfluous in Yorkshire business. Similarly, the only contemporary record after 1462 that mentions or even implies the existence of the younger man makes no attempt to distinguish him from his father. It is the report, in a chronicle, of his death fighting for Robin of Redesdale at the Battle of Edgecote in July 1469.[67] Chronicles do not normally aim at the precision of estate records, and this one calls him simply William Malory esquire. The earliest genealogy said that he died childless.[68]

Much less is known about the other sons. Robert is known only from the genealogies, which say that he was the son of both William and Denise, and that he died as a boy. There is no reason to doubt this, and his death before 1462 would explain why the settlement then does not mention him. Henry, Christopher, George, and Richard are known from the genealogies and are named (in that order) in the 1462 settlement as the sons of both William and Denise, and (in the same order) in William's will, made in 1472 and proved in 1475. The order may well be that of their birth. Henry is otherwise unknown. Christopher was a legal witness in 1469, as a gentleman in rank was admitted to a York guild in 1473, rented a house in Ripon in 1478/79, married Isobel Malthouse in 1486, with George was sued for detention of deeds by his nephew Sir John Constable the Younger of Halsham in 1487/79, paid tithes in Ripon in 1502/3, and rented a grange there in 1503/04.[69] George was sued with Christopher in 1487/89, was a collector of customs in Hull in 1497, as an esquire was granted with his brother Richard the administration of the property of one of their sisters in 1498, as an esquire proved Richard's will in 1507, and paid a small sum to Ripon Minster in 1511/12.[70] Richard as a gentleman in rank was admitted to a York guild in 1474, with George was granted the administration of their sister's property in 1498, as an esquire had a dead man's goods committed to him in 1504, and died in 1506/07.[71]

Thomas presents a quite different picture. He was amerced in the Hutton Conyers manor court in 1444, and was not mentioned in the 1462

---

66 Matthews, p. 167.
67 The 1468 document cited by Matthews (p. 167) as referring to a William Malory senior is a bibliographical ghost: an eighteenth-century copy of that cited in n. 32 supra. The copy is dated correctly by regnal year in its text but wrongly by year of grace on the dorse. For the younger William's death, see John Warkworth, *Chronicles of the First Thirteen Years of the Reign of King Edward IV*, Camden Soc. 1st series, 10 (1839) p. 6.
68 Matthews, p. 167.
69 *Acts of Chapter*, 227; *Register*, 87; *Memorials*, iii 257; *Testamenta Eboracensia*, i, Surtees Soc. 4 (1836) p. 350; P.R.O. C1/126/65; *Memorials*, iii 265, 166.
70 P.R.O. C1/126/65; C.F.R. (1485–1509) p. 265; Walbran, ii 316; *Acts of Chapter*, 329; *Memorials*, iii 269.
71 *Register*, 97; *Walbran*, ii 316; *Acts of Chapter*, 293, 329.

settlement, cited a troublesome neighbour before Ripon Minster Chapter in 1471, and was not mentioned in the 1472 will. Of his seven brothers, only Robert, who died as a child, is recorded fewer times than Thomas, and four who had no rank higher than esquire or gentleman are much better recorded than Thomas is. This group of records is an unpromising basis for belief that Thomas was knighted, and doubts increase when the records are looked at more closely.

The first document is an extract – apparently a contemporary working copy – from a Hutton Conyers manor court roll for 5 November 1444.[72] Tenants are recorded as paying individually or in groups: the Rainton tenants paid one shilling as a group with no names mentioned, and the Copt Hewick tenants another shilling similarly. The name *Thomas Maillore* occurs as that of one of twenty-four men who were supposed to pay twopence each, although one of them did not; the entry in the receipts column is therefore three shillings and tenpence, the largest single sum in that column. The men were probably the demesne tenants of Hutton itself. The next two items read *de Willelmo Py quia defec' in lege versus Willelmum Mailliore ij.d* and *de Willelmo Py versus Willelmum Mailliore ij.d.* The William Malory in both cases will be Denise's husband, the lord of the manor. The natural first assumption is that Thomas is his and Denise's third son. He would necessarily have been a minor; but mediaeval English law allowed minors to hold land under certain exceptional conditions,[73] and a prudent father with a suitable piece of land might settle it on a younger son very early rather than leave him to the charity of his elder brother. Such a settlement could lead to amercements in the father's manor court. However, if Thomas were the third son, he would have been aged between 18 and 27 at the time of the 1462 settlement, and between 28 and 37 at the time of the 1472 will. As an adult or near-adult, it is all the odder that he should have been left out of them. It is worth considering individually the possible reasons for this.

First, he might have been dead. This is impossible for 1462, with the 1471 citation still to come; but there is no reason against it for 1472; and an early death would help to explain the poverty of reference to him.

Second, he might have been thought dead either in 1462 or in 1472. One has to assume an extremely convincing mistake, since both documents are cast in the form they are principally to allow for permutations of death among the beneficiaries, and his parents would have lost nothing by including his name. This hypothesis can hardly explain both omissions: with the 1471 citation between them, the double error required passes the bounds of credibility.

72 MS. V.R. 5278 (olim 51/39).
73 W. Holdsworth, *A History of English Law* (London 1919–72) iii 510–20; F. Pollock and F.W. Maitland, *The History of English Law* (London 1985) ii 437–42.

Third, he might have been disinherited. There is no direct evidence, but it would be untypical of the age, and an estate that would provide for six sons would provide for seven. It would be untypical of his parents, in that it would require them to discard an extra chance in their elaborate plan for family survival, and to do so at a time when they had only one adult son (or, if Sir John was still alive, only two) to continue the family, and it would also require them to remain firm in this decision for between ten and thirteen years – for William lived three years after he had made his will, and did not revise it. It might even be untypical of Thomas: the one certain record of his adult life, the 1471 citation, hints at a peaceful and law-abiding character, more likely to be sinned against than to sin in a way that would make his parents cut him off from the family; and despite the proverbial toughness of Yorkshiremen, it would be surprising to find – as the 1471 citation, on this hypothesis, requires – the disinherited son living cheek by jowl with his parents ten years after they had cut him off.

Fourth, Thomas might have been William and Denise's eldest son, to whom Studley was being left by primogeniture by not being mentioned in the 1462 settlement, and Hutton similarly by not being mentioned in the 1472 will. It then has to be assumed that Thomas and any legitimate children he had had died before his father, since Sir John's eldest son inherited both Hutton and Studley. On this hypothesis, it becomes difficult to explain why Sir John's brother William, who shows every sign of being younger than Sir John, was the one who was being built up as First Reserve in 1462; why Sir John (or his son) is left out altogether from both the 1462 settlement and the 1472 will; why Sir John, who was heir to nothing, founded a chantry, married an heiress, and took on the expensive burdens of knighthood, while Thomas, who was the heir to both their parents, made no mark whatever; why Thomas did not witness the 1462 and every other settlement his parents made, to safeguard the rights of his brothers; and why Sir John's son, when he did homage for Hutton, was described as son and heir of Sir John and grandson and heir of William, without Thomas being named at all.

Fifth, Thomas might have been a younger son of William and Denise, who had been given his share of their inheritance before 1462. If he was a younger son, then it looks, as has been said, as if he was the third one. It is difficult to see why, if even the second son had to wait for that careful, elaborate, and seniority-conscious plan of 1462, his next junior brother did not; and if Thomas did have an early, large, and complete settlement, it is even more difficult to see why he did not witness the 1462 and other land settlements, to safeguard the rights of his brothers.

Sixth, Thomas might have been William's son by another marriage. Since Denise was still alive in 1472, a later marriage is impossible; and since they were very probably married by the time William was five, an earlier one is highly improbable. However, since the dates of William's

birth and marriage to Denise are less than certain, it is desireable to consider the possibility that he might have been married before. Thomas and
Sir John (and after Sir John died, his son) could have been left out of the
1462 settlement and the 1472 will in the knowledge that primogeniture
would take William's property to Thomas and Denise's to Sir John or his
son. It then has to be assumed also that Thomas and any legitimate children he had died before William, since Sir John's eldest son inherited Hutton
as well as Studley. This hypothesis does not explain why later generations
should suppress or forget William's earlier marriage; why Thomas, who
would have had the whole of William's estate, did not keep up in conspicuous consumption with Sir John, who had to share Denise's estate,
albeit larger, with five brothers; why Thomas did not witness every land
settlement the family made, to safeguard the rights of his half-brothers;
and why Sir John's son was able to do homage for Hutton without Thomas
being named.

Seventh, Thomas might have been William's illegitimate son. This con-
tradicts the genealogies, but at the same time provides possible reasons for
the contradiction. Later generations could have suppressed and eventually
forgotten the illegitimacy of a half-uncle who might have been too near
home for too long for the family to suppress or forget his existence; and
they might have wanted to avoid any possible fuss over keeping his
property, such as it was. Illegitimacy would explain why Thomas was
neither a beneficiary nor even a witness in the 1462 settlement, although
William and Denise had then at most two legitimate adult sons to ensure
the continuance of their family. Illegitimacy would also mean that there
may have been more than the late-mediaeval legal instinct for comprehensiveness in the description of the five named sons as '*our* sonnes', in the
tautological assertion that William and Denise are making the indenture
'by th'assent and the agrement of the sayd William', and in the careful
detailed remainders to Denise's family if the lawful heirs of her body
should fail.[74]

---

[74] William may also have had an illegitimate daughter. The genealogies give him and
Denise five daughters, of whom two are said to have died young, and two others are
given dowries in his will. The fifth is not, even though by Professor Matthews's account
she seems to have been alive and unmarried three years after this will was made: Isobel
Malory, perhaps of Clint, was assessed for tithes in Monkton in 1475 (Matthews, p. 168,
dated from Bodleian MS. Dodsworth 50, fol. 63ᵛ). Matthews's dating is questionable,
since the MS. dates itself (fol. 39) 'before' not 'in' 15 Edw. IV, and the Bodleian *Summary
Catalogue* dates it 1468. However, if this is William's daughter (and there is no sign that
she is not), it is surprising and at least compatible with illegitimacy to find an unmarried daughter in her father's lifetime actually possessing property rather than merely
having the promise of a dowry.

A sixth daughter, Jane, attributed by Walbran (ii 316) appears to be of another generation: cf. *The Visitation of Yorkshire* [1584–85], ed. J. Foster (London 1875) p. 61.

Thomas's legitimacy affects the conclusions one may draw about his birth and death. If he was illegitimate, the only basis for calculating when he was born will be his father's date of birth – rather less firmly established than Denise's – together with an estimate of when the fifteenth-century Englishman reached puberty. The dates of birth of Denise and of Thomas's legitimate half-brothers will not help. Illegitimacy might also explain why he was not mentioned in his father's will. However, it might not be a sufficient explanation: some contemporaries at least, including Henry Lord Grey of Codnor, Elizabeth Lady Latimer, and Margaret Paston, spoke freely in their wills about their illegitimate descendants; and Sir Robert Bracken-bury's legitimate daughters even obtained a special grant from Parliament making his bastard son heir to his estate after them.[75] Even if Thomas were William's bastard, the most cogent explanation for his absence from his father's will is his own death.

Eighth, Thomas might have been the child of neither William nor Denise. His surname, however, shows that his father was a Malory, and there is no trace of any other Malory family in Yorkshire at the time. If there were one and he belonged to it, it is difficult to see how he came to be described as William and Denise's child by their own descendants, and described in that way repeatedly, since the discrepancies show that the genealogies are at least partly independent of one another.

It is not certain why Thomas was left out of the 1462 settlement and the 1472 will, but there are strong probabilities. Illegitimacy is by far the most plausible explanation for 1462, and death only a little less so for 1472. A cautious gambler might put a saver, but no more, on disinheritance in 1462. One negative conclusion at least is certain: Thomas was not the legitimate eldest son of William Malory of Hutton, whether by Denise or by another wife. If, less probably, he was a legitimate younger son, it is very improbable that he was a knight. Knighthood was such an expensive burden that late-mediaeval English governments were able to rely on an income from men willing to pay taxes rather than take up knighthood, and only at or near the level of the peerage do gentry families have more than one knight at a time – a knight who is almost invariably the head of the family or his heir. There are occasional exceptions, one of them among the fifteenth-century Malorys: Sir Robert Malory of Litchborough took to politics in the lifetime of his elder brother (who was not a knight) and was beheaded for treason at Coventry in 1495.[76] One exception is a useful reminder of the line

---

[75] *Complete Peerage*, s.v. Grey of Codnor; Matthews, p. 176; *Paston Letters and Papers*, ed. N. Davis (Oxford 1971–6) i 388; *Rot. Parl.*, vi 434.

[76] Sir Robert was given no rank when he witnessed a deed in 1481 or when attainted as 'of Fawsley, Northants.' in 1487, but was a knight when executed at Coventry in 1495: *Abstracts of the Ancient Muniments of the Whitgift Foundation*, ed. C. Paget (Croydon 1934) pp. 77–8; George Baker, *The History of the County of Northampton* (London 1822–41) i 406;

between improbability and impossibility; but there is not a shred of evidence that Thomas Malory of Hutton took the more improbable road. If, as is more probable, he was a bastard, it is almost certain that he was not a knight: not so much because the theorists disapproved (although they did),[77] as because he would lack the necessary income and social consequence. Kings' bastards might become peers, and peers' bastards might become knights – the Duke of Exeter had one who did[78] – but a country squire's byblow was and would remain nothing.

To believe that Thomas Malory of Hutton was a knight, therefore, it is necessary to pile the improbability of a legitimate younger son being knighted on top of the improbability of his being legitimate in the first place. But to believe that he was the author of the *Morte Darthur*, it is necessary to heap a third improbability on top of the others: one must disbelieve the evidence of his rank provided by the 1471 citation. The Act Book of Ripon Minster records that on 28 May 1471, William Monkton of Sharow failed to appear before the chapter court on the citation of Thomas Malory.[79] Malory is given no rank, and it is therefore highly probable that he was not a knight at the time, whereas the author of the *Morte* was a knight by 3 March 1470 at the latest.

Appellations of rank are the qualifiers most commonly found in fifteenth-century documents after the names of men of sufficient social standing to be thought as having a rank at all. This frequency is partly caused by a second function of appellation of rank, which overlaps with individuation. A man's rank was thought of as an important part of his identity, and so the appellation was a proportionately important part of his name. The higher the rank, the stronger this feeling. With peerages and knighthood, it was reinforced by administrative responsibilities and moral prestige, and by definite forms of initiation that made it plain who held that rank and who did not. A knight's title thus became part of his name in

---

[W. Reader], *The History and Antiquities of the City of Coventry* (Coventry 1810) p. 32; and cf. *Chronicles of London*, ed. C.L. Kingsford (Oxford 1905) pp. 201–7, 324–5. The estate of his dead brother Edward was committed to Robert Malary (no rank) and John Risley knight after 18 November 1496, which I take to mean that Risley executed for both of them a will made before Sir Robert was knighted: see London, Guildhall Library, MS. 9168/1 fol. 5ᵛ, a reference I owe to Mr C.R.H. Cooper, Keeper of Manuscripts at the Guildhall. Prior Robert Malory (on whom see Chapter V below) is not relevant here: his knighthood is a consequence of his membership of his order, not of the status of his family. Matthews (p. 163) attributes a second knight to the Hutton family in 1423 on the basis of a will catalogued as of that date, but the text of the will (MS. V.R. 1674, olim T/63) reads 1523, and the knight named in it is the then head of the family.

77 E.g. *The Book of the Ordre of Chyvalry*, trans. W. Caxton, ed. A.P.T. Byles, E.E.T.S. o.s. 168 (1926) 57.

78 *Rot. Parl.*, v 477–81.

79 *Acts of Chapter*, p. 151. The text makes the date clear, although Matthews (p. 167) was only able to date it as after the preceding item, of 13 May.

a way that titles of lower ranks did not; and in 1436 the courts decided that it must be included in all writs and indictments because it was 'a parcel of [the knight's] name', but that the titles of esquire or gentleman need not so be included.[80] So it came about that a knight's rank was almost never omitted even from those documents in which there was no need to guard against ambiguities, and where the rank of esquire was omitted often, and that of gentleman more often still.

The Ripon Act Book is a particularly improbable place for a knight's rank to be omitted. It is a legal record, albeit for a petty local court dealing exclusively with ecclesiastical business: oath-breaking, matrimony, probate, and church discipline. Legal records are fuller and more detailed in relevant particulars than records of any other type; and the records of this court are kept with some care, although without the fulness and formality of the king's courts. Moreover, the Act Book for the most part chronicles pretty small beer: small penalties on small people for small crimes like ribaldry, trading by clerics, incontinence, and working on Sundays. The plaintiffs, defendants, witnesses, and jurors it records are humble people. An analysis of four 15-page sections reveal the names of one peer, two knights, three esquires, two gentlemen, 74 clerics, 52 other people described by occupation, and 309 others.[81] Apart from a doctor and a schoolmaster, the people described by occupation consist almost entirely of craftsmen, tradesmen, and servants. The 309 'others' look as though they were socially on much the same level as the 52: most are described by place of origin or by relationship to someone else. The eight 'persons of quality' make up less than 2% of the whole, and the peer and the two knights together much less than 1%. In this company, a knight stands out, and his title is even less likely to be omitted by accident. It is therefore extremely unlikely that Thomas Malory of Hutton was a knight when the Act Book recorded him.

Indeed, although contemporary record evidence is of its nature stronger than that of later genealogies, there is no reason to doubt the unanimous testimony of the genealogies that Thomas was never a knight at all. Not only, as Professor Matthews himself pointed out, are these genealogies in general more authoritative than most, but the people responsible for them in each case took the trouble to record Sir John's knighthood. Had the family gained additional prestige from a second knight in the same generation, there is every reason to suppose that the family would have remembered and the heralds recorded it. The genealogies therefore resemble the Ripon Act Book in this: their not saying that Thomas was a knight amounts to saying he was not one. And whereas a statement in a genealogy that a

---

[80] Sir Nicholas Harris Nicolas, *History of the Orders of Knighthood* (London 1842) vol. i, p. iii.
[81] *Acts of Chapter*, pp. 1–15, 51–65, 101–15, 151–65.

man was a knight might perhaps be only the product of snobbery, a statement that he was not one falls under no suspicion. And if Thomas was
never a knight, or even if he was simply not a knight until after the 1471
citation, he was not the author of the *Morte Darthur*.

Professor Matthews did not appreciate the importance of Thomas' status
among William and Denise's sons. He mentioned in passing at various
points nearly all the possibilities reviewed above, and finally settled, without reasons, on calling Thomas the son – by implication a younger son – of
William and Denise.[82] He did, however, appreciate the importance of the
citation, and responded to it by saying that in the fifteenth century English
scribes applied titles of rank, specifically the titles of knight and esquire,
indiscriminately to the adult male gentry.[83] This is so improbable and so
false that it would not be necessary to do more than contradict it, had not a
book depending on it been widely accepted. In these circumstances, the
obvious asks for elaboration.

The administrative records of any period must guard against confusing
different people of the same name. The fifteenth century was very conscious of this problem,[84] and having no social security numbers and no
really precise addresses, generally solved it by using appellations of rank,
place, office, occupation, generation, or legal or blood relationship. The
number of appellations used varies in general with the width of context in
which the record is conceived: perhaps few or none in a private will as
against two or more for each person in a record of the king's courts. But
when appellations are used at all, those of rank are the commonest for men
at the higher levels in society. Huge sums can depend on documents that
use these appellations, which therefore engaged the attention of the most
expert lawyers. Had rank been indefinite, its inclusion would have been an
irrelevance; and mediaeval English law had a powerful antipathy to irrelevance: mistakes in irrelevant as well as relevant matter could lose cases.
This sense of relevance can produce an elegant economy in the records of
the king's courts; and the same sense controls the use of appellations,
including those of rank, firmly enough in legal documents for a variety of
inferences to be drawn from them. Other records do not always aim at the
same standards: a chronicler, for instance, may not know or care how many
other John Does and Richard Roes there are besides the ones in his story.
Different kinds of records also vary in the accuracy with which they are
copied out: a newsletter, a genealogy, or a diplomatic report for a distant
country will not normally be as reliable as a Chancery pardon paid for by a

---

[82] Matthews, pp. 124, 126, 136, 154, 167.
[83] Matthews, pp. 152–3.
[84] For instance, in 1413 the Statute of Additions enacted that any action at law that could
lead to the defendant being outlawed should fail unless his rank and domicile were
both specified in the writ that initiated the action: *Statutes of the Realm*, ii 171.

beneficiary whose life may depend on it. Error may appear anywhere – *humanum est* – but in general mistakes and fraud in appellations of rank in a document are proportionate to mistakes and fraud in the document as a whole. Had appellations, including those of rank, not been reliable at least in legal and administrative records, no mediaeval man could have been secure in his property or other rights; nor, in later times, could Dugdale, Nichols, Baker, and others have undertaken to disentangle the history of English counties through their families, estates and politics.

Knowledge of which records are reliable and to what extent is largely a matter of experience. Professor Matthews did not have sufficient experience; and that produced his assertion that fifteenth-century appellations of rank are effectively meaningless. Since he does not give proper references, the handful of examples he proposes in support of his assertion cannot be properly checked, but where examination is possible, all but one of the inconsistencies he alleges seem to be of his own making.[85] I have not found in the documents he cites or elsewhere any confusion between Sir Thomas Malory of Newbold Revel's father John and probable great-grandfather Sir John other than Matthews's own, nor any description of Sir William Malory of Papworth as an esquire even before the date at which he is called knight, let alone after it.[86] The John Malory of Hutton who is called esquire in 1510 does not seem to have been called a knight in 1505.[87] Professor Matthews did discover a genuine mistake when he pointed out that Denise Malory's husband is called esquire in his will in 1472, and knight in his writs of *diem clausit extremum* in 1476.[88] Although the natural inference from this would be that William, after a lifetime's resistance, had given way and taken up knighthood, what proves the 1476 writs wrong is the record of William's grandson doing homage for Hutton, a document that Professor Matthews overlooked.

Mediaeval documents made mistakes about rank, but they are very much more often right than wrong. A scholar can only postulate a mistake

---

[85] Matthews, pp. 153, 157–8, 169.

[86] Sir William was a knight by 8 May 1411: *C.P.R.* (1408–13) p. 319.

[87] Matthews says (p. 169) of this John: 'in Memorials of Fountains (iii 198) he is entitled *miles*, but in 1509–10 he is called *armiger* (iii 173).' He has left out the date of the first item, but his text (p. 153) suggests 1505. In a different set of books, the Memorials of Ripon (cf. nn. 61 and 69 supra) there is a John Malory knight on iii 198 and a John Malory esquire on iii 173. The latter entry is dated 1509–10 but the former only as from an 'imperfect' roll, c.1505. The printed scraps of the roll suggest that it would not be easy to date it within five years, but even if it were firmly dated to 1505 it would still remain to be shown that the two documents referred to the same man. The John Malory whom Matthews intends had an uncle of the same name (Matthews, p. 166): part of the pattern produced by the head of the family calling his eldest son after his father and his second son after himself (cf. Ch. n. 22 infra). The second John may be the man in *The Historians of the Church of York*, ed. J. Raine (1879–94) iii 361, 365, 367.

[88] *C.F.R.* (1471–85) pp. 100, 119, 126.

when a document is demonstrably unreliable or when it is overborne by external evidence. The philological evidence might have done this, if it had pointed to the author of the *Morte* coming from near Ripon. In fact it does not, and there is no reason to doubt the conclusions suggested by the documents considered above. The four contemporary documents that certainly concern Thomas Malory of Hutton confirm the later genealogies of his family. They show beyond reasonable doubt that he was never a knight, and so that he was not the author of the *Morte Darthur*.

II

Identification

Besides the documents that certainly concern Thomas Malory of Hutton, there are four other contemporary documents that may do so. William Matthews argued that they all do: I shall argue that none of them do, but that, notwithstanding, they show who wrote the *Morte Darthur*. They are an English newsletter of 1462, the Yorkist exclusions from pardon from 1468 to 1470, a Milanese diplomatic report of 1469, and the *Morte Darthur* itself. It will be convenient to take the third first, and then the others in the order of their composition.

In a daring attempt to locate the place of composition of the *Morte*, Professor Matthews argued that since the only library in Europe known to have possessed copies of all the French romances that Malory used was that of Jacques Count of Armagnac, since the count was an Arthurian enthusiast responsible for the composition of a number of Arthurian works including an approximate French equivalent of the *Morte*, and since the *Morte* shows local knowledge of the principalities of south-west France around Armagnac, the author of the *Morte* might have been one of the two thousand English prisoners of war reported by the Milanese ambassador at Tours on 30 April 1469 as having been captured near Bordeaux and imprisoned.[1] In the form suggested, this idea is certainly untenable. In the first place, there is every reason to think that the raid the ambassador reported never took place: reputable historians have gone out of their way to comment on the amount of sheer invention in the Milanese dispatches in general and in this report in particular, and they seem agreed that the English did not land on that coast of France in that campaigning season.[2] Second, if the raid had taken place and Malory had been on it, he would not have had time to write the *Morte* after landing: he would have had less than ten and a half months to write a book that on Professor Matthews's

---

[1] C.S.P. (Milan), i 129–30.
[2] C.L. Scofield, *The Life of Edward IV* (London 1923) i 489–90; Ross, pp. 113–14; J.R. Lander, *Crown and Nobility* (London 1976) p. 227; and cf. J.H. Ramsay, *Lancaster and York* (Oxford 1892) ii 334–5.

own estimate must have taken something like two years.[3] And third, however low the rather thin records may make one pitch one's estimate of the probability that a given English library had all the French romances that Malory used, there must be an even lower probability of any Continental library having a single romance in English – and particularly one of the obscure poems in difficult language that Malory most made use of. However, the Milanese report is a reminder of the need to account for the knowledge of south-west France in the *Morte*. Only one Sir Thomas Malory is known to have had a connection with that area: Sir Thomas Malory of Newbold Revel. His first cousin, Sir Philip Chetwynd, was commissioned on 29 July 1442 to recruit soldiers to defend Bayonne, of which he was the mayor.[4] Sir Thomas seems likely to have been available: the first known public record of his life is, as we shall see later, a settlement of Sir Philip's estates that he witnessed in 1439.

The next document demands detailed scrutiny. It is part of a short, scrappy, and conspicuously Yorkist chronicle partly in English and partly in indifferent Latin. Those qualified to judge have not given any very precise opinion of its reliability. Gairdner, who edited it, remarked on its jumbled order, wrong dates, and other errors: of those it lists as killed at Towton, at least seven peers and two knights survived.[5] Its author made some attempt at accuracy, discovering and correcting his mistake over one of the Towton knights; but on the whole Gairdner valued it rather for reporting the ways things were thought to have happened than for reporting the way they had. Kingsford felt much the same, but added that the chronicle was a useful contemporary record containing a number of new and important historical details.[6] Miss Scofield apparently agreed, since she used it without comment in her monumental life of Edward IV.

It appears therefore that the veracity of each statement in the chronicle must be weighed up as far as possible on its own. In this respect, the passage mentioning Malory is reassuringly detailed.[7] It purports to be a list of the peers and knights who accompanied Edward IV on 30 November 1462, when he was on his way to beseige the Lancastrian-held castles of Alnwick, Bamburgh and Dunstanborough. Each rank from duke to knight is neatly listed, and the total number of names in that rank noted in the margin. There are 59 *milites*, of whom 11 have *Ser* in front of their names and 48, including *Thomas Malery*, do not. Early comment on this passage

---

3   Matthews, p. 139 (and cf. *Works*, p. xx). Armagnac was not the only place where writing romances like Malory's was in fashion: see Benson, pp. 17–36.
4   *Proc. & Ord. P.C.*, v 193–4.
5   'Brief Notes', pp. 157–8, and cf. pp. xv–xx.
6   C.L. Kingsford, *English Historical Literature in the Fifteenth Century* (Oxford 1913) p. 161.
7   'Brief Notes', pp. 157–8. The detail impressed Charles Ross: 'Rumour, Propaganda, and Popular Opinion during the Wars of the Roses' in *Patronage, The Crown, and the Provinces*, ed. R.A. Griffiths (Gloucester 1981) pp. 15–32, at pp. 17–18.

was largely devoted to needless debate as to whether or not *milites* meant 'knights' rather than 'soldiers'. It plainly does: not only does the series 'duke, earl, baron . . .' demand 'knight' to complete it, but the only person in England who would have used *miles* to mean anything but 'knight' in 1462 would have been that very rare bird, a humanist writing neoclassical prose, and such a man would have died rather than write the Latin of this chronicle.

The chronicle therefore says that all 59 men were knights. It does not, however, follow that they were. This document, unlike those previously considered, raises serious questions of authorial probity. The chronicler himself was committed to King Edward and an enemy of 'Kyng Herry late kyng of Inglond in dede but not in ryth, and sche that was Queyn Margarete hys wyf, and Edward hyr [sic] son;'[8] and the friend who sent him the list of names is unlikely to have been less partisan. If the list is accurate, it is too detailed not to have been compiled by someone who was with King Edward, in which case the compiler was presumably willing to face war and a Northumbrian winter to keep King Edward on his throne, and might have been willing for the same purpose to tell lies that made King Edward's support among the nobility and gentry look more solid. If he was absent, he must have been lying. The only way to decide on the reliability of his list is to check the names individually as far as possible. The controversy over Malory shows that individual findings may be challenged, but the total pattern will be more reliable than any of its parts.

Professor Matthews, to his credit, was the first person to check the names of the knights.[9] However, he took the compiler's veracity for granted, and devoted himself, on that assumption, to establishing how many of the knights came from the northern counties of England, and in particular from Yorkshire. The results of a re-examination of the evidence made to test the compiler's reliability are set out in Appendix I below. They suggest that both the compiler and Professor Matthews missed some things and suppressed others, the compiler to increase the number of Yorkists, Professor Matthews to increase the number of Yorkshiremen. However, whereas the compiler seems to have been right most of the time, Professor Matthews not only entirely overlooked the compiler's failings but also himself failed more often than not to identify the man the compiler intended.

The list of knights contains, as has been said, 59 names. In 36 cases, one, and only one, knight of that name appears to have been alive at that time. I have assumed in all but two cases that this was the man the compiler meant – one man who was not and one who may not have been a knight

---

[8] Ibid., p. 158. *hyr* is not used for 'their' in this text: the implied defamation is official (cf. the Act of Attainder against the Lancastrian royal family in *Rot. Parl.*, v 479).

[9] Matthews, pp. 127–30, 171–4.

seem more plausible politically than their namesakes who were certainly knights. One knight the compiler intended seems to have been elsewhere: as the chronicle itself records, shortly afterwards he was commanding one of the castles that King Edward's army was on its way to beseige, and his known life leaves insufficient time for him to have travelled up with them and then deserted. The remaining 23 cases present the main problem by their sheer number: it is incredible that there should be so many entirely unrecorded knights in late-fifteenth-century England. In fact, in 21 cases the person intended can be identified, and in nearly every case with something approaching certainty. In seven cases, the compiler has given the man a wrong name (usually the Christian name): in ten others he has named a man who was not or may not have been a knight, to two of whom he has also given a wrong name. The first set of mistakes suggests carelessness, the second, fraud. Fraud is confirmed by the four remaining discrepant cases: a baron already in the list of barons under his title, and three dead men. (All four had been knights, and the baron in a sense was still one.) This leaves two men unidentified. The identifications do not apparently throw any light on the distribution of the title *Ser*, and I would guess it to have been the product of scribal impulse tempered by boredom.

Of the 59 knights, then, 5 were certainly absent – one as the ghost of his baronial self, one as an enemy captain, and three as dead. Of the 54 remaining, 40 were knights, 9 were not, and 5 (including the two unknowns) may or may not have been. Of those who were not or may not have been, at least five were summoned for knighthood at the coronation of Edward V. The list looks dishonest, but dishonest within careful limits. The compiler was not conjuring names out of the air or conferring improbable knighthoods on nobodies: he was supplementing a genuine list of knights with the names of men who, because of their rank, property and consequence, could have been knights. Anyone far from the northern sieges who knew one or two of the men on the list as not being knights would not have been suspicious: he would have assumed that the king had knighted them. He may indeed have done so with Geoffrey Gate and Christopher Conyers, and perhaps with others.

This helps in identifying the Thomas Malory on the list. As a first step, probabilities adducible from the pattern as a whole can be applied to any one doubtful case, and on those grounds the odds are better than two to one that the Malory on the list was a knight, and so, as the only known man of that name and rank at the time, Sir Thomas Malory of Newbold Revel. If, however, he was not Sir Thomas of Newbold Revel, he is most likely to have been a man of the wrong rank and the right name and standing, for which Thomas Malory of Papworth is the only plausible candidate; or one of the right rank but the wrong name, either Christian name or surname. If the former, Sir John Malory of Hutton is the only possible man, if he was still alive; if the latter, there is no obvious person.

The compiler would not, however, have included on this list a nobody – the bastard, or even the legitimate disinherited younger son, of a country squire.

The compiler lied about rank, and he could (and in the last five cases did) lie about presence as well. It is therefore desirable to estimate a second probability: that those named, and Malory in particular, were really there. In four cases I have found reasonably direct evidence of men's presence: for the others I have had to depend on a preliminary investigation of family connections and political commitments. By the time of the expedition, some 24 of the 54 possibles appear to have been Yorkists, from the king's closest supporters to men who could have disentangled themselves without serious damage if Lancaster had turned the tables again. The war machine seems to have caught up four men who were Lancastrians, at least in the sense that they would have preferred Lancaster to have been the winning side, and themselves on it. This is in no way implausible: Yorkists had before then been compelled on pain of death to fight in Lancastrian armies.[10] I have not found any sign of political commitment by November 1462 for the remaining 26. Two things, however, suggest that quite a number of these may have been Yorkists. It was only eighteen months since the Yorkists had seized power: many of their sympathisers would have been maintaining the lowest of profiles beforehand, and they and new adherents could easily have remained unrecorded since then in any discernably political act. Also, many of the obscurer men were northerners, and hence particularly likely to have been part of the Neville affinity: two-fifths of the 54 came from the north (and one-fifth from Yorkshire). It seems reasonable to say that more than half of those left after the five known absentees are excluded would have been willing or eager to respond to King Edward's summons. Moreover, the names of the four Lancastrian sympathisers remind us that the proportion of those present has to be increased to allow for those who came unwillingly. This would depend on each man's estimate of King Edward's power to survive and exact retribution. What those estimates were, no-one can tell, but one young man near the centre of things at the time wrote to warn his neighbours who had stayed at home that they had guessed badly wrong.[11] The figures that emerge from this are similar to those that another general factor suggests: if the compiler told the same kind of lies about presence as he did about rank, something between two-thirds and five-sixths of those named will have been there.

There are particular as well as general grounds for supposing the Thomas Malory on the list to have been present: indeed, King Edward's army may have included more than one Thomas Malory. As Professor Matthews pointed out, several of those named were friends and

---

[10] Ross, p. 29.
[11] *Paston Letters*, i 524.

neighbours of the Hutton Malorys, notably Sir John Conyers of Hornby, who was probably the later Robin of Redesdale. The only known political act of this generation of Malorys of Hutton is Denise's son William's going to war with 'Robin' in the Lancastrian rebellion of 1469. The political discrepancy, which led Professor Matthews into some confusion,[12] can be resolved: Conyers was a follower of Richard Neville, Earl of Warwick, who was a Yorkist in 1462 and Lancastrian in 1469. He might have had every adult male Malory of Hutton with him on both occasions. Thomas Malory of Papworth also had a connection with Warwick: one of the two supervisors of his will was a partisan of the Earl's.[13] However, the man whose connections with Warwick were the closest of all was Sir Thomas Malory of Newbold Revel. As we shall see, the Lancastrian authorities had kept him in prison without trial for almost a decade, ignoring what was technically a royal pardon and putting enormous penalties on his gaolers to make sure he stayed there.[14] Malory's own attempts to obtain bail seem to have been fruitless, and the only people able and willing to help him were the Yorkist lords. York himself during his protectorate gave Malory the pardon that was ignored. Lord Fauconberg, who was Warwick's uncle and principal lieutenant, and the Duke of Norfolk had him bailed out for short periods; and the end of his imprisonment coincides with the Yorkist seizure of power. Gratitude might have taken Sir Thomas north: Warwick, Fauconberg and Norfolk were all with King Edward. But if he had little sense of gratitude – and he seems to have behaved quite remarkably badly while on bail to Norfolk's men – he had presumably another powerful stimulus for answering King Edward's summons: the fear that if the Lancastrians regained power they would have him put back in prison.

It is therefore very probable that the chronicle is right in naming a Thomas Malory among those who followed King Edward to the northern sieges and that, whatever supposition one makes about his rank, the same conclusion follows: if the chronicle is reliable in calling him a knight, the only available knight was Sir Thomas Malory of Newbold Revel; if it is reliable only in the name it gives, Sir Thomas of Newbold Revel is, of all the men of that name, the one most likely to have been present; if more than one Thomas Malory was there, the Newbold Revel knight must be assumed from his social and political consequence to have been the man intended.

The next documentary item is the Yorkist government's exclusions from pardon. The second pardon roll of Edward IV's reign begins on 14 July

---

12 Matthews, p. 136.

13 P.R.O. Reg. Godyn, fol. 28; Wedgwood, *Biographies*, s.n. John Wake.

14 See below Chapter VII. Malory's principal assistant in crime, his steward John Appleby, seems to have been a Carlisle man: Wedgwood, *s.n.* This might point to an early connection with Richard Neville Earl of Warwick.

1468. It starts with a model pardon that excludes from grace Henry VI and his queen and son, certain office holders and others not specified by name, and Humphrey Neville knight, Thomas Malory knight, Robert Marshall of Culham Oxfordshire esquire, Hugh Mill of London gentleman, Gervase Clifton of London knight, William Verdon of London scrivener, Peter House of London esquire, Morgan ap Thomas ap Griffith of Carmarthen gentleman, Henry ap Thomas ap Griffith of Carmarthen gentleman, Owen ap Griffith ap Nicholas of Carmarthen esquire, Maurice ap Owen ap Griffith of Carmarthen gentleman, and Thomas Philip of Rea Gloucestershire yeoman.[15] Every issue of this pardon should have repeated this part of its terms exactly, and the known exemplars, dated 16 July, 24 August, 1 November and 1 December 1468, and 12 February 1469, do so.[16] On 22 February 1470, Malory, Marshall, Verdon and Philip were again excepted in the model pardon at the head of the third pardon roll; but they were not excepted (no-one was) in the model pardon at the head of the fourth roll, on 25 November 1471.[17]

To exclude a man from pardon, the authorities had to believe he was an exceptionally undesirable character, which in this context meant a dangerous Lancastrian. Practically any other offence could be compounded for: the government was very anxious that no-one should feel that he would be better off with the alternative administration in power. As danger increased, King Edward even had it proclaimed that anyone who could not afford to pay for a pardon should have one for nothing; and when, during Clarence and Warwick's rebellion in the summer of 1469, confidence in the general pardon began to be undermined by rumours that King Edward intended to anull it retrospectively, he issued a another proclamation emphasising that, even though he had proclaimed his brother and cousin traitors for what they had done since it was issued, the pardon itself would stand in full force.[18] The attempts to identify the dangerous Lancastrian Sir Thomas Malory have thrown up some fascinating information about the others excepted and some ingenious speculations about Malory.[19] Professor Matthews argued that within the list Neville and Malory constituted a sub-group of two, and it was therefore probable that Malory was, like Neville, a northern Lancastrian revolutionary: Thomas Malory of Hutton in political guise. But for this to be possible, it would

---

[15] P.R.O. C67/46 m. 39; cf. Gweneth Whitteridge, 'The Identity of Sir Thomas Malory, Knight-Prisoner', R.E.S. n.s. 24 (1973) 257–65, esp. p. 262.

[16] B.L. Add. Ch. 17248; Report on the Manuscripts of Wells Cathedral (London 1895) pp. 183–4; Nottingham Corporation Archives C.A. 4173; Calendar of the Manuscripts of the Dean of Chapter of Wells (London 1907–14) i 407; P.R.O. Chester 2/141 m.9. I discount a homoeoteleuton in the Nottingham copy.

[17] P.R.O. C67/47 m.9; C67/48 m.33; Whitteridge, p. 263.

[18] Scofield, i 510–11; Ross, p. 25.

[19] Wedgwood, s.nn. Clifton, Malory, and Mill; Matthews, pp. 130–7; Whitteridge, p. 262.

Thomas Malory of Hutton might have been a knight in the first place. Had not the contrary been demonstrated already, the exceptions from pardon would themselves prove it. They would also disprove again, if it were necessary, Professor Matthews's assumptions about fifteenth-century ranks. Most important of all, however, they can identify with certainty the true author of *Le Morte Darthur*.

Pardons and exceptions from pardon could be a matter of life and death. Their importance is shown by the number of people who subscribed to and paid for them, individually or corporately, and by the care with which, since English law was and is very literal, the beneficiaries ensured that they were all described by every imaginable alias of ranks occupied, offices held, and places lived in.[20] It was widely known that the pardon issued to Jack Cade under that name was invalid because 'Jack Cade' was a pseudonym.[21] Since the exceptions from pardon would also be interpreted according to the literalness of the law, the phrase *Thomas Malory miles* among the exceptions excluded from pardon every Thomas Malory knight; if, as Professor Matthews maintained, the ranks of knight and esquire were interchangeable, every man who held either rank; and if, as his argument really implies, titles of rank were meaningless, every living man called Thomas Malory. The same applies *mutatis mutandis* to Humphrey Neville, although the authorities had for some reason taken the precaution of providing an appellation of place for the third knight, Gervase Clifton,[22] as well as for the three esquires, four gentlemen, and two others excepted, a precaution which would presumably have prevented anyone other than those intended from suffering from the exclusions in those cases. If titles of rank were really meaningless, the official phrasing might have excluded half a dozen Thomas Malorys from pardon; if, less drastically, *knight* and *esquire* were interchangeable, the ban would at least have excluded Thomas Malory of Papworth, Sir Thomas Malory of Newbold Revel, and of course, if Professor Matthews's contentions about him were correct, Thomas Malory of Hutton as well.

These sober and consequential documents make sense only on the assumption that the authorities were very sure at any one time who were knights and who were not. If they had the slightest doubt, all they had to do was to follow the procedure as they did with the men of lower rank and

---

20 E.g. the pardon under 36 very similar aliases to Thomas Foster of Caysho: P.R.O. C67/46 m. 13.

21 I.M.W. Harvey, *Jack Cade's Rebellion* (Oxford 1991) pp. 78, 97–100. Cade may have known it too: he acted, as Harvey points out, as if he did not trust the pardon.

22 Sir Robert Clifton of Clifton, Notts. (d.1478) was son and heir of Sir Gervase Clifton of the same (d.1453), had a next youngest brother Sir Gervase (the man excluded from pardon, d.1471) and a son and heir Gervase (b.1438): Wedgwood, *s.nn.* The youngest Gervase may have been thought to have been considering taking up knighthood at this time.

expend a little ink on specifying domiciles. That the ink was not used is a measure of their confidence that from at least 14 July 1468 until at least 22 February 1470 there was only one Sir Thomas Malory. Confidence can be misplaced, as can be seen from the 1476 writs of *diem clausit extremum* that call William Malory of Hutton a knight. Such mistakes, however, are very rare even with routine documents like the 1476 writs, and are even less likely with exclusions from pardon. It is reasonable to assume that the authorities would have taken some additional trouble over what amounted to a list of their most dangerous enemies. Their list then became part of every general pardon; and those pardons were going out all the time to a representative cross-section of the most important individuals and corporate bodies in the country. The recipients had every reason to check the wording with care. If there had been a second and unrecorded Sir Thomas Malory besides the one from Newbold Revel, then the one not intended (whichever that was) would certainly have come to hear of it before he had been blacklisted for eighteen months, and would have had the erroneous wording corrected. Since this did not happen, the Yorkist government must have been right in its assumption that during the period of the known exceptions there was only one Sir Thomas Malory.

The Sir Thomas Malory who was excepted from pardon must have been the author of the *Morte Darthur*. No other conclusion is possible, even if one exchanges normal canons of probability for those of detective fiction, and tries to maintain that the knight excluded from pardon died on (say) 23 February 1470 and that the author was knighted (in prison) on one of the thirteen days left before the end of that twelve-month period in which the *Morte* was completed. The author of the *Morte* calls himself a knight not merely at the end of his book, but also at the end of the first tale, in a passage that implies that that is all he has written so far:

> This book endyth whereas Sir Launcelot and Sir Trystrams com to courte. Who that woll make ony more lette hym seke other bookis of Kynge Arthure or of Sir Launcelot or Sir Trystrams; for this was drawyn by a knight presoner, Sir Thomas Malleorré, that God sende hym good recover. Amen. Explicit.[23]

Therefore, even if that unknown day between 3 March 1469 and 4 March 1470 on which the author of the *Morte* completed it and described himself as a knight-prisoner fell after 22 February 1470, the author must also have been a knight for a long enough period beforehand to write six-sevenths of the *Morte*. It may be added that he variously says or implies that he was a knight or a prisoner or both at the end of the fourth, fifth, sixth, and

---

[23] *Works*, p. 180.18.

seventh of the eight tales in the book.[24] He must therefore have been a knight during the period of the exclusions from pardon, and since there was only one Sir Thomas Malory alive then, he must have been the man excluded. But Sir Thomas Malory of Newbold Revel was alive then: he died on 12 or 14 March 1471.[25] Therefore Sir Thomas Malory of Newbold Revel must have been both the man excluded from pardon and the author of the *Morte Darthur*.

Presumably the Warwickshire knight who followed the Earl of Warwick to the northern sieges in 1462 later took the same course as Warwick did, back to the cause of Lancaster and of the king who may well have knighted them both.[26] That, in the late 1460s, was a short road to prison: when King Edward was at last dislodged, Sir Geoffrey Gate, who had made himself Warwick's lieutenant in London, went round the gaols of the capital letting out the imprisoned members of his own party, and there were a good many of them.[27] It is reasonable to assume that one of them was the distinguished author from Newbold Revel, and that he had recently completed his book in Yorkist custody.

The final document is the *Morte Darthur* itself. What it reveals about its author was set out at the beginning of the previous chapter. It is the criteria that the *Morte* provides, that its author was a knight and a prisoner between 3 March 1469 and 4 March 1470, that establish his identity. The documents considered in that chapter showed that Thomas Malory of Hutton, like his namesake from Papworth St Agnes, was not a knight, and so not the author. If the Warwickshire knight had also been ruled out, it would have been necessary to explore the claims of their obscure namesakes from Tachbrook Malory and Long Whatton, and perhaps even in desperation those of the rector of Holcot. There is, however, no reason to doubt the claims of the Warwickshire knight. The four debateable documents considered in this chapter do more than show that he is likelier to

24 *Works*, pp. 363.19, 845.29, 1037.12, 1154.19.

25 12 March according to his *inquisitio post mortem*, 14 March according to his epitaph: P.R.O. C140/36/12 and E149/224/18; B.L. MS. Cotton Vitellius F.xii, fol. 284ʳ. The epitaph is more likely to be right.

Mrs Whitteridge (p. 263) provides what looks like converging evidence, arguing that the Malory excluded from pardon must have died during the currency of the third roll (a period including March 1471) since he was excluded at the beginning of it, not pardoned on it, and not excluded at the beginning of the next roll. Unfortunately the system was not that watertight: Mill, for instance, excluded on the second roll and neither pardoned on it nor excluded on the third, survived for years (cf. Wedgwood, *s.n.* Hugh Mill).

26 For who could knight whom see Nicolas, vol. i pp. i–ix; cf. Matthews's contention (p. 136) that the Hutton Malory might have been dubbed by a mere knight bachelor.

27 Robert Fabyan, *The New Chronicles of England and France*, ed. H. Ellis (London 1811) pp. 658–9; Scofield, i 540–1.

have been the author than any other man of that name known to have been alive at the right time: they show that there is no longer a place in Malorian biography for the Fair Unknown. No-one but Sir Thomas Malory of Newbold Revel could have written the *Morte Darthur*.

III

Ancestry

In the fifteenth century, the English gentry had every reason to be interested in their own ancestry. The pleasures and burdens of family pride aside,[1] knowledge of one's ancestry might at any time provide unpredictable but very tangible benefits in law. It is widely agreed that their first concern was for the preservation of their estates,[2] and none of them could tell when a defence of those estates against an unexpected lawsuit or a claim for a windfall inheritance from a remote cousin might depend on the ability to prove some family relationship. Their disagreements over inheritance could last for centuries, as the great Berkeley inheritance dispute did, and the greatest of them engulfed the whole country – the Wars of the Roses can be seen in this context as a dispute between the heir male and the heir general of Edward III.[3]

It is clear that Sir Thomas Malory shared this interest in ancestry. His grandson had an armorial window constructed in the parlour at Newbold Revel that included the arms of Sir Peter Malory the judge, who had died eight generations earlier.[4] That would not have been possible unless the necessary records had been preserved and transmitted down the generations by successive members of the family, including Sir Thomas. In the *Morte Darthur* too, he often shows himself conscious of his characters being 'of jantill strene of fadir syde and of modir syde.'[5] If therefore we turn next

---

1   For one example, see Simon Payling, *Political Society in Lancastrian England* (Oxford 1991) p. 26, n. 34.

2   Christine Carpenter, 'The Duke of Clarence and the Midlands', *M.H.* 11 (1986) 23–48, at p. 24; Edward Powell, *Kingship, Law, and Society* (Oxford 1989) p. 90. For some qualifications, see M.A. Hicks, 'Piety and Lineage in the Wars of the Roses: the Hungerford Experience' in *Kings and Nobles in the Middle Ages*, ed. R.A. Griffiths et al. (Gloucester 1986) pp. 90–108.

3   See J.R. Lander, 'Family, "Friends", and Politics in Fifteenth-Century England' in *Kings and Nobles in the Later Middle Ages*, ed. R.A. Griffiths et al. (Gloucester 1986) pp. 27–40.

4   Dugdale, *Warwickshire*, p. 83; *Cal. I.P.M.*, v 131. The coat of arms is identified as Sir Peter's in the Parliamentary Roll of Arms: *Parliamentary Writs and Writs of Military Summons*, ed. F. Palsgrave (London 1827–34) i 417. It is discussed in Anthony R. Wagner, *Historic Heraldry* (London 1939) pp. 24–5, a reference I owe to Professor W.H. Dunham.

5   E.g. *Works*, p. 62.23.

to his own ancestry, we are not merely sketching in background for con-
trastive effect: we are defining what Sir Thomas plainly felt himself to be, a
'jantyllman that bore olde armys.'[6] Without access to his own muniments,
we cannot know how much he himself knew of his ancestry. We can only
say that in the nearer parts of his pedigree it must have been more than we
can prove from the only solid evidence, the armorial window, and that in
the remoter parts it may well have been less than can be established from
modern archives.

Since Sir Thomas assumed that the social distinctions of his time would
last until the Day of Judgement,[7] he no doubt also assumed that they were
as old as human society itself. He would have been surprised to hear that
his own ancestry could be traced back to a time when the word *gentleman*
had not been invented,[8] and when knights did not usually bear heraldic
arms. The first recorded shield of arms is that which Henry I hung round
the neck of Geoffrey Plantagenet when he knighted him before his wedding in 1127, but it was to be a century and more before every knight
would have such a shield as a matter of course.[9] The first Malory to whom
we can give a name must have been alive at the time of the Plantagenet
wedding: he was Aschetil Malory, whose son Robert early in the reign of
Henry II is the first known Malory of Tachbrook Mallory in Warwickshire.[10] There is evidence of one kind or another that four-fifths of the
approximately four hundred known mediaeval English Malorys descended from Aschetil (or perhaps one of his immediate ancestors) in one of the
eight branches of a single family. In fact it seems likely that all of them did
so, with perhaps two or three early exceptions,[11] and that all that stops us
proving it is the limitations of the surviving records. Several branches of
the family used the first name Aschetil or one of its variants – Anschetil,
Anketil, Anketin, or Anquetin.

Part of the evidence for their interrelationships is set out in Appendix I, a
summary account of the successive heads of the various branches of the

6 See *Works*, pp. 375.23–4.
7 See *Works*, pp. 375.24–6, 683.1.
8 *O.E.D.* cites *gentleman* from 1275. It first applied to all men in 'noble' society: for the
   process by which it came about 1400 to mean a man in the lowest rank of that society,
   see Payling, pp. 76–7
9 Wagner, *The Records and Collections of the College of Arms* (London 1952) p. 33.
10 B.L. Harl. Chart. 47599, 47600, printed in *Documents Illustrative of the Social and Economic
   History of the Danelaw*, ed. F.M. Stenton (London 1920) pp. 245–7.
11 The most likely exceptions are Geoffrey Maloret who held the manor of Todbere in
   Dorset of William de Mohun in 1086; Laurence Mallore of Bristol who owed 10 marks
   under the forest laws in 1176, which he eventually paid off in 1196; and Pigot Malore
   who in the late twelfth century is recorded as having previously occupied a dwelling
   house in Seaton Ross in Yorkshire: *V.C.H., Dorset*, iii 92; *Pipe Roll for 1176–77*, Pipe Roll
   Soc. 26 (1905) 44; *Pipe Roll for 1197*, P.R.S. 46 (1931) 127; *Pipe Roll for 1198*, P.R.S. 47 (1932)
   5; *Early Yorkshire Charters*, ed. W. Farrer et al., 12 vols (1904–65) x 133.

family, but to give, let alone to interpret, all the evidence is impracticable. Some of the problems involved are as complicated as the problem of the authorship of the *Morte Darthur* itself, and the only history of the Malory family is too brief to have solved all the problems.[12] Fortunately, our present purposes do not require the establishment of precise relationships in every case. This much, however, may be said for assuming kinship of some kind between all mediaeval English Malorys, *exceptis excipiendis*. The surname *Malory*, meaning 'unlucky', is a derogatory Norman name of a type coined only when French was a living language in England. Partly because of its alien origin, few other mediaeval surnames can be confused with it, even when both are misspelt. Paradoxically, whereas possessors of unflattering English surnames generally managed to lose them in a generation or two, many of the French ones endured, probably because their bearers soon ceased to understand them.[13] A few instances of *de Malory* indeed suggest that this happened to the Malorys. No mediaeval Malory achieved the sort of eminence that would make people wish to pretend kinship with him (although a number of them came near it), so, once it was no longer fashionable to coin unflattering French names, inheritance was the only reason for anyone to be called Malory.

If Sir Thomas Malory of Newbold Revel had wanted to trace his ancestry, it is not unlikely that he might have been able to name names about as far back as Aschetil. Although, as a cadet branch of a family with senior branches still flourishing, the Malorys of Newbold Revel probably possessed few original family documents from the years before their branch of the family began, Sir Thomas and previous heads of his branch must in their own interest have kept as much information about their origins and land holdings as they could. However, even if he had had originals or copies of every document ever issued for every parcel of land and office his family had ever held, his only information about the period before Aschetil is likely to have come from that uncertain medium, oral tradition. Before Henry II's administrative reforms, records seem to have been fewer and certainly give fewer precise dates and unambiguous names than those of later times. Time and again, modern scholars find that even very good sets of records effectively end about 1166. The fact that the Malorys can be traced two generations further back is due largely to two exceptional factors, a relationship, of which we will see more in a moment, with the great magnate family of the Earls of Leicester, and the fact that, at a time when surnames were not well established at any social level, the Norman sense of humour had firmly imposed a particularly distinctive one on them.

If Sir Thomas had tried to take the story of his family back beyond

---

12 Sheila Mallory Smith, *A History of the Mallory Family* (Chichester 1985).
13 See P.H. Reaney, *The Origin of English Surnames* (London 1967) pp. 256–66.

Aschetil, 'grete clerkes' learned in history might well have told him that one of his ancestors had fought for William the Conqueror at the Battle of Hastings. Copies of the alleged 'Roll of Battle Abbey' purporting to record the names of those who fought at Hastings were widely available at the time, and half the copies of the roll now extant include the name *Malory*. The roll in all its versions is spurious, but distinguished historians believed in it as late as the nineteenth century,[14] and Sir Thomas would have had no way of knowing better.

However, although the alleged roll is a fraud, the conclusion that he would naturally have drawn from it might well be true. In 1204/8, a certain Anquetin Mallore held a fief in Tessancourt in the Vexin of Philip Augustus of France.[15] In the Conqueror's time, the Vexin was ruled by Roger 'de Beaumont' Count of Meulan, and conspicuous among the thirty or so of Duke William's supporters for whose presence at Hastings there is solid historical evidence is Roger's son Robert, later himself Count of Meulan and first Earl of Leicester. In 1118, Earl Robert was succeeded as Earl of Leicester by his second son Robert,[16] and the document that records Robert son of Aschetil Malory is a charter he witnessed with members of the second earl's household. It implies that he is an undertenant of the earl,[17] and he may well have been a member of his household. Another member of the second earl's *curia* was a Richard Malory, perhaps the earl's chamberlain, and Richard's younger brother Anschetil was a member of the household of the earl's son Robert, who succeeded his father as third earl in 1168, and who made Anschetil his seneschal.[18] Given the naming customs of the time, it would be odd if this Anschetil Malory were not the son of Robert son of Aschetil Malory. If we add that Tessancourt stands in much the same geographical relationship to Meulan as Kirkby Mallory in

14 See D.C. Douglas, 'Companions of the Conqueror', *History* 28 (1943) 129–47; and for the roll itself, see J. Hunter, *Sussex Archaeological Collections* 6 (1853) 10; Catherine Powlett Duchess of Cleveland, *The Battle Abbey Roll*, 3 vols (London 1889); John Brompton, *Chronicon* in *Historiae Anglicanae scriptores decem*, ed. R. Twysden (London 1652) at col. 963; William of Worcester, 'Anecdota' in *Liber niger de scaccarii*, ed. T. Hearne, 2 vols (London 1771) at ii 522–4; John Leland, *De rebus Britannicis collectanea*, ed. T. Hearne, 6 vols (London 1774) i 206–9; John Foxe, *Actes and Monuments*, ed. Josiah Pratt, 8 vols (London 1877) ii 136–8; Richard Grafton, *A Chronicle at Large*, 2 vols (London 1568–9) ii 5; Raphael Holinshed, *Chronicles*, 2 vols (London 1577) ii 293–7; John Stow, *The Annales or Generall Chronicle* (London 1615) pp. 103–8; Edouard [Drigon, comte] de Magny, *Nobiliare de Normandie*, 2 vols (Paris 1863–4) i 2–6.
15 *Recueil des historiens des Gaules et de la France* 23 (1876) 713c. *Mallore* is probably the commonest single spelling of the family name in the Middle Ages. For the same man witnessing an Avranches deed of about the same date see R. Fawtier, *Handlist of Charters in the John Rylands Library*, 3 vols (Manchester 1925–37) i 59.
16 See David Crouch, *The Beaumont Twins* (Cambridge 1986).
17 L.C. Loyd, *The Origin of Some Anglo-Norman Families*, Harleian Soc. Pubs 103 (1951) 56.
18 Crouch, pp. 142, 157 & n, 175.

Leicestershire to Leicester, and that Kirkby Mallory, which the Malorys held of the Honour of Leicester, seems to have been the principal Malory manor from at least this time until it was sold to Leicester Abbey in the late fourteenth century,[19] it is not surprising that historians have been inclined to suppose that the Malorys originated in Tessancourt.[20]

All this does not prove that the Malorys had an ancestor with Duke William at Hastings. Although Robert de Beaumont was certainly at Hastings, and Count Roger no doubt sent every able-bodied man he could spare from the Vexin with him, some must have been left at home, and after the historic battle, with a sizeable kingdom to hold down, the victorious Normans in England were in no position to reject volunteers who had not fought with them at Hastings. The most we can say is that Sir Thomas Malory of Newbold Revel is very much more likely to have had an ancestor at Hastings than most of those whose names have been bandied about in that connection in the Middle Ages and later. That ancestor, however, might not have been called Malory: the exceptional bad luck, whatever it was, that gave the family its name may have come later.

When Sir Thomas looked back over his ancestry, he will have seen, probably from the eleventh or twelfth century, certainly from the time when his own branch of the family established its identity in the early thirteenth, a succession of knights holding land in the English midlands. He no doubt thought of his ancestors as he thought of the knights who followed King Arthur to the Roman War, as 'oure noble knyghts of mery Ingelonde',[21] although he will have had less evidence for their following their lords to war, whether with the king or against him, than for the material stake they had in merry England through their lands. Whatever else his muniments recorded, they will have shown land being bought, acquired by marriage, inherited, and disposed of to support younger sons or to provide dowries for daughters. Sir Thomas would certainly have been able to trace his ancestors down from the first Simon Malory, who established their branch of the family at Swinford, to the second, who married Beatrice de Bockervile and established them at Winwick, and on to the third, who in 1329/30 had demonstrated that the enfeoffment by which his cousin at Litchborough held land of him was older than those by which the cousin held of his other lords, thereby establishing his right to the wardship of his cousin's heir.[22] No doubt Sir Thomas could done the same from the same documents in his own generation. He will have known something of Sir Peter Malory, Justice of the King's Bench, who in the

---

[19] Nichols, *Leicestershire*, iv 761–6.
[20] Loyd, loc. cit.; Crouch, p. 157n.
[21] *Works*, p. 209.10.
[22] For references for this and for what follows, see Appendix 1.

generation between Simon II and Simon III, at a time when much the best way to found an enormous landed estate was to become a judge,[23] had disappointingly left his family little more than a coat of arms, albeit a coat of arms they were very proud of.

He will also have known something of Simon III's son and successor, Sir Stephen Malory, lord of the manors of Draughton and Winwick, who flourished 1332–62. Sir Stephen seems to have been very little in the public eye: he is recorded mainly as a landowner, although as he grew more senior in county society he did occasionally find himself with a few minor public duties. Sir Thomas may have known a good deal more about his ancestor than we can, because Sir Stephen was just about within living memory in his time, but he will certainly have known that Sir Stephen married Margaret, daughter of John Revell of Newbold Revel, and that in the next generation, when the Revell family failed in the male line, that marriage brought the Malorys his own principal residence, Newbold Revel. He will have known of Sir Stephen, if in no other way, through the deed by which Stephen's father Simon granted Draughton to Stephen and Margaret at Winwick on 3 September 1332.[24] There can be little doubt this was immediately occasioned by Stephen and Margaret's marriage, and that Sir Thomas would have recognised it as such. It was a familiar technique with many advantages for the lord of two or more manors, when his son and heir married, to grant him and his wife and their future children what might be thought of as a junior manor. Not the least of the advantages was that without it the bride's father was unlikely to be willing to part with her or her dowry. Sir Thomas, as we shall see, may himself have benefitted from this custom when he married, and later followed it on the marriage of his son Robert.

Sir Thomas will naturally have known a good deal more about Sir Stephen's son and heir Sir John, who flourished 1362–93, which was well within living memory for his generation. Sir John apparently began by following in his father's footsteps as a country landowner with no involvement in local or national politics, although he made a drastic reorganisation of the family land-holdings, selling – in an age when the outright sale of such land was not common – the manor of Draughton, and in the same year, 1366–7, buying Sir Peter Malory of Litchborough's lands in that place for himself, Agnes his wife, and Nicholas their son. He remained, however, lord of the manors of Winwick and of Stormsworth in Leicestershire, and must at some time have come to anticipate that (as came to pass) he would inherit a third of the Revell estates in the right of his mother Margaret. When the estates were partitioned in 1383, his third was the manor of Newbold Revel itself and associated lands nearby.

23 See for instance Payling, pp. 31–41.
24 B.L. Add. Ch. 21753.

The inheritance seems to have transformed Sir John's life. He promptly moved from Northamptonshire to Warwickshire, since in 1386 he witnessed a deed as of Fenny Newbold (i.e. Newbold Revel).[25] A grander style of living is hinted at by a licence in 1384 for private oratories – something no member of his branch of the family is known to have had before.[26] He also about this time, perhaps partly because of his abilities but no doubt also because of the increase in consequence provided by his new inheritance, caught the government's eye in a way that no-one in his branch of the family except Sir Peter had ever done before. He was associated in military recruitment with the king's friend Robert de Vere Earl of Oxford in 1386, and was given a series of major appointments in local government: justice of the peace for Warwickshire and commissioner to enquire into the lands of the alien priory of Monks Kirby in 1389–90, Sheriff of Warwickshire and Leicestershire in 1391–2, and Sheriff of Northamptonshire in 1392–3.

In 1391–2, he made a new disposal of a part of his inheritance, settling Newbold Revel and its associated lands on himself and Alice his wife in tail.[27] In 1366/7, as we have seen, he had had a wife called Agnes and a son called Nicholas, who as a party to the deed was presumably adult at the time. Nicholas was probably born about 1345, and Sir John about 1325.[28] Given that Sir John did not dispose of his other lands (they descended to later Malorys of Newbold Revel) and that they were not included in the settlement, it looks as if, when he married Agnes, those lands were settled on her and their children, and one or more of those children still survived. Now, twenty-five years later, when he was nearing seventy, he was remarrying and settling his new inheritance on himself, his new wife, and, by the entail, the children of his new marriage. Unless Alice was past childbearing and the entail a mere lawyer's reflex, his surviving offspring must have trembled for their inheritance: there were spectacular cases in the period of fathers attempting, sometimes in outright defiance of the law, to disinherit the children of earlier marriages so as to endow favourites from later ones.

In the end, Sir John's hopes, if that is what they were, came to nothing. He is last recorded accounting as Sheriff of Northamptonshire in 1393: in August 1406 his successor in the family lands, John Malory, was party to a

---

25 For Fenny Newbold as Newbold Revel, cf. Chapter I above.

26 The parish church at Monks Kirby is a mile and half (two miles by modern road) from Newbold Revel, whereas the parish church at Winwick is just over the garden wall from the manor house, but the licence is for 'oratories' in the plural.

27 *Feet of Fines, Warwickshire*, ed. Ethel Stokes et al., vol. iii, Dugdale Soc. Pubs, 18 (1943) no. 2330.

28 As great-grandson of Sir Roger Malory, who was born 1250/51 (*Cal. I.P.M.*, v 131), Sir John can hardly have been born much before 1325.

Stretton-under-Fosse deed as *dominus de fennynewbold*.[29] There is no explicit contemporary evidence of the relationship between them: a particular misfortune after six generations with contemporary evidence of relationship between each head of the family and his successor. Since John inherited both parts of Sir John's lands and used the Revell coat of arms as his heraldic device,[30] he must, like Sir John, have been a descendant of Sir Stephen and Margaret. The most economical explanation would make him son of the Nicholas who was son of Sir John and Agnes in 1366/67. That would also help explain why the last male Malory of Newbold Revel was called Nicholas: Sir Thomas called his grandson after his grandfather, a tempting idea, since the Malorys of all branches liked giving their children established names. None of this, however, can rule out the possibility that John was the grandson of an unidentified younger brother of Sir John. He can not, however, be the child of Sir John and Alice: the son of a marriage contracted in 1391 could not be legally of age thirteen years later.

That thirteen-year gap in the records is worth setting against the records of the successive heads of the Malorys of Stormsworth, Draughton, Winwick, and Newbold Revel from the mid-thirteenth century onwards. There are 8 known contemporary records of Sir Richard Malory, dated from 1235 to 1264, 22 of Simon II his son (1264–77), 16 of Sir Roger his son (1279–1311), 26 of Simon III his son (1312–34), 18 of Sir Stephen his son (1332–62), and 23 of Sir John his son (1362–93). The longest gap between successive sets of records is two years: the thirteen-year silence between Sir John and John, followed by 50 records of John over the period 1406–34, suggests very strongly that John's father, whether Nicholas or another, died in Sir John's lifetime, that John inherited as a minor, and that the beginning in 1406 of the series of records that name him marks his coming-of-age. If that is so, he will have been born in 1385, and inherited when he was about eight.

For the English gentry in the late Middle Ages, a minority could be a disaster: the law did little to prevent the wardships of minors being exploited like other financial resources, and the longer the wardship the worse the effects were likely to be. The heir's family could of course themselves bid against other interested parties, but their bid might itself strain the family finances for years. Since John apparently held the manor of Winwick of Coventry Priory by an enfeoffment older than that by which he held any other manor,[31] the prior was presumably his guardian in the first

---

29 Warwick C.R.O. D19/730. A transcript of the proper names from this at the Society of Genealogists is misdated 4 August 1401: London, Soc. of Genealogists, Tweedale Annexe, Warwickshire file, under Monks Kirby.

30 For heraldry, see Chapter X.

31 P.R.O. E164/21 (account book of William Haloghton, Pittancer of Coventry Priory) fol. 48ᵛ–49. For the Malorys' tenure of Newbold Revel, see Appendix III below.

instance, and he would normally have disposed of John's wardship and his marriage (unless John was already married at eight) to anyone who was prepared to offer more than the prior could expect to make directly. A marriage during his minority is more likely than not, and if it was to the only wife of his that we know of, it was certainly a marriage as the law required, 'without disparagement'. Whether they got on in ways of which the law took less account is harder to tell. We know even less about who actually undertook John's guardianship or how he exercised his trust: we can only say that the records of John's adult life do not suggest that his minority left him in financial straits.

The 1406 deed also suggests that John had escaped dangers that could be even more serious than those of a minority, the dangers of dower and jointure. A widow was entitled to a third of her husband's estate in dower, but it was not uncommon for husbands to settle larger parts, even the whole, of their estates jointly on themselves and their wives in survivorship, and since widowers were regrettably frequently (from their heirs' point of view) inclined to marry much younger women, the heirs to rich estates could find themselves living in poverty for years, even for generations. Warwickshire husbands have been thought to be particularly indulgent in this respect.[32] In the next generation, Sir Thomas was to see and perhaps suffer from a spectacular example of this among his Chetwynd cousins, but in the present case John Malory escaped lightly. Since the deed calls him lord of Fenny Newbold, he must have been in possession of this part of the family's lands in 1406, which he would not have been had either Alice or any child of hers by Sir John survived.

This John Malory is the ancestor Sir Thomas will have known best of all: his father. Once again there is no explicit contemporary evidence of relationship, but that Thomas was John's son is established by Thomas's inheritance of the family estates when, as will appear later, John's daughters were still alive.

John, like Sir John, had an importance in local and national affairs that must have been the product partly of his personality, but no doubt also partly of his social importance, an importance that might not have reached critical mass without the Newbold Revel estate. That importance is clearly implied by the surviving record evidence. In September 1406 (as John Malory of Newbold, to distinguish him from his namesake at Welton in Northamptonshire), he was a feoffee for a man from Yelvertoft in that county.[33] In 1407, he witnessed a grant by William Mountford of Coleshill

---

[32] See Payling, pp. 54–62, esp. p. 57.

[33] *Ancient Deeds*, iii 262. The deed is dated Wednesday before Holy Cross 7 Hen. IV: 8 Sept. if Holy Cross is the Exaltation, 28 Apr. if it is the Invention, which would make this the first record of John Malory of Newbold Revel.

of rights in the manor Bedworth, Warwickshire.[34] In 1410/11, he held the manor of and land in Winwick of Coventry Priory.[35] In August 1411, with Simon Malory his brother, he sued the parson of Withybrook, Warwickshire, for debt.[36] In 1412, he was assessed as having lands worth over £20 annually in Winwick, and other lands of unspecified value in Warwickshire.[37] In November 1412, he, Richard Chetwynd, John Chetwynd, and William Purefoy bound themselves to agree to a settlement to be reached later that month by arbitrators in a dispute between them.[38] Since Richard and John Chetwynd were the surviving sons and John Malory and William Purefoy the sons-in-law of Aline, widow of Sir William Chetwynd (d. 1396) of Ingestre, Staffordshire, and Aline is known to have died about this time, the dispute is most likely to have been over the partition of her lands.[39] In the years 1412–14, a dispute between Richard and John Chetwynd and John Malory and William Purefoy on the one hand and James Pulteney is alleged to have led to an assault on Pulteney at his home at Misterton in Leicestershire.[40]

In April 1413, John was elected M.P. for Warwickshire.[41] On 12 and 22 August 1413 and 10 February 1414, he witnessed three more Bedworth deeds, the third at Ruthin Castle in North Wales; and in July 1414 as lord of Winwick, and in 1415 as John Malory gentleman of Newbold Revel, he acquired land in Draughton.[42] In 1416–17, he was Sheriff of Warwickshire and Leicestershire.[43] In January 1417, he and Simon his brother witnessed a Swinford and Yelvertoft deed, and in April 1417, he witnessed a Baginton, Warwickshire, deed.[44] In the Hilary Term of 1418, the Court of King's Bench ordered him to be arrested for something he had done or failed to do as Sheriff of Leicestershire, but his successor failed to produce him, despite which in May 1418 he was appointed a commissioner of array for

---

34 P.R.O. E326/10765.
35 P.R.O. E164/21, fol. 48ᵛ–49.
36 *C.C.R.* (1409–13) p. 236.
37 *Feudal Aids*, vi 493.
38 *Ancient Deeds*, ii 117. Dr Carpenter takes this agreement as a sign of social cohesiveness: Christine Carpenter, *Locality and Polity* (Cambridge 1992) p. 312n. It seems more likely to imply the opposite.
39 H.E. Chetwynd-Stapylton, *The Chetwynds of Ingestre* (London 1892) pp. 65–8, 87–95, and passim. Chetwynd-Stapylton puts Aline's death-date at 1411/18, but if my inference is right, it should of course be 1411/12.
40 Carpenter, *Locality*, p. 365.
41 *Return of Members*.
42 P.R.O. E326/10788, E327/214, and E326/9045 (cf. *V.C.H., Warwicks.*, vi 28 and Carpenter, 'Warwickshire', Appx p. 68); B.L. Add. Ch. 21823, 21820–1.
43 *List of Sheriffs*, P.R.O. Lists and Indexes 9, *s.v.*
44 *Ancient Deeds*, iv 264; Stratford-upon-Avon, Shakespeare's Birthplace Trust, MS. ER1/65/466.

Warwickshire.[45] At an unspecified time in 1419, he, as John Malory of Newbold Revel esquire, with John Malory of Walton and two priests, conveyed two parts of the manor of Saddington, Leicestershire, to William Malory and Margaret his wife; and on 4 January 1419, as John Malory of Newbold Revel esquire, he and the two priests quitclaimed Saddington to William Malory.[46] In June 1419, he witnessed a Lapworth, Warwickshire, deed.[47]

In October 1419, he was elected M.P. for Warwickshire again, which led to a commission in November and in January 1420 to raise a loan for the king in the county.[48] Having been named as one of the thirteen knights and esquires in his county most able to defend the realm in the king's absence, he was summoned to discuss this with the king's council in February 1420.[49] On 12 and 14 August 1420, he witnessed two Wolfhampcote charters for Sir William Peyto of Chesterton.[50] In April 1421, he was elected M.P. for Warwickshire for a third time, in May he witnessed another deed concerned with an Astley manor (Alcott Hall) and in December a deed for William Lord Astley's widow: in February 1422 he was appointed a justice of the peace for Warwickshire; he was reappointed to every commission until he died.[51] As John Malory of Winwick esquire, he granted out two properties in Draughton on 1 September 1422, and one in Monks Kirby on the following day.[52] In August 1423, he and Simon his brother witnessed a Little Lawford, Warwickshire, deed; in October of that year, he was elected M.P. for Warwickshire for a fourth time; and in November, he, John Chetwynd, and others were sued by members of the Alspath family over land in Alspath, Warwickshire.[53] He was escheator for Warwickshire and Leicestershire in 1423–4 and sheriff of those counties again in 1424–6.[54] In

---

[45] P.R.O. KB 27/627/Rex rot. 18; *C.P.R.* (1416–22) p. 198. The commission is addressed to – Malory and six others, but John Malory of Newbold Revel, a recent ex-sheriff, is much the most likely candidate.

[46] Nichols, *Leicestershire*, iii 497–8 (giving both John Malorys' surnames as *Mowbray*); Leicestershire C.R.O. MS. DE 2242/6/63. The absence of John Malory of Walton from the second document suggests Nichols may have erred in dating the first, perhaps turning a regnal year carelessly into a year of grace.

[47] *Ancient Deeds*, iv 313.

[48] *Return of Members*, *C.P.R.* (1416–22) p. 461, *C.F.R.* (1413–22) p. 318.

[49] Dugdale, *Warwickshire*, p. 83.

[50] Warwick C.R.O., Wolfhampcote deeds of title, L.4/32–4.

[51] *Return of Members*; P.R.O. E326/6831; Warwick C.R.O., CR 136/C149; *C.P.R.* (1416–22) p. 461 and passim. I am obliged to Mr Christopher Jeens of the Warwickshire Record Office for details of CR 136/C149.

[52] B.L. Add. Ch. 21832, 28647; Martin, p. 173.

[53] Warwick C.R.O., MS. CR 162/123; *Return of Members*; *The Genealogist*, n.s. 17 (1900–1) 19–20, from P.R.O. CP40/651/494.

[54] *List of Sheriffs*; *List of Escheators*, P.R.O. Lists and Indexes 72, s.vv. For a commission to him as sheriff of Leics. in February 1426, see J.E. Stocks, *Market Harborough Parish Records*, 2 vols (London 1890–1926) i 87.

February 1425, as lord of Winwick he witnessed a Watford, Northampton-shire, charter for George Burneby, lord of that place.[55] As some time before September 1425, he and Simon were involved in a two-stage transaction over lands in Coleshill and Marston Green.[56] On 16 January 1427, he witnessed a Withybrook deed, and in 22 January he and Simon witnessed a Swinford and Yelvertoft deed for the same parties as the deed they had witnessed in 1417.[57]

In September 1427, he was elected M.P. for Warwickshire for the fifth and last time, despite an attempt to rig the election against him.[58] In 1431, he and Simon were put on the panel for a jury to try Joan Lady Bergavenny on a charge of conspiring to assault and wound a number of men from Fillongley and Birmingham, though they did not in the event serve on the jury itself.[59] In October 1433, he was re-appointed a justice of the peace for the last time; in November, he, William Purefoy, and others witnessed a grant of the manor of Newnham Paddox; and on 4 December he granted out rents in Cosford.[60] This is the last record of him as alive: he was dead presumably by 16 February 1434, when he was replaced as a justice of the peace, and certainly by 8 June 1434, when his wife Philippa was recorded as his widow.[61]

These then are the surviving documents recording John Malory of Newbold Revel. There is one non-documentary witness, but before turning to it we should consider what the written records imply.

John was plainly known from early in his adult life as energetic, efficient, and fair: given his relatively modest estates, only a reputation of that kind with the king's government and the community of the county can explain his many commissions and other offices. The charters he witnessed suggest that his neighbours felt the same way. We may suspect a relish for work and a sense of responsibility in the fact that after being M.P., sheriff, and J.P. he was willing to take on the humbler post of escheator, before another turn-and-a-bit as sheriff. Something similar may underlie the habit of hearing mass before dawn. A certain practicality might explain why he, unlike his two predecessors as heads of the Newbold Revel branch, resisted the glamour of knighthood.

55 P.R.O. E41/100.
56 Birmingham Reference Library, MS Wingfield Digby A485. I am obliged to Patricia Coleman of the Birmingham Central Library for details of this deed.
57 Stratford-upon-Avon, Shakespeare's Birthplace Trust, MS. ER1/68/628; *Ancient Deeds*, v 94.
58 *Return of Members*; Carpenter, 'Warwickshire', p. 115.
59 *Rot. Parl.*, iv 410–13.
60 C.P.R. (1429–36) p. 626; Bodl. MS. Dugd. 13, p. 343; P.R.O. Wards/2/1/3/2.
61 C.P.R., loc. cit; C.C.R. (1429–35) p. 314. John Malory's death may well have been the main reason for the new commission of the peace: cf. Payling, p. 168.

It may, however, be possible to go well beyond this. A recent study by Dr Christine Carpenter, first as a doctoral thesis and then as a book, has added greatly to knowledge of Warwickshire society in the fifteenth century.[62] Dr Carpenter brought together an enormous range of material, examined it minutely and with great learning, and gave it (where the material allowed) competent statistical analysis. The heart of her study is a comprehensive political history of the Warwickshire gentry, which, since fifteenth-century English political life was generally strikingly un-ideological, means the history of the competition for power, through patronage, administrative office, and land, each as a means to the others. In fifteenth-century England, as Dr Carpenter observes, power was to be found above all in those transient non-exclusive magnate affinities that as a system have come to be called 'bastard feudalism': there was no other form for such power to take.[63] Her history is therefore a story of the rivalry of magnate affinities for the control of the county, and of the efforts of each magnate to control his affinity. It is plain both that insofar as fifteenth-century Warwickshire has a political history, these are the two most important factors in it, and also that they could only be elucidated by an approach like Dr Carpenter's and by someone with her abilities: both the aims and membership of affinities can be very elusive.

This is partly a consequence of their nature. To be effective, affinities had to contain members with a spread of commitment, from the feudal tenant retained exclusively for life and the household servant on the one hand to the mere 'well-willer' on the other. This was part of Sir Thomas Malory's mental world: describing a murderous ambush Mordred sets for Lancelot, Malory adds to his source that all Mordred's men are his elder brother Gawayne's fellow-countrymen, kinsmen, or 'well-wyllars'.[64] The commitment of real-life 'well-willers' must have varied in nature, intensity, and duration: not all will have been prepared to commit murder. Moreover, although lords naturally wanted exclusive commitment, clients equally naturally wanted more benefits than one lord could provide. Some well-placed gentry – lawyers were particularly successful at this – were able to get magnates to accept them as formal members of rival affinities, and many mere 'well-willers' must have dangled their good will under the nose of any lord whose attention they could attract. It must often have been difficult at the time to be sure who, among the less formally committed, belonged to which affinity. Five hundred years on, it will be still more difficult, since documents recording formal commitment have often perished, and good will is unlikely ever to have been recorded at all.

---

[62] Carpenter, 'Warwickshire', in 1976; *Locality* in 1992. The latter does not entirely supersede the former.

[63] 'Warwickshire', pp. 66–7.

[64] *Works*, p. 1164.17.

A full history must attempt to detect 'well-willers', but that can only be done by indirect evidence, particularly by unambiguous evidence of association in actions of the affinity. Unfortunately the lives of fourteenth- and fifteenth-century gentry are so sparsely recorded that (as we have seen) it can be hard to be sure who is referred to in a document and harder to divine its purpose. Dr Carpenter has done wonders in accumulating and interpeting material, but sometimes, and particularly in her thesis, she is too ready to assume that actions by members of the gentry are political and that political activity is that of a magnate affinity. The problem is particularly acute in the early fifteenth century, before the civil war that gave men stronger reasons for seeking protection from a lord's affinity. Given that even in that century, when we so rarely know anyone's thoughts, there is some evidence of a kind of gentry class-consciousness, of a reluctance in principle to commit oneself to any kind of overlordship beyond the minimum,[65] there is a possibility that some of the gentry, if they were skilful and lucky, may have succeeded in politics precisely by avoiding commitment to any lord sufficiently deep and lasting to count as membership of an affinity.

In the fifteenth century, Warwickshire affinities were created out of a rural society of a dozen peerage families and 120 gentry families, the latter's income varying a great deal but well below that of all but one of the peers.[66] Within that society, one peer, Richard Beauchamp Earl of Warwick (d.1439), stands out because he was much richer than any other peer primarily based in Warwickshire, because his family had been established in the county for generations and much of his income came from Warwickshire land, because he maintained generally good relations with the king's government, and because of his competent management of an affinity proportionate to his wealth. Even that affinity, however, manifestly could not control the county without alliances with other peers and their affinities, sometimes by incorporating them into the affinity, sometimes by more temporary alliances to share the spoils.

For all that, the Warwickshire gentry may have been less difficult to manage than those of some other counties. Only half-a-dozen families, including the Mountfords and the Peytos, were wealthy, well-endowed with Warwickshire land, and primarily committed to that county.[67] Whether because of the distractions of properties in other counties or for other reasons, those families did not dominate major political office in the

65 K.B. McFarlane, *England in the Fifteenth Century*, ed. G.L. Harriss (London 1981) p. 256n. Cf. Susan Wright, *The Derbyshire Gentry in the Fifteenth Century* (Chesterfield 1983) for the temporary and limited nature of all but the closest commitments between members of the gentry there.

66 Carpenter, 'Warwickshire', pp. 5–37.

67 Ibid., p. 26.

county as their counterparts did, for instance, in Nottinghamshire.[68] Major offices went to a very wide range of families, but one small group of men, not (except for Mountford) outstandingly rich, had far more than its share. One of them was John Malory of Newbold Revel.

In her thesis, Dr Carpenter argued that all these men were members of the Beauchamp affinity, but that John Malory in particular owed his success in Warwickshire politics to being a member of two affinities, Beauchamp's and that of the Duke of Norfolk, a powerful land-owner in the area round Newbold Revel.[69] There is little evidence, however, for his membership of either affinity,[70] and her book effectively drops both claims. Instead, she argues, largely from his involvement with Bedworth, which belonged to William Lord Astley of Astley, that at the beginning of his career John Malory was a member of a group of gentry from the north and east of Warwickshire that revolved around Lord Astley and lapsed when he died (c.1417): she does not say that he was a member of Astley's affinity.[71] This cautious formulation is very persuasive. She thinks he probably then moved, perhaps through the mediation of Lord Clinton, another member of Astley's circle, to Warwick, although his connection with Warwick may (also) have been 'informal'.[72] In support of such a connection, she rightly stresses that he must have had powerful political support of some kind to have been elected so often as an M.P. Nevertheless, it is unfortunate that in the only event of his life that is both clearly political and reasonably fully recorded, the disputed election of 1427, her own account shows Malory apparently supported by a faction opposed to Beauchamp and certainly strenuously (and unsuccessfully) opposed by the earl's affinity, who tried to substitute the name of one of their own number, Sir William Peyto.[73] This does not invalidate her hypothesis that Malory

[68] See Payling, pp. 109–10.

[69] Carpenter, 'Warwickshire', p. 52.

[70] John does not appear in her list of members of Beauchamp's affinity: ibid., Appendix, p. 102. No Malory appears in the lists of Mowbray affinities in Rowena Archer, 'The Mowbrays, Earls of Nottingham and Dukes of Norfolk, to 1432', D.Phil. thesis (Oxford 1984) pp. 336–54. In Dr Carpenter's list of the affinity of the relevant Duke of Norfolk (Appendix, pp. 108, 114), her major piece of evidence is that John witnessed a grant involving other men of Norfolk's affinity. None of the other men named in the deed appears in her lists of that affinity, but even if they had been its leading members, Malory could have witnessed for reasons other than being one of them: because of his reputation in the county, presumably then at its height, or because, a peasant or two aside, he was the new owner's next-door-neighbour. Given the mediaeval gentry's liking for rounding off their estates, a prudent purchaser would want his neighbour as a witness so that if he had designs on the property the others present could swear he had taken part in the transaction without objection: to have refused an invitation to do so might have been deemed a hostile act.

[71] Carpenter, Locality, p. 314, relying particularly on Warwick C.R.O., CR 136/C149.

[72] Ibid., pp. 361, 319n.

[73] Ibid., pp. 385–7.

had connections of some kind with Beauchamp: it is entirely plausible that the faction opposing Beauchamp might have put up a man generally respected and personally acceptable to him, in order to demonstrate some independence without provoking a state of war.

The electors who supported Malory came largely from east Warwickshire, where he lived and where Beauchamp's power was at its weakest, and between them had connections not only with Lord Grey of Ruthin, who had succeeded to Astley's estates, but with Lady Bergavenny and Norfolk. Whether he or they were egged on by one or more of those magnates or others or none is unknown, a circumstance not uncommon in fifteenth-century history.

The other surviving witness to John Malory's life, apart from the record evidence, is an engraved copy in Dugdale's seventeenth-century *Antiquities of Warwickshire* of a lost stained glass window in the church at Grendon in Warwickshire, portraying John and his wife Philippa.[74] Since the original is the only known visual image of any mediaeval Malory made during life, its loss would be a singular misfortune if it conveyed anything of the psychological individuality of its subjects. Dugdale's engraving however shows that the picture's purpose was not psychological, and that what it aimed to do is likely to have been done equally well by a copy, particularly a copy made under the auspices of England's senior herald, Garter King-at-Arms. The picture was one of a set representing the family of John Malory's mother-in-law, Aline Lady Chetwynd. The Chetwynds were a knightly family from Shropshire and Staffordshire with a pedigree nearly as old as the Malorys',[75] and it was their descent that made it possible for Sir Thomas to see himself, like his characters, as 'of jantill strene of fadir syde and of modir syde.' Sir William's mother had been a Grendon of Grendon, and the Chetwynds had spent much of the fourteenth century trying to gain possession of Grendon, finally succeeding in 1393. Aline had a life interest in the manor, and presumably commissioned the windows in the church.

The pictures celebrate with elaborate symmetry the place of Aline, her two sons and their wives, her two daughters and their husbands, and two past rectors of Grendon, Master John Abingdon and John Pulford, in the spiritual and secular worlds. The lay people are portrayed in the body of the church, the two priests in the chancel. Those in the north windows look right, those in the south windows left, so that all face the altar. All kneel,

---

74 Dugdale, *Warwickshire*, p. 1105.

75 Chetwynd-Stapylton, pp. 65–8 and passim. This chronically careless book contains important material not in the more reliable 'Chetwynd Chartulary', ed. G. Wrottesley, *William Salt Archaeol. Soc. Trans.* o.s. 12 (1891), and here pp. 243–336, esp. 257–60, 298–310.

their hands joined or held up in prayer. The women wear identical hats and long cloaks, the laymen identical full plate armour with swords and spurs, but (since they are in church) no helmets or gauntlets. Three of the pictures as Dugdale gives them invite the viewer's prayers: presumably all once did so. The married couples are carefully balanced: a son and his wife in front, a daughter and her husband behind in the north windows, the same in the south. Although each couple is identified by the husband's coat of arms on his back and breast plates and on his wife's cloak, the patterning of the set implies that this element of individuality is far less important than what they share as gentlemen and gentlewomen in this world, and as souls before God in the next.

The couple in the north window nearest the altar bear the arms of Chetwynd quartered with Grendon. The man is presumably Richard Chetwynd of Ingestre (d.1417), who as Sir William's eldest surviving son was the head of the family, and who also had rights in Grendon.[76] His wife Thomasina (née Frodsham) kneels behind him. The Frodsham arms were displayed elsewhere in the church, but have no place in this picture. In the next north window, and therefore notionally behind Thomasina comes John Malory, and behind him his wife Philippa (Chetwynd), both in the arms of Revell of Newbold Revel. They are distinguished from the other couples in two ways, one of which may record a real-life difference: John has a beard, whereas all the other men, both lay and clerical, are clean-shaven. The other is almost certainly an accident: beneath the picture is the legend, 'Orate pro Iohannem Malorey et Philippa uxore eius.' Similar legends no doubt originally identified the other lay people, although they had disappeared by Dugdale's time. The legends under the pictures of the priests, which survive almost complete, are quite different, asking, with death-dates, for prayers for their subjects' souls. The different formulas and the absence of any picture of Sir William Chetwynd or those of his children who had died suggest that the lay men and women pictured were all alive when the pictures were made.[77] Since the second rector died in 1407, and Aline herself, we have seen, was apparently dead by 1412, that will have been in the years 1407–12. It is easiest to understand why the priests pictured were John Abingdon and John Pulford if the work was at an advanced stage when the latter died.

The couple in the south window nearest the altar, in the arms of Chetwynd without quarterings, will be Richard Chetwynd's younger

---

[76] He had presented John Pulford to the living in 1404: Dugdale, p. 1104.

[77] Sir William's eldest son Roger died *s.p.* in 1397, and a daughter, Christian name unknown, may have married a Mountford: cf. Chetwynd-Stapylton, pp. 81–7 and the shield in Dugdale p. 1105 showing (apparently) the arms of Mountford impaling Chetwynd between similar shields showing Malory impaling Chetwynd and Chetwynd impaling Shirford (for Purefoy).

brother John Chetwynd of Alspath and his wife. Who she was is unknown.[78] Behind them in the next window, in the arms of Shirford quartering Purefoy, are William Purefoy of Shirford in Warwickshire and his wife Margaret (Chetwynd).[79] The symmetry suggests that Margaret was younger than Philippa. Aline herself was pictured in another north window, in a cloak in the arms of Chetwynd without quarterings.

After this view of Sir Thomas's mother's family, we must turn at last to him.

---

78 Given the inconsistency of husband's side and wife's side in the impalements in the previous note, there must a possibility that this John's wife was a Mountford. Dr Carpenter identifies her as Rose daughter and heir of Roger Wasteness esquire of Staffordshire; but the husband of Rose Wasteness was John Chetwynd of Tixall, Staffs, who died in 1433/4, whereas John Chetwynd of Alspath survived until at least 1448 (Carpenter, 'Warwickshire', Appx p. 119; P.R.O., Prob. 11/3, fol. 142; Chetwynd-Stapylton, pp. 114–15). Rose, who was pensioned in 1429 for good service to the infant king Henry VI, remarried by 1437 John Marston, later a knight, treasurer of the king's chamber and keeper of his jewels; she was one of the *damicelle* of Queen Margaret in 1452–3, survived Sir John, and in her widowhood in 1469 sold the reversion of Tixall to the judge Thomas Lyttelton: *C.P.R.* (1422–9) p. 525, *C.P.R.* (1436–41) p. 48; A.R. Myers, 'The Household of Queen Margaret of Anjou', *B.J.R.L* 40 (1957–8) at p. 405; Wedgwood, *s.n.* William Merston; *Chetwynd Chartulary*, passim; Sir Thomas and Arthur Clifford, *Topographical and Historical Description of Tixall* (Paris 1917) pp. 2–9; B. Wolffe, *Henry VI*, pp. 36, 45 and n.

79 Chetwynd-Stapylton, loc. cit.; cf. Dugdale, p. 54.

IV

Birth

Having looked at the antecedents of Sir Thomas Malory of Newbold Revel, we must now turn to his life. It will be best to begin by outlining the accepted view, which is based on an essay published by G.L. Kittredge in 1894, which in turn was based on Dugdale's *Antiquities of Warwickshire*.[1] Malory, said Dugdale, served as an esquire in the retinue of Richard Beauchamp Earl of Warwick at the siege of Calais in Henry V's time. He was next recorded, still as an esquire, in 1439, witnessing a land settlement made by his cousin Sir Philip Chetwynd.[2] In the 1440s he behaved like a respectable member of the country gentry, acquiring land and a knighthood, taking part in local politics, serving in parliament for Warwickshire, and towards the end of the decade, begetting a son. At the beginning of the 1450s, however, he suddenly began a spectacular career of crime that led the Lancastrian government to keep him in prison for the rest of the decade. However, he had connections with the then Earl of Warwick and other Yorkists, and the Yorkist seizure of power in 1461 saw him free again. The early 1460s apparently marked a return to respectability, made eventful only by going north with King Edward and Warwick in the winter of 1462 to beseige three Lancastrian-held castles in Northumberland. At the end of the decade, however, when Warwick became estranged from the king, Malory was excepted from Edward's general pardons. While in prison at this time, presumably because of whatever had caused his exclusion from pardon, he completed the *Morte Darthur*. He died on 14 March 1471.

This reconstruction of events is open to challenge at a number of points, but in recent years Kittredge's opponents have made much of one in particular. Oddly enough, there was material in Dugdale's book to have solved the problem, but narrowness of focus prevented Kittredge or any of

---

[1] Sir William Dugdale, *The History and Antiquities of Warwickshire* (London 1656) p. 56. The entry in the edition revised by William Thomas (London 1730) p. 83 is identical. Compare, for instance, the brief account of Malory's life in W.R.J. Barron's excellent *English Medieval Romance* (London 1987) pp. 147–8.

[2] *C.C.R.* (1435–41) 268.

his successors from doing so, which perpetuated a legend about Malory for nearly a century. Kittredge thought that the siege of Calais at which Malory served probably took place in 1415. The gap in the records until 1439 could be plausibly explained by Malory's having taken part in the wars in France under Richard Beauchamp, who died in 1439. A quarter of a century with Beauchamp, whose chivalrous exploits earned him the name of the mirror of chivalry, might even have caused Malory's interest in chivalric romances. Later biographers made a good deal of this connection, even to finding allusions to Beauchamp's life in the *Morte Darthur*.[3] However, if Malory was old enough to go to war in 1415 – say a minimum of sixteen – he would have been at least seventy in 1469/70. If he was in his early twenties in 1415, he would have been nearly eighty. Yet, as various scholars have said, the *Morte* does not read like a book written by an old man. Several authors of the time, notably Hardyng and Rous, wrote at great ages; but, as Kittredge's most persuasive opponent pointed out, they did not in their later years write books like the *Morte Darthur*:

> Fifty-five or so is a mature age to commit rape and to attempt assassination, but is by no means prohibitive. But seventy-five is no age at all to be writing *Le Morte Darthur* in prison. Nothing is impossible; but recalling the ages at which medieval authors normally sank into silence, recalling the vitality, energy, and even occasional gaiety of *Le Morte Darthur* and the long, persistent labor that it represents, one needs hardly to be skeptical to doubt that the work was written by an ancient of seventy-five.[4]

The partisans of the Newbold Revel Malory had one line of defence in arguing that some, perhaps much, of the *Morte* might have been written in the early 1450s rather than the late 1460s. They would have had a much stronger one if they had asked what evidence Dugdale had for thinking that the man who indentured with Richard Beauchamp in Henry V's time was Thomas Malory of Newbold Revel at all.

Dugdale took his information from a retinue roll of Beauchamp's, which still survives.[5] It is undated, but headed 'Ceste la retinue Monsieur le Counte de Warrewyk des gentz darmes et des archiers pour sa demeure a Caleys pur lenforcement de la ville et les Marches illoeques.' This shows that Dugdale went a little beyond his evidence. The 128 names listed are not of men who had already served in a siege, but of men who had agreed to serve in the future, presumably either to resist a siege or to raid French territory, as circumstances required. The roll must have been compiled

---

3 Fullest attempt in Lynn S. Martin, 'Sir Thomas Malory's Vocabulary', Ph.D. diss. (Pennsylvania 1966) pp. 5–22; criticised in Matthews, *The Ill-Framed Knight*, pp. 60–3.

4 Matthews, p. 73.

5 B.L., Cotton Roll xiii 7, m. 2.

between 3 February 1414, when Beauchamp was first appointed Captain of Calais, and 1420, when one of the men named in it died.[6] The document can almost certainly be dated more closely than that. The Great Council of 16 April 1415 settled terms for fighting the war with France that was then imminent, and shortly afterwards the reinforcements that Beauchamp would provide for Calais when the war broke out were specified in an indenture between Beauchamp and the king dated 19 June 1415.[7] The men listed in the roll will be that 'enforcement'. Beauchamp might have begun serious recruiting as soon as he was appointed, but it seems more likely that he would have waited until the terms of his indenture with the king were finally settled. One may therefore suppose that the retinue was re-cruited and the roll drawn up about midsummer 1415.[8]

A dozen of the other esquires in the roll were serving with Beauchamp two years later, when they were recorded on the muster roll for the great muster taken near Southampton.[9] Malory's name, however, does not occur on that muster roll, either in Beauchamp's retinue or anywhere else. It therefore adds little to the 1415 retinue roll. That roll tells us Malory's name and terms of service, and allows us to infer a little about his age, health, social status, and place of origin from his having undertaken to serve Beauchamp in war at that time as an esquire with a lance and two archers. For instance, since many of the names on the roll are Warwickshire ones, he is quite likely to have come from Warwickshire or a neighbouring county. Dugdale, however, went beyond probabilities and identified a particular Thomas Malory. Since his source did not make that identification, he pre-sumably made it as he had to make innumerable others in his book, by naming the least unsuitable man of the right name that he could think of when he wrote. Having no reason to take special note of Malorys, he overlooked the fact that his own book elsewhere recorded a second Thomas Malory, whose dates match up better with the 1415 campaign than do Sir Thomas of Newbold Revel's.[10] This second man appears much later in Dugdale's book, and he had presumably forgotten the earlier passage when he wrote the later one. The second man may not however have been the only other Thomas Malory in the midlands at this time, and we should plainly attempt to identify them all.

After the death of Sir Thomas Malory of Kirkby Mallory, Leicestershire, in 1317/20, no other Thomas Malory is known until a rash of records appears in the years 1373 to 1431. After this, there is a shorter gap until

---

6   J.H. Wylie and W.T. Waugh, *The Reign of King Henry the Fifth* (London 1914–29) i 39–40; Matthews, p. 72.
7   Wylie and Waugh, i 455, 466; Dugdale, *Baronage* (1675–76) i 244.
8   Dr Carpenter prefers 1414: Carpenter, *Polity*, p. 60n.
9   P.R.O. E101/51/2.
10 Dugdale, *Warwickshire* (1730) ii 1122.

1439, when Sir Thomas of Newbold Revel's attestation of a Chetwynd land settlement begins the records of the known mid and late fifteenth-century Thomas Malorys.[11] The records for the years 1373–1431 fall into the following groups:

1. Thomas, son of Sir Anketil Malory of Somerton, Lincolnshire (d.1393) and Alice Dryby his wife, Lady of Castle Bytham, Lincolnshire, is said in his father's inquisition post mortem, taken 6 May 1393, to have been his son and heir and to have been born between 6 May 1380 and 7 May 1381.[12] He is named as a beneficiary in his father's will, made 17 August 1390 and proved 16 April 1393.[13] He was a remainder-man to William his brother in a settlement of the manor of Papworth St Agnes, Cambridgeshire, licensed 12 October 1391.[14] He was a knight when he served from 4 September to 1 December 1400 in the defence of Roxburgh and the Scottish marches under Richard Lord Grey of Codnor, who had married his step-sister (Alice's daughter by a previous marriage).[15] On 6 and 21 May 1401, the property of Walter Prest of Melton Mowbray was committed to Thomas Malory knight.[16] On 9 May 1401, Thomas Malory knight was again mustered with Lord Grey's retinue to defend Roxburgh.[17] On 20 June 1401, Thomas Malory knight witnessed a deed at Countthorpe, Lincolnshire.[18] He may have died soon after this: on 10 May 1404, what had been his property in Melton Mowbray was held by Joan Malory, presumably a kinswoman.[19] The first firm evidence of his death, however, is his mother's inquisition post mortem, taken 17 November 1412, which names her heir as Elizabeth daughter of Thomas Malory knight.[20] His mother's will, made 14 April 1412, is oddly silent about him: it leaves a bequest to Elizabeth daughter of Thomas Malory knight, but does not even provide for prayers for his soul as it does for the souls of Alice's parents, for her three dead husbands by name, and for all the faithful departed.[21] However, although neither inquisition nor will specifies a relationship, Sir Thomas must have been

---

[11] These Thomas Malorys are discussed in Chapters I–II supra.

[12] P.R.O. C136/75/19 (here as sporadically elsewhere Sir Anketil is called Anthony). On the father, Sir Anketil III, see the previous chapter.

[13] *Early Lincoln Wills*, ed. A. Gibbons (Lincoln 1888) p. 57.

[14] *C.P.R.* (1388–92) p. 503.

[15] P.R.O. E101/42/40. For the Greys of Codnor see Simon Payling, *Political Society in Lancastrian England* (Oxford 1991) pp. 90–3, 106 and n. 101.

[16] Philip Hunt, *Notes on Medieval Melton Mowbray* (Grantham 1965) p. 77.

[17] P.R.O. E101/42/38.

[18] B.L. Cotton Charter xxvii 79.

[19] *C.F.R.* (1399–1405) p. 245; but cf. Hunt, p. 80 (two items).

[20] P.R.O. C137/90/15.

[21] *Early Lincoln Wills*, pp. 110–11.

Alice's son, since his daughter was Alice's heir while his brother William was still alive.[22]

2. Thomas Malory esquire is recorded in both the muster rolls that record Sir Thomas as serving with Lord Grey in the marches in 1400 and 1401. He was presumably the Thomas Malory esquire 'of Bytham' who served with the same Lord Grey in the garrison of Harfleur on 1 March 1418.[23] Grey, who was Captain of Argentan in Normandy, died on 1 August 1418, and was succeeded both in his peerage and at Argentan by John his son. Malory may not have followed the new Lord Grey – like most of the Harfleur esquires, he was not in Grey's retinue at Argentan on 2 May 1421.[24]

3. Thomas Malory esquire is recorded in Beauchamp's retinue roll in the summer of 1415, as above.

4. A second Thomas Malory esquire, without a distinguishing place-name, is listed in the Harfleur muster roll of 1418.

5. Thomas Malory (no rank) 'of Catthorpe', Leicestershire, was accused and acquitted in court of having broken into the houses of the Prior of Lenton at Lenton, Nottinghamshire, on 2 October 1391, and of having stolen a bond and £42.[25]

6. Thomas Malory (no rank) was commissioned by Robert Braybrooke, Bishop of London (d. 28 August 1404), and Sir Gerard Braybrooke to give seizin of property in Shackerstone, Leicestershire, to a purchaser in 1403 or 1404.[26]

7. Thomas (no rank) and Margaret Malory (daughter and heir of Sir Thomas Grendon and widow of one Charnells of Snarkeston) had the manor of Bramcote-juxta-Polesworth, Warwickshire, settled on them in Hilary Term 1407.[27] Thomas and Margaret Malory granted the manor to feoffees on 6 October 1411, and Thomas Malory of Bramcote was sued by

---

22 E.g. P.R.O. C138/19/24, dated 1416 and completing the process begun by the settlement of 1391.

23 P.R.O. E101/48/6.

24 Paris, Bibliothèque Nationale, MS f. fr. 25766, no. 800.

25 Farnham, *Notes*, vi 282.

26 *Bedfordshire Historical Record Soc.* 17 (1935) 172. The knight must be Sir Gerard Braybrooke IV of Colmbrook, Beds., after the death, on 1 Feb 1403, of his father Sir Gerard III (*C.P.R.* (1401–5) p. 58), before which time they were distinguished as *junior* and *senior*. In 1398, Sir Gerard IV was a feoffee for the manor of Shelton, Beds., in which Sir Anketil III, not yet knighted, already had an interest, and which eventually came to his son William: *V.C.H., Beds.*, iii 162 and n. 24, whose emendation is wrong. Robert Braybrooke, as a 'courtier-bishop' (A. Steel, *Richard II* (Cambridge 1941) p. 261) would have known both Sir Anketil II and Sir Anketil III. Unfortunately, these connections cannot support the inference that the only Malory the Braybrookes would have employed in their business in Shackerstone would have been one from Sir Anketil's branch of the family.

27 Dugdale, *Warwickshire*, p. 1122.

another man's executors for £26 in Easter Term 1426.[28] He must have been dead when Margaret alone settled the manor on John Charnells, son of her previous marriage, on 6 December 1428.[29] Dugdale noticed the first, second and fourth of these items.

8. Thomas Malory (no rank) and John Pulteney (who will be of the family from Misterton, Leicestershire) sued a man for cutting down and carrying away trees from their close in Edgbaston, Warwickshire, in Trinity Term 1421.[30] Thomas Malory (no rank), Sir John Pulteney, and others brought a plea of novel disseisin against Richard Clodeshale on 20 July 1422.[31] Thomas Malory of Shawell, Leicestershire, and Thomas Pulteney were sued for 10 marks by another man's executors in Hilary Term 1424.[32]

9. Thomas Malory (no rank) witnessed a settlement by the Cheyne family of the manors of Quainton and Overbury in Great Missenden, Buckinghamshire, on 20 September 1431.[33]

10. Thomas Malory of Welton and his brother John were granted goods by their father, Sir John Malory of Welton, in 1373; the two of them were left a bequest by someone else in 1381.[34] This Thomas Malory was dead in 16 March 1430, when a document was made that is worth summarising:

> Thomas Wydevill esquire, John Loudham mayor of Northampton, John Spryng mercer, Henry Caysho draper, Richard Wemmys mercer, Thomas Watford gentleman, and John Bernhill of Northampton affirm that in their presence at Northampton Agnes Malory alias Compeworth daughter of the late John Malory knight and Joan his wife confessed freely and of her own initiative that, Joan her mother having survived John her father, Joan because of her affection for Agnes gave her two charters, one by which Sir John granted his manor of Welton to John Wolf, Nicholas Benet, and John Broun, clerks, and a second by which the said John, Nicholas, and John granted the manor to Sir John and Joan for their lives with remainder to John Malory son of Sir John and Joan and to Elizabeth his wife and to the heirs male of their bodies lawfully begotten, and failing such heirs to the right male

---

[28] *Warwickshire Feet of Fines*, ed. E. Stokes et al., Dugdale Soc. 18 (1943), no. 2463; Farnham, *Notes*, iv 141. Ethel Stokes says the former document concerns Bramcote-in-Bulkington, but her nos 2431, 2463, 2550, and 2680 plainly deal with the same subject, and the text of no. 2550 names 'Bramcote by Pollesworth'. Dugdale, pp. 62, 1122, and *V.C.H., Warwicks.*, iv 189 and vi 52 are therefore right to associate the Malorys with Bramcote-juxta-Polesworth.

[29] Dugdale, *Warwickshire*, p. 1122.

[30] Farnham, *Village Notes*, iii 226. For the Pulteney family, see idem, *Leicestershire Medieval Pedigrees* (Leicester 1925) pp. 52–4.

[31] P.R.O. Just 1/1524/m.28. Since Clodeshale came from Saltley near Edgbaston (Carpenter, Appx p. 45), the same property may have been involved in both cases.

[32] Farnham, *Village Notes*, iii 226.

[33] Devon C.R.O. MS. 1038 M/T 4/24.

[34] P.R.O. E40/15855, *Early Lincoln Wills*, p. 49.

heirs of John Malory knight forever. Agnes kept the two charters for more than twenty years and then gave them to John her brother, and when she asked him for them he refused her, saying that they touched him in law. And afterwards John Malory esquire son of Thomas Malory brother of John Malory son of John Malory knight, cousin and next male heir of John Malory knight sought the two charters from John Malory son of John Malory knight, and the latter denied them to him to his great damage and to the distress of Agnes.[35]

This story of the frustration of an entail is plausible enough and not incompatible with the known history of the Malorys of Welton; but it is difficult to date its allegations. Agnes's father was alive in November 1393,[36] and her mother made a grant as his widow in 1395.[37] The younger John is very solidly recorded as lord of Welton from then until April 1429, but was dead by 6 March 1430, when his widow granted her rights in the manor of Welton to their daughter and son-in-law, which may well have prompted Agnes's testimony.[38] We may guess that his nephew attempted to recover the charters at some time in the years 1415–30, at which time Thomas was presumably dead. The complete absence of any record of Thomas as alive after 1381 might be explained by his having died in the early 1380s. It could also be explained if he had moved somewhere else and become Thomas Malory of that place.

The origins of these men, the knight and Thomas of Welton apart, are very much a matter of speculation. If Thomas of Bytham is not Thomas of Welton, he might be an otherwise unrecorded son of John (fl.1369) son of Anketil (later Sir Anketil) Malory of Sudborough, Northamptonshire,[39] and so first cousin to his knightly namesake. There are, however, other possibilities. Castle Bytham in south-west Lincolnshire was an administrative centre for a part of the estates of Grey of Codnor: for part of our period it was also the home of Joan dowager Countess of Hereford, Essex, and Northampton, who brought up there the children of her daughter Mary Countess of Derby, who included the future Henry IV.[40] There would have been employment opportunities in Castle Bytham, which Malorys already there would have been well-placed to corner for themselves and for cousins from far away. Later in the century, Richard Malory esquire of Radcliffe-on-the-Wreake, Leicestershire (who from his domicile was presumably a Malory of Walton-on-the-Wold in the same county) after

---

35 P.R.O. E40/14829.
36 B.L. Add. Ch. 6047, *Ancient Deeds*, iv 399–400.
37 *Ancient Deeds*, iv 425.
38 *Ancient Deeds*, iv 192, 446.
39 Northants. County Record Office, MS. SS 175.
40 John Wild, *The History of Castle Bytham* (Stamford 1871) p. 61.

allegedly breaking into and robbing Combe Abbey with Sir Thomas of Newbold Revel, found more regular employment with Henry Lord Grey of Codnor: he was Constable of Codnor Castle, Derbyshire, in 1459; was accused of violence in Cheadle, Cheshire, where the Greys had interests, in 1468; and was in Grey's retinue for Ireland at some time in the reign of Henry VII.[41] If Thomas of Bytham was a similarly restless cousin, and had wanted eventually to return to the bosom of his family, he might well have found himself settling in Shawell or Bramcote.

Catthorpe and Shawell are two of a group of obscure hamlets in the southern tip of Leicestershire, where that county meets Warwickshire and Northamptonshire. Malorys are recorded in them sporadically from the early thirteenth century, and in Catthorpe in particular from 1279. The Catthorpe records are too sparse to allow a reliable genealogy to be constructed, but may represent a cadet branch or a succession of short-lived cadet branches of the Malorys of Draughton and Winwick, who eventually became the Malorys of Newbold Revel. Sir Roger Malory of Draughton, a direct ancestor of Sir Thomas of Newbold Revel, held land in Catthorpe in 1279, and is the only ascertainable member of any of the better-recorded branches of the Malorys to have done so.[42] Thomas of Catthorpe, who is the last Malory to be recorded there, might be the son of the Roger Malory who held half a knight's fee in 'Thorpe-by-Lilburne' (i.e. Catthorpe) in 1361.[43]

Thomas of Bramcote's domicile in the extreme north of Warwickshire tells us nothing at all. Since he acquired it by marriage, he could have come from anywhere.

Thomas of Shawell is equally elusive. Dr Carpenter boldly asserts that Shawell was Newbold Revel property and that he was Sir Thomas of Newbold Revel.[44] The inference would be questionable even if the premiss were sound, but the Newbold Revel Malorys are not known to have held land in Shawell at all, the nearest they came to it being apparently the attestation of a Shawell deed by Richard Malory of Stormsworth (modern Starmore, north-east of Swinford) in 1235.[45] The most important of their holdings in the area was Swinford, a mile and a half away, which they held almost from the establishment of their branch of the family to the very last generation, that of Sir Thomas of Newbold Revel's great-granddaughters. It would not be surprising if a junior Malory of Newbold Revel, perhaps a

---

[41] Hicks, pp. 95–6; I. Jeayes, *Descriptive Catalogue of Derbyshire Charters* (London 1906) p. 110; G. Wrottesley, 'Extracts from the Plea Rolls', *William Salt Archaeol. Soc. Trans.* n.s. 4 (1901) 157; P.R.O. E101/55/24; and see pp. 101, 129n below.

[42] *Feudal Aids*, iii 97; Nichols, *Leicestershire*, iv 361.

[43] C.C.R. (1360–64) p. 206.

[44] Carpenter, *Polity*, p. 52n, from Farnham, *Village Notes*, iii 226.

[45] See Appendix I, under Newbold Revel.

son-and-heir in his father's life-time, were on record as lord of Swinford; but Swinford, Stormsworth, and Shawell were distinct entities, even if sometimes aggregated for tax purposes,[46] and in 1421–4, Shawell was surrounded by manors held by different branches of the Malory family: Swinford, Catthorpe, Bredon, and Walton-on-the-Wold in Leicestershire, Welton, Winwick, and Litchborough in Northamptonshire, and Tachbrook Mallory, Botley, and Newbold Revel in Warwickshire. Given the number of recorded younger sons, almost any of those branches of the family may have had an unrecorded one.

The number of men involved in these groups of records could be as low as three or as high as ten, although it is highly unlikely that there were ten different Thomas Malorys in the midlands in the early fifteenth century. The records of the knight are relatively coherent and independent of the others, and his rank should have prevented confusion with others after he was knighted. In fact, it has not always done so: several writers have conflated him and Thomas of Bramcote, thus putting the latter to death some years before Beauchamp's retinue roll was compiled.[47] Had that not happened, the identification of the Malory in that roll as Thomas of Newbold Revel might have been questioned long ago. The other records all suggest men of similar social status, a status that would only rate the rank of esquire in the army, where the word did not carry quite the same meaning as in civilian life.[48] How many men are involved is unclear, and any attempt to group the sets must be very tentative. Of the many possible permutations, perhaps the most tempting is that Thomas of Catthorpe married Margaret Charnells and became Thomas of Bramcote, and that Thomas of Shawell was Thomas of Bytham home from the wars. That could group the first nine sets 1; 3 + 4 + 5 + 6 + 7; 2 + 8 + 9. If this is right, and Thomas of Welton was one of the men involved, he would have to be the second.[49] Both premisses, however, are risky in the extreme.

No interpretation of any of these documents, however, alone or together, suggests that Sir Thomas Malory of Newbold Revel was active in the period that they span. Nor is that conclusion suggested by anything in the overall picture of his life and the lives of earlier heads of the Malory family in Draughton, Winwick, and Newbold Revel from the late thirteenth century. As we have seen in the previous chapter, there is good reason to

---

[46] Nichols, loc. cit.

[47] E.g. Kittredge, *Who Was Sir Thomas Malory?*, p. 90 n. 4; Matthews, *Ill-Framed Knight*, p. 159.

[48] Cf. K.B. McFarlane, 'A Business-partnership in War and Administration', *E.H.R.* 78 (1963) 290–308.

[49] He cannot be the first because of his paternity, and or the third because he was apparently dead in 1430, whereas no. 9 implies life in 1431. The second would fit because no. 7 suggests death 1426/8.

suppose his father John Malory was born in 1385. John's wife Philippa was one of perhaps seven children of Sir William Chetwynd II of Ingestre, Staffordshire, who is said to have been born about 1352; her two eldest brothers were born in 1374 and 1380 respectively, and one of her sisters married in 1397.[50] We might therefore put Philippa's birth about 1380, making her rather older than her husband.

A man born in 1385 would have to have married young and begotten his first child very promptly indeed for that child to have been old enough to go to war in 1415.[51] It may be canonically, medically, and legally possible, but it is hardly likely. There is no evidence that it happened, and some to suggest that it did not. The first documentary evidence of his and Philippa's marriage is a papal indult of 1423 granting them permission to have Mass before daybreak, but they will have been married well before that, since the church window at Grendon, Warwickshire, that portrays them as man and wife seems to have been made in or soon after 1407.[52] One pointer to the date of Thomas's birth may be found in the records of their daughters, whose very existence is the only solid evidence that Sir Thomas was the son of John and Philippa (since Thomas inherited and the daughters did not). Isobel was contracted to marry Edward Dodingsels of Long Itchington, Warwickshire, in 1434, when we might suppose her to have been nearing twenty.[53] Philippa was married to Eustace Burnaby of Watford, Northamptonshire, by 1429 and was widowed in 1464.[54] Helen was married to Robert Vincent of Swinford, Leicestershire, probably by 1441.[55] One might guess at Isobel being born about 1414 or a little later, and Philippa being at least five years older. The accepted picture of Thomas's life would make him fifteen or twenty years older than Isobel. Such an age-gap between the eldest and the youngest child is not impossible, but it too is unlikely.

---

[50] H.E. Chetwynd-Stapylton, *The Chetwynds of Ingestre* (London 1892) pp. 81–95, and cf. 'The Chetwynd Chartulary', pp. 256–311. If Chetwynd-Stapylton is correct about the two successive Sir William Chetwynds he postulates at Ingestre, the younger must have been born within a year either way of 1352.

Philippa's third brother, John, was '50 and more' in 1444, according to an I.P.M. of that year, but seems to have been legally of age in 1411/12, implying birth in or before 1391: 'Chetwynd Chartulary', p. 322; Chetwynd-Stapylton, pp. 111–15; *Ancient Deeds*, ii 117.

[51] If, as Dr Carpenter believes, the retinue roll is from 1414, the difficulty is proportionately greater.

[52] *Cal. Pap. Reg.*, Papal Letters, vii 315, and Dugdale, *Warwickshire*, p. 1105, and cf. Chetwynd-Stapylton, pp. 81–95 and pp. 51–3 above.

[53] *C.C.R.* (1429–35) p. 314.

[54] Ibid. (1422–29) p. 442; *C.F.R.* (1461–71) p. 137; cf. *The Visitation of the County of Warwick in 1619*, Harleian Soc. 12 (1877) 79.

[55] Nichols, iv 361; cf. *The Visitation of Northamptonshire 1564 and 1618–19*, ed. W.C. Metcalfe (London 1887) pp. 149–50, a pedigree of Robert and Helen's descendants compiled by one of them, the great antiquary Augustin Vincent.

Another kind of evidence, however, suggests that, far from begin fifteen or more years older than Isobel, Thomas may have been a little younger. John their father is last recorded making a grant of land on 4 December 1433, and was presumably dead when replaced on the commission of the peace for Warwickshire on 16 February 1434.[56] Records of Thomas begin five and a half years after the land-grant. During the intervening years, Philippa widow of John Malory is recorded as such arranging Isobel's marriage on 8 June 1434.[57] In 1436, Philippa widow of John Malory is recorded in a tax-assessment as holding land worth £60 a year in Warwickshire.[58] On 14 May 1437, Philippa was granted a general pardon as widow and executrix of John Malory.[59] She had presumably recently completed proving his will (which unfortunately does not survive). These records, particularly the tax-assessment, and the silence about Thomas show that Philippa was acting as head of the family during this period. That strongly suggests that Thomas was a minor. Philippa may have held the lands on which she was taxed as her son's guardian,[60] or as her own jointure – her situation is a reminder that jointure could reduce the risks of a minority. However, on 23 May 1439 Thomas witnessed a land settlement for his cousin Sir Philip Chetwynd, and he will then have been of age. From that time until his death in 1471 records of him survive in much the same ratio to the passage of time as they do for previous heads of the family, except that the density naturally increases during his brushes with the law.

If Thomas came of age between the tax assessment and the Chetwynd land settlement, he will have been born about 1416 – more precisely, between the end of 1414 and June 1418. It is therefore more probable than not that at the time when the Beauchamp retinue roll was being drawn up, he was not yet born. Such a birthdate means abandoning the long-cherished notion that Malory spent a quarter of a century at war in the company of that mirror of chivalry, Richard Beauchamp Earl of Warwick, but it gives a more plausible sequence of ages not only for his literary achievement but for his whole life. He will have succeeded his father when he was in his late teens, undertaken his alleged strenuous life of crime in his mid-thirties, been imprisoned by the Lancastrians in his late thirties and early forties, and died when he was about fifty-five. During the period of his exclusion from pardon as a conspicuous public enemy, his subsequent imprisonment by the Yorkists, and the writing of the *Morte Darthur*, he will have been in his early fifties. This is entirely consistent with both the literary and the historical record.

---

56 P.R.O. Ward/2/1/3/2; *C.P.R.* (1429–36) p. 626.
57 *C.C.R.* (1429–35) p. 314. Cf. *Polity*, p. 108n
58 P.R.O. E179/192/59.
59 P.R.O. C67/38 m. 1.
60 See Carpenter, *Polity*, p. 52n.

V

Growing Up

In the Middle Ages, the years when a man's character was formed rarely left any trace. Occasionally, a comprehensive set of account books for a family, perhaps supplemented by private letters, may make it possible to say something about a subject's formative years, but not for Thomas Malory: the first document that names him records him as an adult. For his earlier years, all that can be done is to sketch in some circumstances that may have influenced him, without knowing which of them did so.

At the centre of things we must put his home at Newbold Revel, with his parents, his three sisters, perhaps other unrecorded siblings, no doubt ten or so servants, and a larger number of estate workers living not far away.[1] The family's income seems to have been rather above the average for a Warwickshire squire's family,[2] and John's involvement in local and national affairs, added to the normal complexities of running estates in three counties, will certainly have made their home busier than most – a place where they had to hear Mass before daybreak if they were to hear it at all. The comings and goings of his father and of others to see his father will have accustomed Thomas to power and authority and respect, mostly local but nonetheless real, before he could put a name to those things.

Rather than splashing their way across the sodden landscape that gave Fenny Newbold its name (more sodden then than now, before eighteenth-century field drainage), the great will no doubt have sent messengers, on those occasions when John Malory did not come to them. Humbler people will have come to him on foot and his fellow gentry on horseback, some-times neighbours from Newnham Paddox or Little Lawford, sometimes family, friends, and acquaintances from further away. Among them will have been his brother Simon, Philippa's brothers Richard and John, and

---

[1] Susan Wright notes a contemporary estimate that a knight with an income of £100 a year would have a household of 16: *The Derbyshire Gentry in the Fifteenth Century* (Chesterfield 1983) p. 23.

[2] In 1436, Philippa was recorded as holding land worth £60 a year in Warwickshire, whereas Dr Carpenter estimated the average income of a Warwickshire squire as £52 a year: p. 64 supra, Carpenter, 'Warwickshire', p. 35.

her brother-in-law William Purefoy, but not, in Thomas's lifetime, any of his grandparents, all of whom died before he was born (unless his father's entirely unrecorded mother outlived the others by some years).

Thomas will not have known his uncle Richard Chetwynd either. Richard died, aged about forty-seven, in 1417/18,[3] and within a year his son and heir William had died a minor. About that time, perhaps as a consequence, Thomasina his mother (after whom Thomas may have been named) went mad.

William was succeeded by his brother Philip, then about eighteen, in an estate much encumbered with dowagers: the widows of William his brother, Richard his father, and Roger his father's elder brother, each of whom had her third of the estate as it was when her husband died.[4] Financial encumbrances must have encouraged him to find a patron, and by February 1427 he was associated with Humphrey Stafford Earl of Stafford, from whom he held his principal manor of Ingestre in Stafford-shire, and who now became a feoffee for Philip's Warwickshire lands.[5] He may briefly have served Richard Beauchamp Earl of Warwick, in whose retinue he received a silver collar of the king's livery at court at Christmas 1427.[6] However, becoming Sheriff of Staffordshire in 1428–29 coincides with a fuller commitment to the Earl of Stafford: in 1429/30 he was in Stafford's retinue in Paris for the coronation of the young Henry VI, and in 1431 Stafford doubled his fee to twenty marks a year. The increase in consequence produced by association with Stafford may explain his taking up knighthood, which he had done by 1436–37, when he was again Sheriff of Staffordshire. That association will have helped to make possible his marriage in 1436/8 to Helen, widow of Edmund Lord Ferrers of Chartley. They were members of the same circle: Ferrers had witnessed the deed by which Stafford became Philip's feoffee. Lady Ferrers had borne her first husband four sons, of whom the eldest, being of age when his father died, promptly came into his father's lands.[7] She was nevertheless a desirable match: in addition to her dower, she was an heiress in her own right, and being much the same age as Sir Philip, must have looked a good prospect to give him an heir as well. In fact, she was to die in November 1440; but however this may have affected Sir Philip emotionally or financially, his

---

3 'The Chetwynd Chartulary', ed. G. Wrottesley, *William Salt Archaeol. Soc. Trans.* o.s. 12 (1891) pp. 259–60, 304–10; cf. H.E. Chetwynd-Stapylton, *The Chetwynds of Ingestre* (London 1892) pp. 87–95.

4 From the date of Philip's parents' marriage he cannot have been born (if we rule out his being William's twin) before April 1399; he was of age in 1422: 'Chetwynd Chartulary', loc. cit. For the rest of this paragraph except as otherwise indicated, see 'Chetwynd Chartulary', pp. 261–4, 311–16; and cf. Chetwynd-Stapylton, pp. 95–111.

5 *C.C.R.* (1422–29) pp. 326, 328, 330.

6 P.R.O. E28/50/22.

7 *Complete Peerage, s.v.* Ferrers.

career does not seem to have been damaged at all: he was still in demand among the magnates. In 1441 he apparently entered the service of Lord Bonville, and served under him in Gascony in the following year.[8] In a rank-conscious age, whenever the family came together, Sir Philip's knighthood would have given him precedence over his uncles and everyone else. To his cousin Thomas, half a generation younger, he must have seemed a standing lesson on one way to succeed in life.

Thomas's other Chetwynd uncle, John Chetwynd of Alspath, presented a different kind of model for imitation: he apparently become a lawyer.[9] He was born 1381/91,[10] perhaps right at the beginning of that period if he was of age when Alspath was acquired, about 1402.[11] Most of the few people who have been concerned with his life have confused him with his kinsman and namesake, John Chetwynd of Tixall, Staffordshire, a notable royal servant who fought with Henry V at Agincourt and in later campaigns in Normandy (for which he was granted the serjeanty of Caen), and a member of the household of the infant King Henry VI; he held Tixall in 1431, and died as Constable of Tintagel in 1433/4.[12] His principal connection with the Chetwynds of Ingestre was that in 1427 he became a feoffee for Sir Philip's Staffordshire lands.[13] John Chetwynd of Alspath lived, according to the records, a much more mundane life. He is identifiable as a feoffee with his brother Richard for a Stafford man in 1410, as involved with Richard, John Malory and William Purefoy in several Warwickshire land disputes in 1412–14, as M.P. for Warwickshire in 1422, as putting Alspath in the hands of feoffees in 1429/30, quitclaiming the manor of Shenstone, Staffordshire, to John Verney Dean of Lichfield and others in 1431, as a J.P. (replacing his dead brother-in-law John Malory) in 1434, and as M.P. for Warwickshire again in 1437.[14]

John Chetwynd's landed income was small, less than that of the average gentleman.[15] That is the rank he is sometimes given, but it was presumably the law that, both directly as a respected skill and indirectly

---

8 *Proc. & Ord. P.C.*, v 160, 166; Martin Cherry, 'The Struggle for Power in Mid-Fifteenth-Century Devonshire' in *Patronage, the Crown, and the Provinces*, ed. R.A. Griffiths (Gloucester 1981) pp. 123–44, at p. 125.

9 Carpenter, 'Warwickshire', pp. 48, 72, 82, Appx 101, 108.

10 His elder brother Richard was born in 1380, and John himself appears to have been legally of age in 1411/12: 'Chetwynd Chartulary', p. 259, Chetwynd-Stapylton, pp. 111–15; *Ancient Deeds*, ii 117.

11 Carpenter, Appx 45.

12 'Chetwynd Chartulary', pp. 264–5, 317–23, Chetwynd-Stapylton, pp. 111–15, *V.C.H.*, *Staffs.*, i 241, *C.P.R.* (1429–36) p. 340. For his wife Rose Wasteness, who was also a member of the household of the infant Henry VI, see p. 53n.

13 *C.C.R.* (1422–29) pp. 328, 330.

14 'Chetwynd Chartulary', Chetwynd-Stapylton, locc. citt., *C.C.R.* (1429–35) p. 361, and for the John Malory connection, Chapter III supra.

15 Carpenter, p. 14.

by supplementing his income, increased his status to a level at which he was normally called esquire and was eligible for major offices in his county. Those offices in turn increased his income and his status yet further. A legal training was a well-trodden path to success for younger sons and could be useful to a son-and-heir whose father was still alive, but it would be less attractive to one who had already come into his inheritance. It is not surprising that the *Morte Darthur* shows sporadic signs of knowledge of the law,[16] but not of formal legal training.

Thomas Malory's Chetwynd uncle-by-marriage, William Purefoy, gives less cause for remark, partly because there is a succession of men of that name at Shirford between 1379 and 1466, and it is difficult to make out how many of them there were, or when the records of one stop and the next begin. There are no death-dates and no signs of marked individuality in the run of records. Thomas's uncle therefore cannot be characterised in even the most elementary way. Fortunately the records rather suggest that the Malorys of Newbold Revel were less close to the Purefoys than to the Chetwynds.

Thomas had one other uncle, perhaps two, both Malorys of Newbold Revel. Further consideration of his uncle Simon must be part of an account of the other kinsman, who was politically the most distinguished Malory in the Middle Ages, the only Malory (apart from Sir Peter Malory the judge, who lost his place when he lost his office) to have sat in the upper house of parliament. He was Sir Robert Malory, Prior of the Hospital of St John of Jerusalem in England from 1432 to 1439 or 1440.[17]

Whatever his personal failings and those of his order, the prior of the Hospital of St John of Jerusalem, more than any other man in England in the late Middle Ages, stood for the political standards that were most respected, if not always acted upon, by his fellow-countrymen.[18] He was also one of the great magnates of the kingdom, given power, money, and access to the king by his rich priory based at Clerkenwell, the five preceptories his office entitled him to, and his place in the upper house of parliament and the royal council. What use the priors made of their office and

---

16 See Ernest C. York, 'The Duel of Chivalry in Malory's Book XIX', *P.Q.* 48 (1969) 186–91; 'Legal Punishment in Malory's *Le Morte Darthur*', *E.L.N.* 11 (1973) 14–21; 'Emendable Crimes: Legal Anachronism in Arthurian Literature', *The McNeese Review* 29 (1982–3) 46–52; P.J.C. Field, 'Time and Elaine of Astolat', in *Studies in Malory*, ed. James Spisak (Kalamazoo, Mich., 1985) pp. 231–6.

17 For the Order of the Hospital of St John of Jerusalem, see F. de Hellwald, *Bibliographie méthodique de l'Ordre Souverain de St Jean de Jérusalem* (Rome 1885); E. Rossi, *Aggiunta alla bibliographie méthodique . . . di F. de Hellwald* (Rome 1924); and J. Mizzi, *A Bibliography of the Order of St John of Jerusalem (1925–69)* (Malta 1970).

18 See, for instance, A.B. Ferguson, *The Indian Summer of English Chivalry* (Durham, N.C., 1960).

how they lived up to the ideals they were supposed to embody were therefore, matters of consequence at the time. The surviving records are not abundant, but can provide partial answers to these questions for some of them. Sir Robert Malory attracts attention not only because of his kinship to fifteenth-century England's most famous author, but also because in his case there is enough evidence to hint at answers to those questions. He certainly did his duty in defending Christendom: when the Sultan of Egypt threatened Rhodes, Sir Robert personally organised and commanded the Hospitaller contingent that sailed from Britain to help ward off the attack. In the eyes of his contemporaries it would not have discredited his dangerous enterprise that in the end the enemy failed to come out and fight, and Sir Robert acquired, instead of scimitar scars, yet another preceptory. The severe might have been critical of the oriental fabrics his household wore, the Rhodian wine they drank, and the Turkey carpets they walked on after their return from the Levant, and perhaps also of the promptness with which he defended the rights and privileges of his office. Few would have objected if, as seems to have been the case, Sir Robert occasionally granted favours to his close relatives, who may or may not have deserved them. Among his close relatives was Sir Thomas Malory of Newbold Revel. Kinship with the Prior of St John had no perceptible effect on Sir Thomas's highly-coloured public life, but it may have had some effect on his book.

Very little is known of Sir Robert before he became prior. He could have been the Robert Malory, clerk, apparently of Newbold Revel, who was Rector of Withybrook in Warwickshire from 20 September 1407 until 16 July 1408, and who became a member of the Holy Trinity Guild in Coventry during that time.[19] No other clerk called Robert Malory is known at the time, and a Hospitaller-to-be could hold a diocesan benefice while still a postulant, and resign it when formally received by the order as a

---

19 'Rob. Malorie Cler.' in the episcopal register: Lichfield Joint Record Office, MS. B/A/1/7, fols 19ʳ, 21ʳ; 'Robartus de Kyrkeby, Rector Ecclesie de Withibroke' in the guild register: *Reg. of the Guild of Holy Trinity, Coventry*, ed. M.D. Harris, Dugdale Soc. 1935, p. 58. Miss Harris identified the two, but inferred from 'Kyrkeby' that the subject was a Malory of Kirkby Mallory in Leicestershire. The absence of any other record of such a man is not a conclusive objection to this, even though the records of the Malorys of Kirkby Mallory are unusually full for the generation in question (e.g. *Early Lincoln Wills*, ed. A. Gibbons (Lincoln 1888) pp. 57, 110–11); however, 'Kyrkeby' is plainly Monks Kirby in Warwickshire (see *The Place-Names of Warwickshire*, ed. J.E.B. Gover et al., English Place-Name Soc., 13 (1936), 112. The monks of Monks Kirby, in the name of their mother-house, Axholme, were patrons of Withybrook (Dugdale, *Warwickshire*, p. 215), and the parish of Monks Kirby included Newbold Revel – their neighbour, Sir Thomas Malory of Newbold Revel, was described on his tombstone as 'de parochia de monken-kyrkby': B.L. MS. Cotton Vitellius F. xii, fol. 284ʳ; printed with minor errors in *Collectanea topographica*, ed. J.G. Nichols, 5 (1838) 287. I am grateful to Miss Jane Isaac of the Lichfield Joint Record Office for verifying the entries in the episcopal register.

novice and sent to Rhodes for his noviciate.[20] The date of the next record fits in plausibly with the five-year noviciate in Rhodes customary at this time. But if the Withybrook Malory was another man of the same name, the first records of Sir Robert are as Preceptor of Balsall and Grafton, Warwickshire, witnessing a deed on 11 March 1415, and taking part in an election to vacant preceptories on 8 April 1417, both at Clerkenwell.[21] It is not significant that the second record omits Grafton, which was held as part of Balsall. One author says that Sir Robert was also Preceptor of Greenham, Berkshire, when elected prior, but gives no evidence for this;[22] and, at least in the 1417 election, another knight held that preceptory. On 5 October 1426, he and Simon Malory became feoffees for William Lecroft of Coleshill.[23]

Sir Robert was acting as prior of his order in England by 1432, when he issued a mandate to the order's bailiff in Rainham, Essex, to deliver lands and tenements in Thurrock to a tenant who had come of age.[24] At some time during the year ending 31 August 1432 he was made an honorary member of the Merchant Taylors' Company of London, presumably at the same time as he himself confirmed a previous prior's grant making the Merchant Taylors *confrates* of the Hospitallers.[25] On 3 November, a clerk whom he presented was instituted in Heathfield Durborough, Somerset, and on 12 January 1433, another at Kilmersdon in the same county.[26] A bull of Grand Master Fluvian, dated 4 May at Rhodes, formally elected him as Prior of the Priory of the Hospital of St John of Jerusalem in England.[27] It made him Prior (of the Priory) of England to his order, and Prior (of the Hospital) of St John of Jerusalem to his country. A court roll from the manor of Dunwich in Suffolk, dated 7 January 1433, gives him the more surprising title *magister templi Beate Marie Virginis*.[28] It is worth noticing that he was *not* Prior of Clerkenwell: the Priory of Clerkenwell was a subordinate entity within the Priory of England, having its own prior, subprior, community (*conventus*), and common seal, and contemporary Hospitaller documents carefully distinguish the *prior prioratus Hospitalis* from the *prior ecclesie*

---

20 I am grateful to Fr. Joseph Mizzi for confirming that this could happen.

21 Valletta, Royal Malta Library, MS. Arch. 340, fols 116ᵛ–117, 117ᵛ–118; A. Mifsud, *Knights Hospitallers of the Ven. Tongue of England in Malta* (Malta 1914) p. 153. It is conventional to distinguish Hospitaller *commanderies* from Templar *preceptories*, but both English and Rhodian documents of this time use *preceptor* &c. so consistently that I feel obliged to follow suit.

22 E.J. King, *The Knights of St John in the British Empire* (London 1934) pp. 68–9.

23 Birmingham Reference Library, MS. Wingfield Digby A491. John Malory had been involved with the Lecroft property earlier: ibid. A485.

24 Chelmsford, Essex Record Office, MS. D/DP T1/1023.

25 C. Clode, *Memorials of the Guild of Merchant Taylors* (London 1875) pp. 619, 49–50.

26 John Stafford, *Register*, Somerset Record Soc., 31–2 (1915–16) 129, 136.

27 MS. Arch. 350, fol. 221.

28 B.L. Add. Roll 40724.

eiusdem Hospitalis.[29] Sir Robert's bull of appointment conferred on him the preceptories of Clerkenwell, Cressing in Essex, Sandford in Oxfordshire, Balsall, and Grafton. If, as has often been said, the Prior of England was entitled to five preceptories, Balsall and Grafton must have counted as two in this context; for, although another bull four days later granted him the Preceptory of Buckland and Bothmescombe, in Somerset and Devon respectively, he acquired his right to that by surrendering, most probably at his election by the chapter, the visitation fees he would otherwise have been entitled to on his inspections of the order's properties.[30] A third bull, on the same day, made him, like his immediate predecessor, administrator of the order's bailiwick in Scotland, which needed to be stimulated into paying its dues to Rhodes.[31] His election also gave him some responsibilities for the third member of the English *langue*, the Priory of Ireland: although that priory had been juridically independent of the English one since the thirteenth century, the order had repeatedly to call on the priors of England to try to prevent the Irish houses from becoming entirely independent of Rhodes as well.[32]

Most of what is known about Sir Robert for the rest of 1433 concerns the parliament that met from 8 July to 13 August and from 13 October to about 18 December of that year. He was sent his writ of summons on 24 May; and on the first day of the parliament, the Duke of Bedford was licensed to grant the church of Cheshunt, Hertfordshire, in mortmain to the Prior of St John in exchange for the lands the duke held of the prior in and around Southwark.[33] On 3 November Sir Robert was among those members of the upper house subscribing to an oath not to maintain peacebreakers, and on 27 December, after the dissolution, he and the M.P.s for Middlesex were commissioned to assess in that county the usual rebates on the taxes granted by parliament.[34] In the meantime, the grand master had written to him several times in July, August, and September on routine matters concerned with the collection and dispatch of dues to Rhodes; and on 20 November, he had received the homage of a Northamptonshire tenant at Clerkenwell.[35]

---

[29] *Monasticon Anglicanum*, ed. W. Dugdale (London 1817–30) vi(2) 831; B.L. MS. Cotton Nero E.vi, fols 5ᵛ, 6ᵛ.

[30] MS. Arch. 350, fols 221ᵛ–222; King, *The Grand Priory of the Order of the Hospital of St John of Jerusalem in England* (London 1924) p. 61; Mifsud, pp. 43–4.

[31] MS. Arch. 350, fol. 221ᵛ; Whitworth Porter, *A History of the Knights of Malta* (London 1858) ii 283.

[32] *Cartulaire général de l'Ordre des Hospitalliers*, ed. J. Delaville le Roulx (Paris 1894–1906) vol. i pp. clxv–clxvi, vol. ii no. 1394; Porter, *The English or Sixth Langue of the Order of the Hospitallers of St John of Jerusalem* (London 1880) p. 5; D. Seward, *The Monks of War* (London 1972) p. 198.

[33] *C.C.R.* (1429–35) p. 244; *Rot. Parl.*, iv 460–1; *C.P.R.* (1429–36) p. 296.

[34] *Rot. Parl.* iv 422; *C.F.R.* (1430–37) pp. 188, 195.

[35] MS. Arch. 350, fols 224, 226, 258, 278ᵛ; MS. Cotton Nero E.vi, fol. 114ᵛ.

The records of 1434 and 1435 present a more miscellaneous picture of the actions of a Prior of St John. On 23 March 1434 a clerk whom Sir Robert presented was instituted to the vicarage of Ewell in Kent.[36] He was present at a meeting of the Great Council on 26 April, and perhaps at its other meetings from 24 April to 8 May.[37] Parliament had enacted that an oath not to maintain peacebreakers should be taken throughout the country, and on 1 May Sir Robert, the bishop of London, and the M.P.s for Middlesex were commissioned to supervise its administration in that county.[38] At some time during this year, the Grand Master, alarmed at the political situation in the Levant, issued a general citation calling for a contingent of twenty-five knights or serving brothers from each priory to be in Rhodes by March 1435.[39] This summons may explain the next record: on 13 May the king instructed Sir Robert to receive his obedientiary Sir Andrew Meldrum and six companions when they came from Scotland under a six-month safecon-duct on the order's business, which was also to include a payment of dues and a chapter meeting.[40] Meldrum, however, had already arrived, since a confirmation by the general chapter of the order in Rome in 1446 records that on 12 May, before Sir Robert, Oddo Tradeheik, William Kessill, and others, he granted his chaplain John de Kindeloch certain of the order's estates in Scotland.[41] It seems quite likely that the chapter meeting in-cluded the proceedings of 6 July 1434, when Sir Robert, nineteen of his English preceptors, and a *confrater* called John Stillingfleet made elaborate arrangements to ensure that the Office of the Dead was properly said for deceased members of the Priory of England.[42] At some time during the same year, Stillingfleet also compiled a summary list by preceptories of the properties donated to the Hospitallers, to ensure that deceased benefactors of the priory of England were also properly commemorated in its prayers. This list survives, but unfortunately is not a reliable record of the precep-tories extant in 1434 or their component parts.[43] On 5 October, a clerk whom Sir Robert presented was instituted to Copgrove church in the West

---

36 Henry Chichele, *Register,* Canterbury & York Soc. 45 (1943) 283.

37 *Proc. & Ord. P.C.,* iv 212 (and cf. 304).

38 *C.P.R.* (1429–36) p. 408.

39 MS. Arch. 351, fol. 10ᵛ; Iacomo Bosio, *Dell'Istoria della Sacra Religione et Illustrissima Militia di San Giovanni Gierosolimitano,* 2nd ed. (Rome 1621–84) ii 206; R.-A. de Vertot, *Histoire des Chevaliers Hospitalliers* (Paris 1726) ii 577–8.

40 *Foedera,* ed. T. Rymer (The Hague 1739–44), v(1) 8.

41 *The Knights of St John of Jerusalem in Scotland,* ed. Ian B. Cowan et al. (Edinburgh 1983) p. 165. For an outline of Meldrum's career, see ibid., p. 198.

42 MS. Cotton Nero E.vi, fols 5ᵛ–6ᵛ.

43 *Monasticon,* vi(2) 831–9. Stillingfleet, for instance, makes Sandford part of Cressing, whereas it is a separate preceptory in Malory's bull of appointment (supra), in the 1438 grant, and in his successor's bull of appointment (infra).

Riding of Yorkshire.[44] Sir Robert himself prepared to take the British contingent out to Rhodes, and his passport lists the retinue, money, and the plate that he was allowed to take.[45] The passport is dated 25 January 1435, but his departure was much delayed, and he eventually arrived in Rhodes well after the date the Grand Master had specified. On 11 February, a candidate whom he presented was instituted to Burgham vicarage, Rochester.[46] (It would be reasonable to infer his presence in England then or shortly beforehand from this, even if there was no other evidence, since the methodical Hospitallers distinguished presentations by the prior himself from those made by his deputy.) On 3 March his preparations were advanced enough for him to be granted letters of attorney.[47] On 5 July, he was sent a writ of summons for the parliament that met from 10 October to about 23 December, for part at least of which time he was still in England: another candidate was instituted to Kilmersdon on his presentation on another 13 October, and on 24 November, the king granted Meldrum another year's safeconduct.[48] But Sir Robert may not have attended the parliament of 1435: he is not among the triers of petitions for it, nor in the only known list (for 29 October) of lords present.[49]

Almost every record of Sir Robert for the years 1436 and 1437 was affected in some way by his stay in Rhodes. Some of them show the priory's administration working efficiently in his absence: on 24 January 1436 his attorney sued a chaloner from Ashbourne, Derbyshire, for £12 in the Court of Common Pleas.[50] Fresh letters of attorney were issued for him in England on 21 May 1436; but he was certainly in Rhodes on the following day, when he dissented from a decision by which the Council of the Order settled the conflicting jurisdictions of two of the order's courts.[51] On 29 October he was sent a summons to the parliament that met from 21 January to 27 March 1437; but he was still in Rhodes on 15 December 1436, when the Grand Master was pressing him to have arrears of dues collected in England.[52] On 2 and 3 February respectively, candidates were instituted to the benefices of Tolland in Somerset and Kirkby Fleetham in the North Riding of Yorkshire on the presentation of his lieutenant, Sir Richard Paule,

---

44 'Registers of the Archdeaconry of Richmond', *Yorks. Archaeol. & Topog. Jnl* 25 (1918–20) 220.
45 First issue in the Patent Rolls (*C.P.R.* (1429–36) p. 452) superseded by a second of the same date in the French Rolls (*48th Rpt of the Deputy Keeper of the Public Records*, p. 301).
46 Chichele, 286.
47 *48th Rpt*, p. 302.
48 *C.C.R.* (1429–35) p. 366; Stafford, 187; *Cal. Doc. Scotland*, ed. J. Bain (Edinburgh 1881–88) iv 223.
49 *Rot. Parl.*, iv 484.
50 P.R.O. CP40/700/233.
51 *48th Rpt*, p. 312; MS. Arch. 352, fol. 1.
52 *C.C.R.* (1435–41) pp. 103, 105; MS. Arch. 352, fols 128ᵛ–129.

Preceptor of Eagle, Lincolnshire.[53] The General Chapter of 1330 had enacted that one or two preceptories every ten years could be granted to deserving knights residing at headquarters; and, on 10 June, under this provision, Sir Robert was granted the Preceptory of Yeavely and Barrow, Derbyshire.[54] On 22 July, instructions were sent from Rhodes to his proctors in England to take possession of his new preceptory and to collect arrears from another.[55] On 6–14 August, the fifteen-year-old Henry VI stayed at Clerkenwell Priory on his return from a progress round the English midlands: Prior Robert was of course not there to receive him.[56] At the end of the year, Grand Master Fluvian had died, but fortunately for the order, the danger from Egypt subsided at the same time – sufficiently so for Sir Robert to be allowed to return to England. His permission to leave is dated 30 November,[57] but both he and the order took advantage of his journey to conclude some last-minute business. On the same day he was given permission to exchange Yeavely and Barrow for the Preceptory of Newland in the West Riding of Yorkshire; on 3 December, he, another of his party, and the procurator-general of the order were commissioned to inform Pope Eugenius IV, then in Florence, of the death of Fluvian and the election of John de Lastic in his place, and on the day after that, he was given permission to admit twelve novices into the order.[58]

The records of 1438 and 1439 show Sir Robert first on his way back to England, and then becoming immersed once more in the routine business of the Priory of England. A reference in the proceedings of the English royal council in February 1438 to 'the Maister of St John's' implies that the prior was still abroad.[59] On 11 May the authorities in Rhodes also thought he might not have reached home: a bull issued then to compel an English Hospitaller to honour a letter of exchange is addressed to Sir Robert 'or his lieutenant'.[60] On 29 May the pope confirmed a grant that the Order had made to him; that having originally been granted the Priory of England and its appurtenances for ten years, he should now have them for life.[61] The appurtenances were specified as the Preceptories of Clerkenwell, Cressing, Sandford, Balsall, and Grafton, and included in the priory and preceptories, the manors of Sutton-at-Hone in Kent, Harrington in Northamptonshire, Somptyng, Shipley, and Compton, all in West Sussex,

---

53 Stafford, 202; 'Reg. of Richmond', 224.
54 MS. Arch. 352, fols 132ᵛ–133.
55 Loc. cit.
56 Mabel E. Christie, *Henry VI* (London 1922) p. 377.
57 MS. Arch. 353, fol. 139.
58 Ibid., fols 139, 168, 140. Cf. Bosio, ii 211.
59 *Proc. & Ord. P.C.*, v 93.
60 MS. Arch. 353, fols 140ᵛ–141. The same form of address is used when Malory is known to be in Rhodes, e.g. MS. Arch. 352, fols 128ᵛ–129.
61 *Cal. Pap. Reg.*, ix 3.

Berwick in East Sussex, and Sutton in Essex, each maintaining a chapel with a perpetual chaplain; the estates of Millbrook and Sutton in Bedfordshire ('Mulbroke and Sumpton'), Duxford in Cambridgeshire, Copmanthorpe in the West Riding of Yorkshire, Little Sutton, Cardington, and Preen in Shropshire, Keele in Staffordshire ('Prene' and 'Kele' being run together as 'Proukele'), and 'Colpyt'; and the parish churches of Guilsborough-with-Ravensthorpe in Northamptonshire, Langford in Bedfordshire, Wilbraham in Cambridgeshire, and Standon in Hertfordshire.[62] Sir Robert admitted that he had no documentary evidence that the properties belonged to the priory of England, but asserted that the connexion had never been denied. This papal grant is the most detailed single piece of evidence for the lands that Sir Robert held as prior.

On 28 June a candidate whom he presented was instituted in Salcombe Regis, Devon.[63] Since he and not his lieutenant is named as patron, he was presumably back in England. On 8 July he and his brethren, at a chapter meeting in Clerkenwell chapterhouse, granted a London tailor a fifty-year lease on a house and garden in the parish of St Dunstan-in-the-West.[64] On 10 November the king, at Sir Robert's request, granted Meldrum and his party, now of five, a safeconduct back to Scotland.[65] A writ to the preceptor of Chippenham, Cambridgeshire, on 3 January 1439, includes Sir Robert's name, no doubt as a formality.[66] On 24 February he attended another meeting to the Great Council.[67] Two days later, presumably as a consequence, the king sent him a mandate instructing him to assemble the knights of his

---

[62] All the manors except perhaps Berwick and all the churches except perhaps Wilbraham belonged to the preceptory of Clerkenwell: *Monasticon*, vi(2) 800n. The papal grant gives a county in only one case and some of the properties are difficult to identify. The Order held Berwick in 1434: *Monasticon*, vi(2) 834. My only grounds for assuming 'Sumpton' to be the Sutton near Millbrook are phonology and physical proximity. Little Sutton is near to and was once part of the liberty of Stanton Lacy; it, Cardington, Preen, and Keele followed similar routes from the Templars to the Prior of St John: *The Knights Hospitallers in England*, ed. L.B. Larking and J.M. Kemble, Camden Soc. 65 (1855) 199–200; *Monasticon*, vi(2) 822, 834; *V.C.H., Staffs.*, iii 268; ibid. *Salop*, ii 85–6. Mrs Eileen Gooder suggested to me that 'Colpyt' might be Chilvers Coton, a property near Nuneaton that belonged to the preceptory of Balsall and in which coal was mined in the Middle Ages.

At an unknown but perhaps early date during his term of office, Sir Robert tried to consolidate his prioral rights over the manor of Newington Barrow (now Highbury) in Middlesex by expelling from lands in 'Strode' (now Stroud Green) belonging to that manor a tenant whom his predecessor had installed there in 1422: P.R.O. C1/39/155. He pursued these rights even when he was in Rhodes, when his deputy successfully disputed eightpence-worth of Essex rents against the king in Chancery: MS. Cotton Nero E.vi, fols 456ᵛ–457ᵛ.

[63] Edmund Lacy, *Register*, ed. F.C. Hingeston-Randolph (London 1909) i 235.

[64] *C.C.R.* (1447–54) p. 173.

[65] *Foedera*, v(1) 56.

[66] *C.C.R.* (1435–41) p. 238.

[67] *Proc. & Ord. P.C.*, v 108.

priory at the Palace of Westminster for a further Great Council to discuss certain unspecified extremely important matters.[68] On 25 April the Sandwich customs were ordered to release duty-free to him or to Sir Robert Bootle their armour, and wine, silk, 'chamlet', and Turkey carpets in a carrack from Rhodes lying in Sandwich under the command of Antonio Querini.[69] On 2 May a candidate was instituted to Brendon, Devon, on his presentation; on 30 June, at a chapter meeting, he and his brethren rented out one property in Clerkenwell and accepted the gift of another in exchange for a promise of having the Office of the Dead said annually for the donor in the Clerkenwell church; and on 2 July the king pardoned Sir Robert and the Abbot of Gloucester for a breach of mortmain in a minor agreement about landed property.[70] On 26 September 1439 Sir Robert was sent a writ of summons to the parliament that met from 12 November to 13 December at Westminster, and from 14 January to 15/24 February at Reading.[71] His presence there is the more probable in that he was made a trier of petitions for England, and that a private bill about some Hospitaller property in Fleet Street that had been destroyed in 1381 in the Peasants' Revolt was put forward in his name, and in due course became law.[72] On 19 October 1439, a candidate whom he had presented was instituted at Sherbourne, Warwickshire.[73] On 16 December, the king at Sir Robert's request once more granted a year's safeconduct to Andrew Meldrum, and on the same day Sir Robert himself gave a quittance for rent to a tenant from Holborn Bridge in London.[74]

Sir Robert did not benefit from the pope's extension of his term of office. He must have died by 10 May 1440, when Henry VI wrote to ask Grand Master de Lastic to confirm Bootle, the choice of the brethren, as Sir Robert's successor.[75] On 29 November the Grand Master issued a bull at Rhodes doing so.[76]

Apart from the inconclusive matter of Withybrook rectory, the evidence presented so far leaves Sir Robert, like Melchisidek, without father, without mother, and without descent. A previous chapter has described how the eight branches of the Malory family proliferated from a common ancestor who lived at the beginning of the twelfth century. By the fifteenth century, however, some of the relationships involved were quite remote; and although a relationship of some sort can be assumed between Prior Robert

---

68 P.R.O. E28/59/51.
69 C.C.R. (1435–41) pp. 214–15.
70 Lacy, i 252; MS. Cotton Nero E.vi, fols 11[r–v], 6[v]; C.P.R. (1436–41) p. 290.
71 C.C.R. (1435–41) p. 337.
72 Rot. Parl., v 23.
73 Dugdale, Warwickshire, p. 668.
74 Cal. Docs. Scotland, iv 233; MS. Cotton Nero E.vi, fol. 53[r].
75 Thomas Bekynton, Official Correspondence (R.S.) i 78–9.
76 MS. Arch. 354, fols 206[v]–207.

and any other medieval Malory, it might be one so distant as to be a matter of indifference to both parties. If, for instance, Prior Robert knew of the John Malory who was a Hospitaller serving brother stationed at Newland a century before he acquired it, he may neither have known nor cared that the man would have been his kinsman.[77] The late medieval English Hospitallers always arouse suspicions of nepotism; but proof or disproof of this in Prior Robert's case needs a closer definition of his family ties than could be provided by all English Malorys having a common origin in the generation after the Conquest.

One incident in the received account of Prior Robert's life might have been used to do this, although it points in the opposite direction from the Withybrook evidence. It is said that at some time during his term as prior Sir Robert dedicated a chapel in Clerkenwell Priory to Sts Catherine, Margaret, and Ursula and gave it a processional cross, which was eventually rediscovered and in 1904 presented to the museum of the revived British order at St John's Gate, Clerkenwell, where it now is.[78] On this cross, a small shield beneath the feet of the crucified Christ shows a forked-tailed lion rampant under a chief of the arms of the Hospitallers. Most branches of the Malory family bore *or a lion rampant a queue fourchee gules*, the arms, with the tinctures changed, of Simon de Montfort, whom they had followed in the Barons' Wars.[79] The Newbold Revel branch, however, did not.[80] Sir Robert's origins might have been discovered by eliminating first Newbold Revel and other branches not bearing this device, and then eliminating those that bore it differenced.

However, the Rainham mandate is sealed with Sir Robert's signet, and that has another coat of arms entirely: *ermine a chevron (gules) within a bordure engrailed (sable)*, arms that were also painted on a shield in the church at Balsall, and which, in the light of the mandate we may assume to have been painted for Sir Robert.[81] They are the arms of Revell of Newbold Revel, which in the 1380s when the last male Revell died, came with the manor of Newbold Revel to his sister Margaret's son, Sir John Malory of Winwick.[82] Sir John not only moved to Newbold Revel, but assumed, as

---

[77] *Knights Hospitallers*, ed. Larking, p. 46.

[78] E.g. King, *Knights of St John*, pp. 68–9; G.R. Gayre, *The Heraldry of the Knights of St John* (Allahabad 1956) p. 62; H.W. Fincham, *The Order of the Hospital of St John of Jerusalem* (London 1953) p. 74.

[79] J.W. Papworth, *An Alphabetical Dictionary of Coats of Arms* (London 1874) p. 84.

[80] See W. Birch, *A Catalogue of Seals in the Department of Manuscripts in the British Museum* (London 1887–1900) *s.n.*; F. Palsgrave, *Parliamentary Writs* (London 1827–34) i 417; Nichols, *Leicestershire*, iv 361, 368; Martin, pp. 173–4; and cf. Papworth, p. 505.

[81] King, *The Seals of the Order of St John of Jerusalem* (London 193?) pp. 99–100; Fincham, pp. 79–83; Dugdale, *Warwickshire*, p. 969.

[82] Slightly discrepant accounts in Dugdale, *Warwickshire*, pp. 81–3, Nichols, iv 361–9, and Bridges and Whalley, i 603–4. Cf. *Warwickshire Feet of Fines*, Dugdale Soc., iii no. 2330.

was his right, the Revell coat of arms in place of his previous one. Sir Robert's coat of arms shows him to be a descendant of Margaret Revell, and therefore, a son either of Sir John himself or of an unrecorded brother. The arms on the cross must be spurious, as is the only other known attribution of the Malory lion to a member of this branch of the family.[83]

Sir John's successor in his lands, John, like Sir Robert, had the Revell arms on his seal and in a Warwickshire church – in his case in a stained glass window depicting him and his wife.[84] One of the factors in his notable success in local politics, in which he played a greater part than any of his forbears for generations, is likely to have been the consequence enjoyed by a brother (or cousin) of the Preceptor of Balsall. Had he not died, between October 1433 and June 1434, that consequence would have increased when Sir Robert became prior. John's brother Simon, however, lived longer and gained proportionally more. He was well established in Warwickshire, where he had worked with John: he called himself 'de comté de Warrewyk' when suing (in 1422/26) for the jointure of the widow he had married, lived at Chilverscoton and held land near Coventry in the same county, and acted the part of a member of the local gentry even to the point of having his coat of arms, the arms of Malory of Newbold Revel, displayed on a shield in Chilverscoton church.[85] Nevertheless, despite having an income of £24 from land in various midland counties, he followed Sir Robert to London, where he attested a deed in 1439, and although he remained a layman, when he died, in February or March 1443, he was buried in Clerkenwell priory church, and left a will in which the only places mentioned are in Clerkenwell.[86] It has been thought surprising, given his relatively meagre land-holdings, that Warwickshire should have

---

83 Sir Peter Malory of Winwick, the judge who tried Wallace (*D.N.B.*) bore, according to the Parliamentary Roll of Arms, *or 3 leopards passant sable*: Palsgrave, i 417. However, the antiquary Sir Edward Dering, compiling from the best information available to him in the seventeenth century, a roll of arms for lords and judges who attended the parliament of 1297, wrongly attributed the forked-tailed lion rampant to Sir Peter: 'The "First Nobility" Roll of Arms', ed. J. Greenstreet, *Notes & Queries*, 5th series, 5 (1876) 103–6; and cf. A. Wagner, *A Catalogue of English Mediaeval Rolls of Arms* (Oxford 1950) p. 157.

84 See pp. 51–3 supra.

85 See pp. 45–7 supra; P.R.O., C1/6/110, E326/10762; Birmingham Reference Library, MSS. Wingfield Digby A485, A491; *Warwicks Feet of Fines*, iii no. 2548; Dugdale, p. 1071. His wife, however, came from Ditchford Frary in the extreme south of Warwickshire and her previous husband had been a man from nearby Brookhampton: Carpenter, 'Warwickshire', Appx 121.

86 P.R.O., E179/238/90; C.C.R. (1435–41) p. 333; John Stow, *A Survey of London*, ed. C.L. Kingsford (Oxford 1908) ii 85; P.R.O., Prob. 11/1, fol. 117ᵛ. He may have left Warwickshire by May 1434, when he had a written obligatory to Sir Richard Hastings enrolled in the Court of King's Bench, on which he called himself Simon Malory late of Chiverscoton esquire: P.R.O. KB27/692 rot. 67d. None of the other six men named is called 'late of' anywhere.

been willing to accept him as an esquire:[87] his kinship to Prior Robert provides a plausible explanation.

Prior Robert provided at least one other Malory, perhaps two, with gainful employment. First, in 1445, a William Malory attested a deed at Sutton-at-Hone in Kent, one of the manors which Sir Robert had held as prior.[88] There is no evidence of any other Malory having settled in Kent before this William, and he may be the William Malory gentleman, of Northamptonshire, who was in London on legal business in 1435 and 1438, and the William Malory, late of Northampton, mercer, who in 1457 was pardoned non-appearance in a suit for debt brought by a London mercer.[89] He may also be the William Malory layman, who was also buried in Clerkenwell priory church, on an unrecorded date.[90] Second, at some time between 1431 and 1459, a Thomas Malory was instituted into the living of Holcot in Northamptonshire, of which the Prior of St John was patron.[91] Since the Malorys of Winwick had become a Warwickshire family, we might guess that both Northamptonshire men were from the remaining branch of the family in that county, at Litchborough, and were fourth cousins of John Malory of Newbold Revel, or fifth cousins of his son Sir Thomas.

How far Sir Robert's influence extended to other members of his family is less certain, but it may be presumed with two later Malorys. The first was a later Knight Hospitaller. A John Malory was granted the preceptories of Battisford in Suffolk and Dingley in Northamptonshire on 21 January 1468.[92] He was in Rhodes on 29 December 1469, when he was given permission to revisit England to inspect his two preceptories.[93] He was presumably one of the senior knights of the Priory of England when, on 21 August 1474, he and three other Hospitallers presented a newly elected prior to do homage to Edward IV.[94] He can be assumed to be the John Malory of Clerkenwell Priory and the Order who was buried in the priory church on an unrecorded date.[95] Taken together, these facts suggest he died as Prior of Clerkenwell. His degree of kinship with Sir Robert can only be guessed at. Since the Hospitallers seem to have made some effort to

87 Carpenter, *Locality*, p. 70.
88 I owe this information to Miss Pamela Willis.
89 *C.F.R.* (1430–37) p. 254; *C.C.R.* (1435–41) p. 185; *C.P.R.* (1452–61) p. 318.
90 Stow, loc. cit. The persons and places named in these four records distinguish the William Malory in them from another man of the same name, who was in London on legal business in 1437, died late in 1438, and was buried in St Katherine's by the Tower: *C.C.R.* (1435–41) p. 164; London, Guildhall Library, MS. 9171/4, fols 3ᵛ–4.
91 Bridges and Whalley, ii 145.
92 MS. Arch. 377, fol. 143ᵛ.
93 I owe this information to the late Dr Lionel Butler.
94 *C.C.R.* (1468–76) p. 380.
95 Stow, loc. cit.

appoint preceptors to posts where their family connections would give them local influence, the Northamptonshire preceptory suggests a link with one of the midland branches of the family rather than the Yorkshire one, but that still leaves Newbold Revel, Litchborough, Tachbrook, and perhaps even Papworth St Agnes. His Christian name provides no clue: unlike Simon, which was used at this time exclusively by the Malorys of Newbold Revel, John was popular in all branches of the family. There is, however, one other rather enigmatic piece of evidence: on 14 May 1470, a George Burneby of Sutton-at-Hone, late of Watford, Northants., was granted a general pardon.[96] He must be the George Burneby of Watford who was the son of Eustace Burneby of Watford and Philippa, sister of Sir Thomas Malory of Newbold Revel. George was born in 1439/40, the year in which Prior Robert died.[97] His connection with a Hospitaller property so far from home so long afterwards strongly suggests a continuing connection between the Hospitallers and the Malorys of Newbold Revel. The simplest connection would be with this Sir John Malory, although other more complicated ones are possible. If Sir John was from Newbold Revel, it would be in accordance with mediaeval naming patterns if he were either the younger brother or the son of Sir Thomas Malory of Newbold Revel, named after Sir Thomas's father. We may also notice that a man who was one of the senior knights of the English priory in 1474 might have been one of the novices Prior Robert admitted to the order by virtue of the licence he was granted just before he left Rhodes for the last time.[98]

Surprisingly, however, Sir Robert's most lasting influence may have been exercised through his disreputable kinsman, Sir Thomas Malory of Newbold Revel, the author of Le Morte Darthur. That book for generations of readers of English most fully embodied the romance and ideals of chivalry. It is difficult to think of its author, the most imaginative writer of his century, remaining unaffected by growing up with an uncle (or first or second cousin once removed) who was one of the greatest magnates in the kingdom and a professional crusader, and both these factors may have contributed to the genesis of the Morte Darthur. Sir Thomas's motives for the life of crime that put him in prison where he composed his romance have been the subject of much speculation, but one may include among them expectations dashed by the death of his powerful kinsman.[99] As to

96 P.R.O. C67/47, m.5.
97 P.R.O. C140/15/61, E149/214/8.
98 Dr Butler informed me that there was a Malory in Rhodes during the Mameluke seige of 1444: he might be this Sir John, perhaps late in his novitiate.
99 For notions of kinship and the 'good lord' in Sir Thomas's life and book, see P.J.C. Field, 'Four Functions of Malory's Minor Characters', Medium Aevum 37 (1968) 37–45, and Edward D. Kennedy, 'Malory's King Mark and King Arthur', Mediaeval Studies 37 (1975) 190–234, esp. 209–10 and 223–4.

the ideals of Sir Robert's order, whatever influence the young Thomas Malory imbibed from them is likely to have been strengthened when the imprisoned and much older Sir Thomas was writing the *Morte*: at that very time, another Hospitaller kinsman of his, perhaps a brother or even a son, was travelling to and fro between an embattled Rhodes and the part of England where Sir Thomas's family lived.

The most important part of Sir Robert's influence cannot be measured, or even proved to have existed at all. The political seriousness of Sir Thomas's romance, compared with the amorous frivolities frequent in French and Italian writing in that genre, might only be a matter of personal or national character.[100] Many men hoped that chivalry would redeem the time, but not all of them pinned their hopes on the kind of chivalry professed or practised by the military orders.[101] Sir Thomas himself in the *Morte* presents King Arthur's Round Table as resembling less a military religious order than a secular order of chivalry such as the Order of the Garter. Like the secular orders of chivalry, it has a sovereign ruler at its head, a fixed number of members associated with him as brothers-in-arms, and regular meetings to celebrate their fellowship. But Malory's sources set limits to the ways in which he could present the organisation of the Round Table, as they do the overall sequence of events in his story. Such major components of the Arthurian legend existed in a received version that he could not and probably did not want to alter. He himself emphasised that he had looked for his story in 'authorised' books:[102] not only the famous stories that form the basis of the successive sections of the *Morte*, but, as has recently become clear, also in obscurer works that supplied supplementary details here and there. However, the received version of his story could be presented in different ways; and by small additions and alterations and large omissions, Malory considerably altered the proportions, tone, and interpretation of his story, so that it suggested ideals of man and society more in accord with the ideals of the military orders than is usual in his sources or in romance in general – in, for instance, his apparent indifference to ceremony and conspicuous consumption, his dislike of courtly love, and his presentation of knighthood itself as an 'order' with a moral purpose and a religious justification.

Malory's changes suggest not only chivalric ideals but also specific political aims in accord with and perhaps inspired by those of military Orders. It is natural in a romance for real political aims to remain in the

---

[100] Malory, *Works*, passim; P.E. Tucker, 'Malory's Conception of Chivalry as in Appears in His Story of Sir Lancelot', B.Litt. thesis (Oxford 1954); idem, 'Chivalry in the *Morte*' in *Essays on Malory*, ed. J.A.W. Bennett (Oxford 1963) pp. 64–103.

[101] Ferguson, *Indian Summer*, pp. 116, 141; R. Barber, *The Knight and Chivalry* (London 1970) chs 14–17, 21–2.

[102] *Works*, pp. 1242.3, and cf. p. 1260.8.

background; but crusades and the defence of Christendom against Islam are more conspicuous in the *Morte Darthur* than in Malory's sources or in most other English Arthurian romances. While reducing other things in his sources, he tends to preserve or add to their sporadic references to Islam as a hostile power on the edge of the Arthurian world, so that such references become proportionately more conspicuous. Sometimes they provide an interpretative yardstick, as when, at the beginning of the *Morte*, the wrongness of the rebellion against Arthur is shown by its result, a Saracen invasion.[103] That invasion becomes a campaign of devastation and indiscriminate slaughter, as natural a consequence of the enemy's 'mysbylevyng' as the chivalric virtues were of Christianity. In the second section of the *Morte*, it appears that Malory felt that such behaviour deserved retaliation in kind, for he gives King Arthur an exhortation not in his source: 'Therefore save none for golde nothir for sylver: for they that woll accompany them with Sarezens, the man that wolde save them were lytyll to prayse. And therefore sle doune and save nother hethyn nothir Crystyn'.[104]

Alterations elsewhere also present crusades in a more conspicuous and more favourable light. In the long fifth section of the *Morte*, Malory untangles an episode in the French prose *Tristan* so that his admired Sir Tristram no longer refuses a genuine papal summons to go on crusade to Jerusalem.[105] The climax of the section is the conversion of the Saracen knight Sir Palomides, an episode not in Malory's source.[106] In the last section of the *Morte*, he adds to the famous legend that King Arthur would one day return to Britain the notion that, if he did, it would be to recapture the Holy Cross.[107] The close of the *Morte Darthur* was also altered to introduce the idea of a crusade. In both Malory's sources, when Sir Lancelot is dead his kinsmen retire to a monastery for the rest of their lives, but Malory says instead that they went crusading to the Holy Land, where they 'dyd many batayles upon the myscreantes or Turkes', and there, in the last words of his book, 'dyed upon a Good Fryday for Goddes sake'.[108]

103 Ibid., pp. 37.9, 40.15.
104 Ibid., p. 224.1–3; not in *Morte Arthure*, ed. Mary Hamel (New York 1984) lines 2263–4. Cf. *Works*, p. 997.1–27, esp. 24–5.
105 *Works*, pp. 677–8 and n. to p. 680.1; cf. Kennedy, p. 206.
106 *Works*, p. 1532, n. to pp. 840.16–845.9.
107 *Works*, p. 1242.2–22 and n.; cf. *Morte Arthure*, lines 3214–17.
108 *Works*, pp. 1260.5–15 and n.; cf. *La Mort le roi Artu*, ed. J. Frappier (Paris 1936) §264; *Le Morte Arthur*, ed. J.D. Bruce, E.E.T.S. o.s. 88 (1903) p. 121.

VI

Politics and Private Life

Thomas Malory of Newbold Revel is first recorded on 23 May 1439 as an esquire, witnessing a settlement made by his cousin Sir Philip Chetwynd, who was putting his affairs in order before he and his wife Helen sailed for Gascony.[1] Sir Philip granted Grendon to John Hampden and William Purefoy esquires, Simon Melbourne rector of Grendon, and Robert Whitgreve of Stafford gentleman, in a deed witnessed by Thomas Erdington knight, John Chetwynd and Thomas Malory esquires, Clement Draper of Ardeston, and John Ullenhall. Sir Thomas Erdington and others connected with the lords Ferrers of Chartley no doubt represented Lady Chetwynd's interests, but their presence has been thought to show that Malory too was a member of the Ferrers of Chartley affinity.[2]

This view needs to be taken seriously, since the scholar who advanced it, Dr Christine Carpenter, knows more than any other scholar of the surviving evidence about the fifteenth-century Warwickshire gentry. In a recent essay, she reconsidered the principles by which such judgements can be made from the principal legal acts by which members of the gentry engaged with one another: retaining, service, witnessing, enfeoffment, and benefitting from wills.[3] She recognised that such evidence was 'problematic' and that retaining in particular need not imply an important bond – that some men might even have links with several lords precisely in order to avoid being bound too closely to any one of them. However, she argued that despite the 'numerous and obvious pitfalls' in evidence of association, it was axiomatic that 'no family would entrust its lands to feoffees, or use witnesses or executors, on whom it could not place the strongest reliance.' This, for feoffees and executors, will surely be universally accepted, but it is far from obviously true of witnesses. Each case needs to be considered in as much of its context as is discoverable.

In the present case, Sir Philip might have chosen the witnesses he did for

---

1 *C.C.R.* (1435–41) p. 268; 'The Chetwynd Chartulary', ed. G. Wrottesley, *Collections for a History of Staffordshire* 12 (1891) 316–17.
2 Carpenter, 'Warwickshire', Appx 106.
3 'The Duke of Clarence and the Midlands', *M.H.* 11 (1986) 23–48, especially pp. 24, 42.

various reasons, not all of which imply universal trust. He might have
wanted his kinsmen to make sure his political associates, who were also his
wife's family's political associates, did not misrepresent the transaction in
future legal proceedings. On the other hand, since his uncle John
Chetwynd was his heir-presumptive and his cousin Thomas was (jointly
with the Purefoys) the next in line, and since the settlement had put a new
obstacle between them and his estate, Sir Philip might have wanted his
political associates to be in a position to swear that his kinsmen had taken
part in that settlement, and raised no objections. All this settlement implies
about Malory's politics is that he was in the same room with the other men
named on 23 May 1439.

About this time he may have been involved with another kinsman: he is
said to have lent money to his brother-in-law Robert Vincent on security of
of Vincent's manor of Swinford in Leicestershire, and later to have bought
it outright.[4] The first record of him as a knight comes on 8 October 1441,
when he was one of a group of gentry to whom the vicar of Ansley in
Warwickshire granted everything he owned.[5] Ansley being twelve miles
from Newbold Revel, Malory was not an obviously necessary choice for
the group: being asked to take part must therefore have been a welcome
sign of his standing in Warwickshire, particularly since his domicile at the
time may have been in Northamptonshire. On 28 December 1441, he heads
the list of electors in the return for the parliamentary election for that
county.[6] That may be a sign that he had married and that his mother had
settled Winwick on him and his wife, herself remaining at Newbold Revel.
There is no way of telling whether the wife in question was Sir Thomas's
only recorded wife, Elizabeth Walsh of Wanlip, who bore him his son and
heir Robert.[7]

His knighthood also suggests political ambition, perhaps to a degree
that he might have difficulty living up to: his parents' known income, as
we have seen, appears to have been less than half the £165 a year that was
the average for a Warwickshire knight,[8] and his and his sisters' marriages
had hardly increased their family's consequence, particularly in Warwickshire, where his estates and his father's connections gave him his greatest

---

4   William Burton, *The Description of Leicester Shire* (London 1622) pp. 279–80. The sugges-
    tion that the dates Burton gave Thomas Malory in his genealogy (19 Henry VI [= 1 Sept.
    1440 – 31 August 1441] and 27 Henry VI) were for the two stages of the land transaction
    was Eugène Vinaver's: *Malory* (London 1929) p. 121.

5   P.R.O. E326/10717. The gentry were Edward Grey of Ruthin and Thomas Malory
    knights, Robert Grey, Henry Fillongley, and John Payne esquires, and John Hilton,
    William Tandy, and William Brette gentlemen; the witnesses were six Ansley men.

6   P.R.O. C219/15 Pt 1; cf. Wedgwood, *Biographies*, p. 567.

7   For Sir Thomas's wife as a Walsh of Wanlip, see p. 136 below.

8   For the knight's income: Carpenter, 'Warwickshire', p. 35.

chance of making a mark. His wife's family were from Wanlip in Leicester-shire, and in addition the head of the family, Thomas Walsh, was intermit-tently insane at least during the years 1422 to 1449, when his guardian, his brother-in-law Sir Thomas Gresley of Drakelow, who had been robbing the estate, had to be superseded; and Thomas's heir-apparent, his brother Richard, had an income of only £13 a year and had to pay the endowment for the marriage of his son and heir incrementally.[9] The description of Richard Walsh's son Thomas in 1456 as 'kinsman and heir of Thomas son of Thomas Walsh knight' suggests his unfortunate uncle was still alive then.[10] Not surprisingly, none of the Walshes held any offices of any im-portance during this period even in their own county. Sir Thomas's wife was presumably of the same generation as Richard's son Thomas, and if she had been the daughter of Thomas the lunatic, she would have been the heir. The most straightforward assumption is that she was Richard's daughter.

Helen Malory married into a Leicestershire family too, and an even more obscure one. The Vincents' sale of Swinford, although they reserved an annuity that passed down the family until the Malorys of Newbold Revel bought them out in 1518/19,[11] seems almost to have lost them their gentry status. Robert became clerk to the kitchens to Richard Neville Earl of Warwick,[12] but they held no public office at all in the years when Thomas was beginning of his public life. Thomas's sister Philippa also married 'abroad'. The Burnebys of Watford were more important than the Walshes or the Vincents, but very much a Northamptonshire family. Philippa Malory's husband Eustace was born in 1398/9 (being therefore much older than Thomas) and married Philippa about 10 September 1428.[13] His father died in the following year, but he did not come into possession of Watford until his step-mother died in 1431. He was Sheriff of Northamptonshire in 1439 and 1448, a J.P. there from 1448 to 1452, and died in 1463: Philippa

---

9 George Farnham, *Medieval Leicestershire Pedigrees* (Leicester 1925) p. 141, Nichols, *Leices-tershire*, iii 1095; *C.P.R.* (1416–22) p. 409; (1436–41) p. 424; *C.C.R.* (1447–54) p. 108; P.R.O., E179/192/59.

10 *C.C.R.* (1454–61) p. 131.

11 Burton, loc. cit.

12 *The Visitations of Northamptonshire 1564 and 1618–19*, ed. W.C. Metcalfe (London 1887) pp. 149–50.

13 P.R.O. C139/39/29, C139/54/34. The assumption that Philippa was Thomas's sister depends on the close association between the Malorys of Newbold Revel and the Burnebys from 1433, when Eustace witnessed a land-grant by John Malory of Newbold, to 1470, when Eustace's son and heir George was living at the Hospitaller property of Sutton-at-Hone in Kent; on Philippa's Chetwynd Christian name; and on the assertion in the 1619 visitation of Warwickshire that she was the daughter of Thomas Malory: P.R.O. Ward 2/1/3/2, C67/47 m. 5 (and cf. p. 80 above), *The Visitation of Warwickshire in the Year 1619*, ed. J. Fetherston, Harleian Soc. Pubs 12 (1877) p. 79.

survived him.[14] Isobel Malory's husband Edward Dodingsells was a Warwickshire man, but a younger son of a family that slipped into obscurity in his generation, perhaps because it took on too many financial commitments to younger sons and a dowager, perhaps because his father Sir Edward deliberately opted out of politics.[15]

On 28 June 1442, Sir Thomas witnessed a second Chetwynd settlement. Helen Chetwynd had died and Sir Philip had married again, presumably at this time, to Joan daughter of William Burley (d.1459) of Broncroft, Shropshire.[16] He was about forty-three, she was sixteen. The feoffees of 1439, witnessed by William Mountford and Thomas Malory knights and three esquires, granted Ingestre and Grendon to them and the heirs male of their bodies, and failing that ('quod absit') to the right heirs of Philip.[17]

Sir Philip, however, was urgently needed elsewhere.[18] His services in Gascony had given the English government confidence in him, and he had been created Viscount Tartas in 1440 and appointed mayor of Bayonne the following year, but while he was in England, French armies had captured the whole province except Bayonne, which was beseiged. The government looked to Sir Philip, and on the day after his marriage settlement he was made mayor of Bayonne again, with effect from August, and given money to recruit soldiers. Bayonne surrendered before he could take up his post, but he got to Gascony in October, and the city expelled the French and accepted him as mayor. The English cause, however, was doomed: Gascony was soon permanently lost, and by February 1444 Sir Philip was back in England. His part in the last days of English Gascony is unknown, but may have been highly creditable, since what reveals his presence in England is an appointment to the country's most important remaining military post in France: an indenture with the Governor of Calais, the Earl of Stafford, to be his lieutenant-governor.

It would have been in keeping with the customs of the time for Sir Philip to have recruited his junior officers among his family and friends, and for Malory to have increased his reputation and income by serving with his cousin in Gascony. There is a little evidence to suggest that this happened. In one passage near the end of the *Morte Darthur* Malory shows a familiarity with the numerous little lordships of Gascony of a kind that in an age before maps were common would normally have been gained by direct

14 *C.F.R.* (1437–45) p. 129; (1445–52) p. 103; *C.P.R.* (1446–52) p. 592; P.R.O. C140/15/61, E149/214/8, C.C.R. (1461–8) pp. 218, 220.

15 Carpenter, 'Warwickshire', pp. 49n, 210–11; *Locality*, p. 215. Cf. *C.P.R.* (1441–6) p. 438.

16 *Complete Peerage, s.v.* Ferrers for Helen's death (4 November 1440); Wedgwood, *Biographies, s.v.* Burley.

17 'Chetwynd Chartulary', loc. cit.: the esquires were Thomas Standley, Hugh Erdeswick, and Ralph Egerton.

18 'Chetwynd Chartulary', loc. cit.; H.E. Chetwynd-Stapylton, *The Chetwynds of Ingestre* (London 1892) pp. 95–111; *Proc. & Ord. P.C.*, v 121.

experience, and earlier he pays what looks like a chivalrous compliment to one of the enemy commanders, Poton de Xantrailles, by renaming a minor Arthurian knight in his source after him.[19]

If Malory was with his cousin on his last journey to Gascony, he was back by 10 August 1443, when he witnessed the sale of the manor of Botley, Warwickshire, by the feoffees of John Malory of Tachbrook Mallory to Richard Archer and others.[20] Sir Thomas's father had been a party to the Tachbrook Malorys' acquisition of Saddington, Leicestershire, in 1419, and his own participation now need not imply more than keeping up the connection with his cousins. On 10 October, however, he and Eustace Burneby were accused of having insulted, wounded, and imprisoned Thomas Smythe of Spratton, Northamptonshire, and stolen £40-worth of his goods.[21] It is difficult to know how much truth there was in this, since the accusation is something of a formula, the case never came to trial, and allegations like it are not unusual: the Warwickshire gentry accused one another of scores of comparable crimes during the fifteenth century.[22] True or false or somewhere in between, however, this accusation provides a context for later accusations against Malory, making it less easy to believe that the first of them were wholly invented by his enemies, and the others simply the product of despair at being outmanoeuvred earlier on.

The following summer saw an event of great importance to Malory: on 10 May 1444, Sir Philip Chetwynd died (presumably at Calais).[23] For Malory, a connection of enormous potential was replaced by a kind of vacuum. Joan Chetwynd, who had not borne her husband a son, quickly took her life interest in his lands to a second husband, whose connections were in Worcestershire and London. That husband, the judge Sir Thomas Lyttelton, wrote what was for centuries known as the greatest work on the English law of land-tenure: it is hardly surprising that when Sir Philip's heir, his uncle John Chetwynd, challenged the 1442 settlement, he lost.[24] Until Lady Lyttelton's death, sixty years later, the Chetwynds of Alspath lapsed into an obscurity so deep that there are problems in discovering their descent, but which certainly included a mid-century minority of some length. If they had wanted to help their Malory cousins, they were hardly in a position to do so.

---

[19] *Works*, pp. 1205.2–21, 432.13; and see P.J.C. Field, 'Fifteenth-Century History in Malory's *Morte Darthur*' in *Cultural Intermediaries in Medieval Britain*, ed. Françoise Le Saux, forthcoming.

[20] Stratford-upon-Avon, Shakespeare's Birthplace Trust, MS. D.R. 37 Box 50/2938.

[21] George Lyman Kittredge, *Sir Thomas Malory* (Barnstaple, Mass., 1925) p. 8, from P.R.O., De Banco Roll 731 m. 278 d. (Mich. 22 Hen. VI [1443]), 732 m. 414 (Hil. an. cit [1444]); Hicks, pp. 4, 54; Baugh, p. 4; Matthews, p. 14.

[22] Carpenter, 'Warwickshire', Appx 150–6.

[23] For this paragraph, 'Chetwynd Chartulary', Chetwynd-Stapylton, locc. citt.

[24] P.R.O. C1/14/28.

Sir Philip's death, however, did not immediately deprive Malory of local influence. On the contrary, in 1444/5, Monks Kirby priory paid him an annuity of £2, presumably for his good-will in their affairs; he also paid them £5 for farming the tithe-corn of Stretton-under-Fosse, the village nearest Newbold Revel.[25]

An even more significant sign of influence is that early in 1445 Malory was elected an M.P. for Warwickshire. The date of the election is unknown, because the return is lost: the election of Malory and his colleague Sir William Mountford (who had served with John Malory in 1423 and 1427) has to be deduced from their appointment to a commission to assess exemptions from the taxes granted by that parliament.[26] The election will have been held between the summoning of parliament on 13 January and its first meeting on 25 February, by Sir Robert Harcourt, then Sheriff of Warwickshire and Leicestershire, who is associated with Malory later.

The favour of his father's old parliamentary colleague and of the sheriff may have been helpful, but more important still would be that of the county's two leading magnates, both new faces since John Malory's time. They were rivals, but there is some reason to suppose Malory may have been acceptable to both of them. Henry Beauchamp had succeeded his father Richard as Earl of Warwick in 1439, at the age of fourteen: in 1445, he was just beginning to take a part in Warwickshire politics.[27] In 1446, as will appear, the custodians of his estate were paying Malory a sizeable annuity. If the same payment was being made in 1445, Malory must have been formally one of Earl Henry's retainers.

The second magnate was Humphrey Earl of Stafford, who had been created Duke of Buckingham in 1444. He had been trying to increase his power from Staffordshire in Warwickshire since at least 1433, and in 1438 had obtained by exchange the strategic north Warwickshire castle of Maxstoke.[28] The most direct way for Buckingham to achieve his aims was to entice members of Warwick's affinity into his own. The attractions of Warwickshire for Buckingham must have included the convenient placement of Sir Philip Chetwynd's lands, which gave him a strategically placed retainer in his target county. Sir Philip was dead, and although Buckingham maintained good relations with the Lytteltons, it must have been obvious that their commitments elsewhere would make them unable to exercise that influence which Sir Philip had at least sometimes been able to

---

25 P.R.O. S.C.6 1039/18: ministers' accounts for Monks Kirby 31 July 1444 – 31 July 1445. Dr C.C. Dyer first drew my attention to this document. It does not call Malory a knight, but Dr Dyer confirms that absence of ranks is not significant in an account.
26 So deduced by Dugdale, *Warwickshire*, i 83, and by Colonel Wedgwood, *History of Parliament: Register* (1938) pp. 53, 63.
27 Carpenter, 'Warwickshire', p. 135.
28 See Carpenter, pp. 119–35.

exercise by his presence in the county. It must also have been obvious that
Sir Philip's young cousin was ideally placed to fill his shoes. Malory may
therefore have found himself being courted by two of the most powerful
men in England.

Parliament met on 25 February 1445 and was dissolved on 9 April 1446.
It was a very long parliament, the longest of Malory's lifetime and the first
ever to extend to a fourth session.[29] As part of its business, Malory, Sir
William Mountford, and Buckingham were on 3 June 1445 commissioned
to allocate tax-exemptions among the impoverished towns of Warwickshire.[30] That on its own hardly makes Malory and Buckingham intimates,
since the duke could not be expected to take much part in the commission's
day-to-day work, but he and Malory must have been in some sense political associates: the very fact that Buckingham was replaced in the following
year shows his appointment was not entirely nominal.[31] Another item in
the business of that parliament was of particular concern to the Warwickshire members: Earl Henry was created Duke of Warwick, and he and
Buckingham quarrelled over precedence. Buckingham had been given the
rank first, but King Henry's inability to refrain from giving things away –
even things he had already given to someone else – had led him to give the
new Duke of Warwick precedence over Buckingham. The matter was settled temporarily by parliament arranging for the two dukes to take precedence of one another in alternate years, and permanently by Warwick's
death without a male heir two months after parliament was dissolved.[32]

The other item may have mattered to few but Malory himself: parliament enacted that no man should be a knight of the shire unless he was 'a
notable knight' of the county he represented, or at least a gentleman of it
who was 'able to be a knight'.[33] The income that for a century and a half
had been associated with knighthood, the income that must in most
people's eyes have made a man able to be a knight, was £40 a year.[34] Most

---

[29] Sessions were 25 February – 15 March, 29 April – 5 June, 20 October – 15 December, and
24 January – 9 April. The parliament of 1463 was and that of 1453 may have been longer
from assembly to dissolution than that of 1445–6, but both spent much less time in
session and all others were shorter in both respects. For the fourth session and for
mid-century parliaments generally see J.S. Roskell, *The Commons and Their Speakers in
English Parliaments, 1376–1523* (Manchester 1965) pp. 227, 225–47.

[30] *C.F.R.* (1437–45) p. 330.

[31] The new commission was to the Bishop of Worcester and the two M.P.s: *C.F.R.* (1445–52)
p. 36.

[32] *Complete Peerage, s.v.* Buckingham [1444]. For a comparable case involving Sir William
Bonville and the Earl of Devon in 1441, see R.L. Storey, *The End of the House of Lancaster*
(London 1966) p. 87.

[33] *Statutes of the Realm*, ii 342 = 23 Hen. VI, c. 14.

[34] This is revealed by distraint of knighthood and royal grants. In the thirteenth century,
the king had distrained at a variety of annual incomes on men deemed able but unwilling to take on knighthood. Higher figures were sometimes used, but £20 was common,

knights, however, had much higher incomes. We have no reliable estimate of Malory's income, and although his widow's inquisition post mortem gives hers as only half the required sum,[35] his at this time may have been higher than that, not only because inquisitions post mortem are notoriously unreliable, but because this one postdates the vicissitudes of the 1450s. But even if Malory enjoyed the income that his mother was assessed at in 1436, parliament's link between office and income would still have reminded him uncomfortably that compared with others of his rank he was still, as Dr Carpenter has called him, 'a poor knight'.[36] It is not surprising that the *Morte Darthur* shows more often than most romances an awareness of financial insecurity and its consequences, or that it contains a sympathetic picture of a knight at court who

> for he was poore and poorly arayde, he put hymselff nat far in prees. But in hys herte he was fully assured to do as well, if hys grace happed hym, as ony knyght that there was.[37]

A knight's landed income might be his official income, but he would expect to supplement it from other sources, and, since it sometimes required very little in return, an annuity from a magnate could the most

and it has been assumed that this was still the rate in 1445: W. Stubbs, *Select Charters* (Oxford 1929) p. 448; T.P. Taswell-Langmead, *English Constitutional History* (London 1960) pp. 97–8, 203–4. But the rate during the fourteenth and fifteenth centuries was consistently £40: C.C.R. (1307–13) p. 543; (1333–7) pp. 93, 362; (1341–3) p. 134; (1343–6) p. 450; (1354–60) p. 319; (1364–8) p. 266; (1476–85) p. 305; (1485–1500) p. 350; T. Rymer, *Foedera* (London 1816–30) iv 23; *Tudor Proclamations*, ed. P.L Hughes and J.F. Larkin (New Haven, Conn., 1964–9) i 10–11. An exception of £50 in 1316 seems to have been specially agreed with parliament: C.C.R. (1313–18) p. 327. Grants 'to maintain knighthood' are particularly common on the mid fourteenth-century Patent Rolls, and the standard rate is £40, even if it has to be made up of several smaller grants: C.P.R. (1354–8) p. 580; (1358–61) p. 370; C.C.R. (1349–54) p. 310. The only exceptions, of higher grants to peers' sons or lower grants 'towards maintaining' rather than 'to maintain' knighthood, confirm £40 as the norm.

35 P.R.O. C140/75/46, translated in Hicks, pp. 108–11. This gives Malory's annual income from land as £19 0s 4d from Newbold Revel, Winwick, and Stormfield (modern Starmore), and £2 13s 4d from Swinford. The lands at Swinford, which his brother-in-law apparently mortgaged to him in 1441 and then sold to him in 1449 would therefore have raised his annual income above £20, the income the law after 1439 required in a justice of the peace: *Statutes of the Realm*, ii 309 = 18 Hen. VI, c. 11. Malory's real income even from land may of course have been more or less than £21 13s 8d, but it was his notional income that would have determined his legal status. His father had been a J.P., but if Thomas acquired the Swinford lands to help him follow in his father's footsteps, something must have persuaded the authorities that he was unsuitable.

36 Carpenter, *Locality*, p. 52.

37 *Works*, pp. 62–3 and nn., where Professor Vinaver pointed out how Malory emphasises that chivalry is a matter of inner worth not conspicuous consumption. Malory also adds the embarrassment felt at being visibly poorer than the company one is in: cf. *Merlin: Roman en prose du XIIIe siècle*, ed. G. Paris and J. Ulrich (Paris 1886) i 215.

desireable alternative source. The only record of Malory receiving such an annuity comes just after the death of Duke Henry. He was paid £4 15s 0d for the accounting period from the duke's death to Michaelmas.[38] The duke died on 11 June, and the annuity was of twenty marks. There is a small anomaly in that: Malory received something over eighteen-weeks-worth of annuity for a period of sixteen weeks. That suggests the completion of a commitment instituted by Duke Henry rather than one that the keepers of his lands began, whether in their own interests or in what they believed to be the interests of his infant daughter.

One other record needs to be considered here, because of a controversial dating affecting its interpretation. It is a petition by Katherine wife of Sir William Peyto to the Archbishop of Canterbury as Lord Chancellor, accusing Sir Thomas Malory of Fenny Newbold of having stolen four oxen from her estate at Sibbertoft, Northamptonshire, and driven them to Fenny Newbold, and when Lady Peyto's bailiff attempted to stop him, of having threatened to maim or murder the man.[39] As a postscript to the usual closing phrase she adds that she had 'put up a bille of this said mater to my lord of Warrewyk now late being in countrey and can have no remedie.'[40] Dr Carpenter takes this as part of a two-part document of which the second part is a similar petition by Lady Peyto to the Archbishop over a raid on her manor of Camden, Gloucestershire, and concludes that together they record 'a two-pronged assault' on Lady Peyto's lands in 1444,[41] at the very beginning of the period in which Henry Beauchamp could have been directing the Warwick affinity rather than having it act in his name.

Both conclusions need examination, and it will be convenient to take the second first. In the Camden petition, Lady Peyto says she had held that manor in dower from Thomas Stafford her first husband for 'nineteen years and more', and that it was attacked 'on the Tuesday before St James last'. The date when she was assigned dower is unknown, but Thomas Stafford died on 11 December 1425,[42] and the first Tuesday-after-St-James that comes more than nineteen years later is 20 July 1445. That must be the date intended: 19 July 1446 would have produced 'twenty years and more', and so on with later dates. Moreover, the attackers told her steward they were acting for the Abbot of Pershore, which, she complained, meant they were retainers of 'my lord of Warwick'. On 19 July 1446 Duke Henry had been dead for five weeks. Lady Peyto's lawyers might not have realised

---

[38] P.R.O. E368/220/107–8.

[39] P.R.O. C1/15/78, printed in Baugh, p. 19.

[40] *in countrey* = 'in the provinces': the dictionaries are not helpful but cf. *Excerpta historica*, ed. S. Bentley (London 1831) p. 281, and *Paston Letters*, ed. N. Davis (London 1971–6) ii 313.

[41] Carpenter, 'Warwickshire', pp. 135–6; *Locality*, p. 416, referring to P.R.O. C1/15/77.

[42] P.R.O. C139/22/18.

that the Archbishop of Canterbury had ceased to be Lord Chancellor on 11 June 1446, but they and the Warwickshire attackers (most were from other counties) would certainly have known Duke Henry was dead and that it would have been pointless for the attackers to suggest the duke was supporting them or would support them retrospectively, or for Lady Peyto to imply (if that is what she is doing) that she needs the chancellor's support because the duke's power is preventing her from obtaining justice.

The importance of this document lies not who was in the right in the theft (or pledge-taking or forcible repossession) of sheep at Camden. It is, as Dr Carpenter says, that both sides were associated with Duke Henry. Sir William Peyto was not only one of Duke Henry's retainers, but he had been Earl Richard's retainer before him; and at the time of the attack he was probably a prisoner-of-war in France.[43] One of the principal functions of a good lord was to keep his affinity harmonious, and make it unnecessary for them to go to uncertain and perhaps ruinously expensive law. It looks as if the duke visibly failed in this, the more shamefully in that Lady Peyto's husband was unable to help her. If Duke Henry allowed it to happen twice, the failure would have been more than twice as serious, particularly in the case of a concerted simultaneous attack. He would have been proclaiming to the world that, as Dr Carpenter put it, he 'pandared to' strong retainers like Malory by allowing them to prey on weak ones.

This view, however, depends entirely on the simultaneity of the two attacks. On its own, the Camden petition does not imply that Lady Peyto or anyone else had grounds for dissatisfaction with Duke Henry. No magnate, not even John of Gaunt at the height of his power,[44] could realistically be expected to keep every member of a large affinity under control all the time, still less his retainers' retainers, even those who might falsely imply that he supported them in their crimes. Except in cases more serious than sheep-stealing, the most that could be expected was a stiff warning to the intermediate retainer and letting the law take its course with the criminals themselves. There is no evidence that this did not happen: for all we know to the contrary, Lady Peyto might have drafted her Camden petition with the help of Duke Henry's lawyers.

It is therefore a matter of some importance to establish the dates of the two raids. Dr Carpenter apparently assumes they are simultaneous because they are described in a single document, but they are not. The petitions are separate documents, each complete in itself. The Public Record Office numbers them consecutively, but that does not imply anything. The internal evidence, such as it is, points the opposite way: within the norms for such petitions, these two are in different styles. Lady Peyto sought redress for legally identical crimes in manors to which she had

---

43 Carpenter, 'Warwickshire', loc. cit. and Appx 103.
44 For Gaunt's affinity, see Simon Walker, *The Lancastrian Affinity 1361–1399* (Oxford 1990).

legally identical rights, but only with Camden did she say how long she had held the manor and exactly when it was attacked, and only with Sibbertoft did she mention an appeal to Warwick. If the attacks were even within a few days of each other, then during the time when she was appealing to Warwick and taking legal advice about the first attack she would have heard about the second. Her decision to appeal to Chancery on both counts would presumably have been taken on a single occasion, and although she might have been advised to petition separately for separate crimes, the two documents would presumably have been written and verified in immediate succession. From that, one would expect a more uniform style.

If the two petitions do not constitute one document, they need separate dating, which for the Sibbertoft one is difficult. The four periods during the adult lives of Malory and Lady Peyto when there was an earl or duke of Warwick and when the Archbishop of Canterbury was Lord Chancellor are 13 May 1443 – 11 June 1446, 23 July 1449 – 31 January 1450, 21 July 1452 – 22 March 1454, and 7 March 1455 – 11 October 1456. The fourth period is the least likely: as we shall see, Malory was in prison and the authorities were taking particular care to keep him there. The second period is unlikely too: Malory was accused of a variety of crimes at an inquisition at Nuneaton on 23 August 1451, and someone took a great deal of trouble to make the indictment comprehensive. They would hardly have overlooked a crime like this. The first period is also unlikely, for a reason we cannot now rule out, that Malory and Peyto were members of the same affinity. For part of the third period, however, they were politically opposed: Peyto had become a supporter of Buckingham, and Malory was at odds with him.[45] These considerations cannot be conclusive, but they make it most likely that the attack on Sibbertoft took place ten years after that on Camden. If that is so, the 'my lord of Warrewyk' Lady Peyto appealed to was Richard Neville, who was later called the Kingmaker. We will have to return to this.

When Duke Henry died, his heir was his sixteen-month-old daughter, whose wardship went to King Henry's favourite, the Duke of Suffolk. The child, however, died just before her fourth birthday and was succeeded by Richard Neville, her father's sister's husband. He was 'confirmed' as Earl of Warwick on 23 July 1449, but later surrendered his earldom to the king and received it back on slightly different terms on 2 March 1450.[46]

The period has been plausibly portrayed as one of increasing uncertainty in Warwickshire, with Buckingham trying to establish himself as the dominant power in the county, and being resisted first by senior members of

[45] Carpenter, pp. 198, 207, 210, Appx 103.
[46] *Complete Peerage, s.v..*

Duke Henry's affinity, and then by the new earl.[47] The records of Malory's life, however, do not reflect that uncertainty. First, a record from a later period asserts that his son and heir Robert was born in 1447/8.[48] Second, on 9 October 1448 Malory, Sir Robert Harcourt, and others sued three obscure Leicestershire men for unspecified transgressions; the sheriff failed to produce them and the plaintiffs had to start again a year later.[49] Harcourt had connections with the royal court, where he may have been a friend of Suffolk, but in Warwickshire he had become notorious by killing Richard Stafford of Grafton, with whose family his had a long-standing feud, in Coventry the previous May.[50] Association with Harcourt will have presented risks for Malory. In particular it could have damaged him in Buckingham's eyes: Buckingham was a Stafford and Staffords tended to stick together. The third record is less ominous: it is the suggestion outlined at the beginning of this chapter that Malory acquired Robert Vincent's property in Swinford outright in 1448/9.[51] Finally, on 9 October 1449, Malory, Harcourt, and the others began their lawsuit again, with exactly the same result as before.[52] However, whereas the lawsuit got nowhere, the relationship between Malory and Harcourt seems to have flourished: on 27 December 1449, Malory's brother-in-law Thomas Walsh of Wanlip contracted to marry Harcourt's sister-in-law Margery Byron.[53]

At this point, however, Malory's ambition appears to have involved him in national politics. The 1440s had been troubled years for the whole country, and by the autumn of 1449 the conspicuous incompetence and corruption of Suffolk's government was beginning to create a united political opposition; an uneasy situation in which magnates on all sides gathered retainers.[54] In Warwickshire the new earl must have found his inheritance in some confusion, but Buckingham was more firmly established, and his loyalty to King Henry did not bind him to all the policies that ministers or the queen might foist on his inept monarch.[55] This may have had a direct effect on Malory. A new parliament was summoned on 23 September and met on 6 November, and a Thomas Malory was returned to it as M.P. for the borough of Bedwin in Wiltshire.[56] There do not appear to have been

---

[47] Carpenter, 'Warwickshire', pp. 140–56.

[48] Sir Thomas's inquisition post mortem: P.R.O. C140/36/12. It says Robert was '23 and more' on 6 November 1471, which implies birth 7 November 1447/5 November 1448.

[49] P.R.O. KB27/750 m. 48d: Thomas Malory and Robert Harcourt knights, William Belgrave, John Danet, and Nicholas Maune against William Lussell of Walcote and William Reynold of North Kilworth husbandmen, and Robert Milner of the same miller.

[50] Storey, pp. 57–8.

[51] In 27 Henry VI (1 September 1448 / 31 August 1449).

[52] P.R.O. KB27/754 m. 61d.

[53] C.C.R. (1447–54) p. 108; Wedgwood, s.v. Harcourt; Farnham, *Pedigrees*, p. 141.

[54] J.H. Ramsay, *Lancaster and York* (Oxford 1892) ii 111–13; cf. Storey, pp. 9–17, 26–8.

[55] Storey, pp. 183–4.

[56] *Return of Members*, which calls him *Malery* and does not give him (or most of his fellow

any Malorys living in Wiltshire in the fifteenth century, and the small south-western boroughs often elected non-residents with money or influence who wanted a parliamentary seat.[57] The problem is knowing which Thomas Malory this borough elected.

Buckingham was in a position to exercise two sorts of influence in Bedwin, because his family had been lords of Bedwin for three-quarters of a century,[58] and because of his exceptional wealth. Roger Virgoe has pointed out that it would be unusual at this time for the lord of a borough to use his influence in the choice of an M.P. for the borough, and surprising for a knight to be a borough M.P., or if he were, for him to be given no rank on the sheriff's return and to have his name, as is the case here, second to that of a member who was not a knight.[59] Against this, late 1449 was an exceptional moment, Sir Thomas's connection with Buckingham gives him a link with Bedwin, and he is the only man of his name known to have had an interest in politics. If, as has been argued above, fifteenth-century governments generally knew the names of every knight in the country, the absence of Malory's rank from the return might have been a deliberate subterfuge. It was illegal for any constituency, county or borough, to elect a non-resident M.P.,[60] and whereas the breach in the law would be undetectable with most men, it would be flagrant with a knight.

The provable connection between Malory and Buckingham – their membership of the 1445 parliament and the subsequent committee – is not strong, but many other possibilities are opened up by Malory's relationship to Sir Philip Chetwynd and the fact that he had been a figure of some importance for ten years in a county in which Buckingham was trying to increase his power. These things make it easy to believe that Buckingham, having found Thomas Malory of Newbold Revel useful in the parliament of 1445, used his influence to get the Warwickshire knight into the new parliament to provide another voice in the Commons for the policies that Buckingham favoured.

The only plausible alternative has been proposed by Dr Virgoe, who suggested that the M.P. elected on this occasion was Thomas Malory of Papworth, who was twice in 1449–51 involved in property-dealings with a Northamptonshire client of the Beaufort family, much of whose power lay

M.P.s) a rank. The return for Wiltshire and its boroughs was made by John Norris of Bray, Berkshire, retiring sheriff of Wiltshire, at Wilton on 14 October; the other member for Bedwin was Thomas Wells of Eastleigh, Hampshire.

[57] V.C.H., Wilts., v 77–8.

[58] J. Aubrey, Wiltshire: The Topographical Collections (Devizes 1862) pp. 373–80; cf. Wedgwood, Biographies, p. 567.

[59] Dr Virgoe in a private letter.

[60] S.R., ii 170.

in Somerset and adjacent counties.[61] Another man involved in those property dealings was M.P. for Bedwin in the parliament of 1453–4.[62] These are considerations of some weight, but Thomas Malory of Papworth is not known to have taken an interest in politics at any other time, and if he was sufficiently interested at this time to take the trouble, on a patron's behalf or his own, to get himself elected by a constituency far from home to a parliament far from home, it is odd that during the final session of parliament – the session that voted the taxes – he was proving his age in Shrewsbury, a chore he could have undertaken at any time in the previous three-and-a-half years.[63]

It will be best to suspend judgement on this question and turn to the most sensational event in Malory's life, which happened shortly after the prorogation of parliament on 17 December 1449. On 4 January 1450 (so it was later alleged), Sir Thomas Malory of Fenny Newbold and twenty-six other armed men laid a murderous ambush in the abbot's woods at Combe in Warwickshire for the Duke of Buckingham.[64] It is the first of a series of crimes that were to be laid at Malory's charge. Even assuming that Malory was the M.P. for Bedwin, the remaining evidence is insufficient to allow us to say whether he had been driven by some personal quarrel to desert in a spectacular fashion a patron who only three months before had got him into parliament, or whether he was merely expressing political dissent in a manner that was becoming only too common. A month before the alleged ambush, the Duke of Suffolk was said to have had a fellow-member of the royal council beaten up outside the council chamber itself, and five months later Suffolk himself was waylaid on his way to exile and murdered.[65] Both his chief associates in power, though bishops, were murdered by the mob during the same year: one in Portsmouth a few days after Malory's ambush, the other in Wiltshire some months later.[66] In the latter case, the bishop was dragged from the altar where he was saying mass and killed as if he were a wild beast, with cudgels and boar-spears. There was also plenty of non-political violence about, well away from the court: at about this time Buckingham was the target of an attempted assault by eight members of the Ferrers affinity.[67] It is understandable that, as his household accounts show, he kept some scores of men available on his estates

61 C.F.R. (1445–52) pp. 101–2, 197. For the Beaufort client, Thomas Crosse, clerk to Thomas Thorpe, see Wedgwood, s.vv.

62 See Wedgwood, s.v. Thomas Humfrey.

63 P.R.O. C139/144/45, dated 18 May 1450; cf. Martin, pp. 167–70.

64 P.R.O. KB9/265/78; Hicks, pp. 34–5, 93–7; A.C. Baugh, 'Documenting Sir Thomas Malory', Speculum 8 (1933) 3–6.

65 Ramsay, ii 113, 121; I.M.W. Harvey, Jack Cade's Rebellion (Oxford 1991) pp. 62–3, 73.

66 Storey, pp. 62, 66; Harvey, pp. 63–4, 123.

67 Carole Rawcliffe, The Staffords, Earls of Stafford and Dukes of Buckingham 1394–1521 (Cambridge 1978), p. 178.

from the spring of this year onwards, and called them out when there was likely to be trouble.[68]

The opposition to Suffolk eventually forced the king to dismiss him. The means by which this was achieved included disturbances in the provinces and insistent demands from the House of Commons during the second session of parliament (22 January – 30 March 1450).[69] Sir Thomas had shown some talent for both kinds of activity, and there is no sign of his having been in Warwickshire during that second session. On 29 April parliament was adjourned to the Lancastrian stronghold of Leicester, and it was after that that Malory (so it was said) committed rape on 23 May and extortion on 31 May, both at Monks Kirby, fifteen miles down the road from Leicester to Newbold Revel. In the former case, it was said, accompanied by William Weston of Fenny Newbold gentleman, Thomas Potter of Bernangle husbandman, and Adam Brown of Coventry weaver, he broke the close and houses of Hugh Smith and feloniously raped and carnally lay by Hugh's wife Joan. *Raptus* could mean simple abduction, but in this case the wording of the charge shows it did not: the charge was sexual assault. In the latter case, he and John Appleby are said to have used threats and oppression to extort a hundred shillings from Margaret King and William Hale.

Parliament was dissolved about 6 June, and during the following weeks, Malory was alleged to have committed rape and theft on 6 August, and a second extortion on 31 August.[70] The accusations were first, that in addition to having once more feloniously raped and carnally lain by Joan Smith, this time in Coventry, he had also carried off to Barwell in Leicestershire goods and chattels belonging to her husband Hugh to the value of £40, and second, that he and Appleby by threats and oppression had extorted twenty shillings from John Milner at Monks Kirby. His freedom of action was the greater because the court and Buckingham were kept occupied in the south-east by various affairs, including Cade's and other risings and the Duke of York's return from Ireland.[71]

All over the country private quarrels were polarizing into political ones, and if Malory's disagreement with Buckingham had ever been merely personal, it was bound to become more than that. There is evidence to suggest that this had happened by the autumn of 1450. A new parliament was summoned on 5 September, and met on 6 November. The magnates brought small armies to London to support them, and there were riots

[68] K.B. McFarlane, 'The Wars of the Roses', *P.B.A.* 50 (1964) 91.
[69] Ramsay, ii 111–20; Storey, pp. 43–53.
[70] Dissolution 5–8 June (Wedgwood, *Register*, p. 115); crimes in Hicks and Baugh, locc. citt.
[71] Ramsay, ii 125–36; Storey, pp. 61–8. It is one of the ironies of the situation that Cade's rebels wanted to prevent magnates from putting their nominees into parliament.

there among their partisans.[72] Some of the lords, notably York and his only major supporter at the time, the Duke of Norfolk, had worked hard and successfully to procure factions in the House of Commons as well as outside.[73] Over the three sessions of parliament, 6 November – 18 December 1450, 20 January – 29 March, and at least 5–24 May 1451, York's supporters gained control of the Commons, and on 24 May they presented the government with an ultimatum, refusing to transact any more business unless the duke was given the succession to the throne. Within a week, parliament was dissolved.[74]

In that parliament, Wareham in Dorset was represented by a Thomas Malory.[75] Since there were no Malorys living in Dorset at the time and no other Thomas Malory is recorded in the entire *Return of Members*, it is generally agreed that the M.P. for Wareham must have been the Thomas Malory who was previously M.P. for Bedwin. If the one was Sir Thomas Malory of Newbold Revel, so was the other. The arguments for and against are similar to those that bear on Bedwin but slightly weaker in both directions. The borough of Wareham belonged to the Duke of York,[76] and if Sir Thomas Malory of Newbold Revel was the new M.P. it will have been because he belonged to York too. Once again it would be surprising to find the lord of a borough influencing its parliamentary electoral process, to find a knight as its M.P., and to find his title suppressed and his name put second to that of someone who was not a knight. Once again it can be said that the time was exceptional, and that Sir Thomas of Newbold Revel has the advantages of a connection (although not a strong one) with the lord of the borough, and of being the only man of his name with a known interest in politics.[77] There is the same possible explanation for the absence of his rank. The connection with York was indirect: he apparently held Newbold Revel of York's ally Norfolk,[78] and although in the fifteenth century the feudal link need not amount to much, there was also to be, as we shall see, a strong connection between him and Norfolk a few years later, whose basis may already have existed in 1450. Moreover, the indirectness of the connection between Malory and York is compensated for by York's known

---

72 Ramsay, ii 137.
73 Storey, pp. 78–9. For York, see P.A. Johnson, *Duke Richard of York 1411–1460* (Oxford 1988); for lords' electioneering, cf. McFarlane ut supra, pp. 90–1 and nn.
74 Wedgwood, *Register*, p. 147.
75 *Return of Members*. The return for Dorset and its boroughs was made by John Austell of Churchill, Somerset, retiring sheriff of Somerset and Dorset, at Dorchester on 2 November; the other member for Wareham was Robert Browning of Winterbourne Stapleton, Dorset.
76 Wedgwood (*Biographies*, p. 567) noticed the patron here; and cf. *V.C.H. Dorset*, ii 141.
77 See a sceptical view, see Johnson, pp. 105–6.
78 See Appendix III.

need for men with Sir Thomas's abilities, and by Sir Thomas's urgent need for protection against Buckingham.[79]

As in the case of Bedwin and for much the same reasons, the only credible alternative is Thomas Malory of Papworth. The arguments for and against him are much the same as they were with Bedwin, except that no associate of his is known to have been M.P. for Wareham, but then neither was he demonstrably elsewhere while this parliament was in session. Judgement may again be suspended for the moment.

The next document concerning Sir Thomas Malory of Newbold Revel may have been an attempt to get rid of the member for Wareham as a notorious fomenter of trouble. A warrant was issued on 15 March for the arrest of Malory, Appleby, and eighteen others for various felonies.[80] Even if Sir Thomas of Newbold Revel was the member, the authorities might not have known where he was, but if he was and they did, it would have been a bold officer who tried to arrest him, and the Controlment Roll indicates that nothing was done. This is confirmed by later accusations of a new series of crimes in Warwickshire within three weeks of the dissolution of parliament.

On 4 June at Cosford in Warwickshire, three miles east of Newbold Revel, Malory and five others were said to have stolen and driven to Newbold Revel seven cows, two calves, 335 sheep, and a cart valued at £22, all the property of William Rowe and William Dowde of Shawell.[81] Malory also seems to have frightened the monks at Monks Kirby, since on 13 July Buckingham, Warwick, and the Sheriff of Warwickshire and Leicestershire were directed to arrest him and John Appleby and make them give security that they would do no damage to the Abbey of Axholme, Lincolnshire, which was the mother-house of Monks Kirby.[82] There is no record that Warwick took any action, but Buckingham gathered sixty mounted yeomen including his receiver for Staffordshire at his manor of Atherston-juxta-Merevale, which was conveniently between the headquarters of his household at Maxstoke and the headquarters of his retinue at Stafford, and himself rode to arrest the wanted men.[83] This is the only recorded occasion on which Buckingham himself rode out with his men on such an expedition, and the band he took with him was larger than that sent from this part

---

[79] For attempts by Buckingham to turn the law on his enemies, see Rawcliffe, pp. 178–81.
[80] Baugh, p. 6.
[81] Hicks, p. 97; Baugh, pp. 7, 14–15. Those accused with Malory were three men from Fenny Newbold (John Masshot yeoman, William Smith labourer, and Geoffrey Griffin yeoman) and two from Leicestershire (John Frisby of Carlton yeoman, and John Arnesby of 'Tyrlynton' [Tur Langton] husbandman).
[82] C.P.R. (1446–52) p. 476.
[83] McFarlane, p. 91; more fully in R.I. Jack, 'A New Reference to Sir Thomas Malory', A.J. 69 (1969) 131–3.

of his estates in 1450 to face Cade's rebels.[84] The size of his following suggests that he expected Malory to have a good deal of support.

While Buckingham was looking for him, Malory apparently broke into Buckingham's park at Caludon on 20 July, stealing six does and doing an enormous amount of damage: the indictment said £500-worth.[85] In this period Caludon is usually said to belong to the Duke of Norfolk;[86] it was the hunting-lodge from which a previous Duke of Norfolk set out for the famous duel with Henry Bolingbroke with which Shakespeare opens his *Richard II*. However, when Malory was brought to book for the Caludon Park offence, the accusation was made by the Duke of Buckingham, the Duke and Duchess of Norfolk, and the Archbishop of Canterbury, who according to their attorneys were the owners of the park. The duchess was Buckingham's maternal half-sister, and the archbishop, as the illegitimate son of Sir Humphrey Stafford of Southwick, was Buckingham's kinsman. The four names suggests some form of displaced ownership, perhaps a lease, perhaps enfeoffment.[87] Even if it was the latter, even a moderate amount of good-will between the joint legal owners, since Norfolk and the archbishop were based in the south-eastern counties, might have made Buckingham the effective occupant of the park in the eyes of Warwickshire. Even if we discount the possibility suggested by the Wareham episode that he and Norfolk may have been on good terms, it is difficult to see why Malory should have vandalised what he believed to be Norfolk's property: he had enough powerful enemies already. The Norfolks' involvement may have dawned on him as an extremely disagreeable surprise. Attacking Buckingham's deer-park, however, would have been a different matter. Buckingham was an established enemy, and attacking deer-parks was a recognised form of magnate-baiting. It had happened to the Duke of Norfolk and the Duchess (she had her own parks), to their enemy the Duke of Suffolk, to Suffolk's rival Lord Cromwell, and in the previous year, a hundred armed men had carried off game from Buckingham's park at Penshurst in Kent.[88] Malory's attack might even have been a copy-cat crime triggered by the last of these, although he was easier to bring to book than his predecessors, because they had put on long beards, blackened their faces with charcoal, and called themselves the servants of the queen of the fairies.

Succeeding events suggest that the two parties may each have been

[84] I am grateful to Dr Rawcliffe for this information.
[85] P.R.O. KB27/763 m. 23d, printed in Baugh, p. 21.
[86] Dugdale, *Warwickshire*, p. 127; *V.C.H.*, *Warwicks.*, viii 121.
[87] I owe this suggestion to Dr Rowena Archer.
[88] Harvey, p. 121; Rawcliffe, p. 178; Simon Payling, *Political Society in Lancastrian England* (Oxford 1991) p. 196.

ignorant of what the other was doing.[89] Buckingham caught Malory at Newbold Revel, and handed him over to the sheriff at Coventry on 25 July for safe-keeping. The sheriff, Sir William Mountford, who had been Malory's colleague as M.P. for Warwickshire in 1445 and had sat with him on the commission of 1445, locked Malory up in the Mountford manor-house at Coleshill on 27 July. That night, however, he allegedly broke out, swam the moat, and on the following night with ten named accomplices and others unnamed battered down the doors of Combe Abbey to steal ornaments and money worth £86, returning the day after that with a hundred armed men to break in again, insult the monks, do a great deal of damage and steal over £40 in money, five rings, a small psalter, two silver belts, three rosaries (of coral, amber, and jet respectively), two bows and three sheaves of arrows.[90]

On 23 August, Malory was charged by a court at Nuneaton with these offences except the one at Caludon. The court was presided over by four justices, among whom, undeterred by any scruples that the first and gravest charge was an attempt to murder himself, was the Duke of Buckingham.[91] Two juries of presentment were required, because Cosford was in Knightlow Hundred and the other charges all involved places in Hemlingford Hundred.[92] The juries considered the charges, and found a true bill on these counts. On 5 October, however, a writ of certiorari called the proceedings into the court of King's Bench in London.[93] Malory may have been out of Warwickshire before 8 November 1451, when Sir William Mountford's term as sheriff of Warwickshire and Leicestershire expired,

[89] For these events see Hicks, pp. 93–6; Baugh, pp. 3–6.
[90] On the first occasion those accused with him were John Appleby of Fenny Newbold gentleman, John Sherd of Fenny Newbold yeoman, William Hall of Stoneleigh yeoman, John Masshot of Fenny Newbold groom, Roger and Thomas Sherd of Fenny Newbold yeomen, John Tyncock of Wolvey husbandman, Gregory Walshale of Brinklow yeoman, Richard Irishman of Fenny Newbold labourer, and Thomas Maryot of Monks Kirby yeoman, and on the second occasion Richard Malory of Radcliffe-juxta-Leicester [Radcliffe-on-the-Wreake] Leicestershire esquire, Appleby, John Sherd, William Podmore of Fenny Newbold yeoman, William Hall (now called 'walker', i.e. fuller), Masshot, Thomas and Roger Sherd, Walshale, Irishman, Thomas Leghton of Fenny Newbold yeoman, Robert Smith of Fenny Newbold smith, John Warwick of Fenny Newbold yeoman, John Harper of Fenny Newbold harper, and John Cook of Fenny Newbold cook. For these man, see Baugh, p. 14, and for Richard Malory in particular, pp. 60–1 supra.
[91] The other justices were Sir William Birmingham, Thomas Bate, and Thomas Greswold: Hicks, p. 93. Hicks (p. 33) wrongly calls Birmingham sheriff-designate: the next sheriff was the 76-year-old Sir Robert Moton, a distant cousin by marriage of Malory's: C.F.R. (1445–52) p. 251; J.S. Roskell, *The Commons in the Parliament of 1422* (Manchester 1954) pp. 205–6.
[92] For juries of presentment see Edward Powell, *Kingship, Law, and Society* (Oxford 1989) pp. 65–71.
[93] P.R.O. KB9/265/77.

and the new sheriff, Sir Robert Moton, took office: he was certainly in London by the New Year, since on 27 January 1452 the sheriffs of London produced him in the King's Bench, where he was accused of all the offences that he had been charged with at Nuneaton, pleaded not guilty, asked for trial by his countrymen, and was committed to the custody of the Sheriffs of London, in other words to Ludgate prison.[94] Four days later, attorneys for the Norfolks, Buckingham, and the Archbishop of Canterbury accused him in the same court of the Caludon Park offence, and he made the same response, with the same result.

With one exception, this was the last time that Sir Thomas Malory of Newbold Revel and the Duke of Buckingham are known to have been concerned with one another. It was also the end of Malory's alleged criminal spree (if not the last crime to be laid against him), and the beginning of eight years spent mostly in London prisons. It is a good point to attempt a judgement on which Thomas Malory was the M.P. for Bedwin and Wareham. Two factors not yet considered need to be taken into account. First, Sir Thomas of Newbold Revel's connections explain why these two particular constituencies were the ones in question: Thomas of Papworth's do not. More important, whereas the parliamentary sessions conflict slightly with what is known of Thomas of Papworth, they dovetail quite remarkably with Sir Thomas's alleged crimes. The crimes are only allegations though well attested, and Sir Thomas's service in parliament only a deduction, however probable, but alien as they may at first sight seem to be, each by chronological dovetailing makes the other more probable. If Sir Thomas were not in parliament, one might have expected the pattern of allegations to be quite opposite, because when the county's magnates (and their retinues) were away in London, a potential law-breaker might have felt more free to do as he pleased.

A combination of crimes and membership of parliament makes a pattern all too familiar to Englishmen in the middle of the fifteenth century. Malory was not the only man who was sometimes law-abiding or even a legislator, but who at other times ignored the law to take what he wanted or what he felt was his due. Sir Robert Harcourt's spell in prison after the murder of Richard Stafford, for instance, did not prevent him from being elected an M.P. or later made a Knight of the Garter.[95] Neither rank or the religious state guaranteed respect for the law; one of the abbots of Combe, which Malory robbed, was himself accused of robbery twice in one decade.[96]

However, what was previously the most favoured hypothesis about the form of Malory's involvement with the politics of his time now appears to be false. It was long assumed that a Warwickshire knight would have

[94] P.R.O. KB27/763 m. 23d, printed in Hicks, p. 97; cf. Baugh, p. 29.
[95] Storey, p. 87; Wedgwood, *s.vv.*
[96] Matthews, p. 13.

given lifelong allegiance to successive earls of Warwick, and that if he opposed Buckingham it must have been on their behalf. It now seems more probable that he followed several different lords in turn. The more astute and self-seeking of his contemporaries were prepared to follow several – even several hostile – lords simultaneously: nine or ten influential lawyers and administrators were still profiting from both Buckingham and York in the late 1450s, when they were definitely at odds.[97] Although, there is no evidence that Malory was ever formally committed to more than one lord at any one time, his actions suggest that he was continually seeking a 'good lord' (a motive that greatly preoccupies the characters in the *Morte Darthur*),[98] and that the great magnates reciprocated by showing a surprising amount of interest in the unruly 'poor knight'. That search seems to have taken him first to Henry Duke of Warwick, but when the duke's lands descended to his daughter, whose wardship and marriage Suffolk had bought, Malory perhaps hesitated between William of Suffolk and Humphrey of Buckingham, before settling for the latter. He deserted Buckingham very suddenly at the end of 1449, perhaps for the Duke of Norfolk, and either directly or through Norfolk found himself in York's party in the House of Commons. When the government called the Commons' bluff in May 1451, York's power collapsed and even Norfolk deserted him.[99] Any efforts York may have made to keep Malory out of prison were fruitless.

There is no apparent connection in all this between Malory and the most famous Earl of Warwick, Richard Neville. Scholars have often been tempted by the hypothesis that the Kingmaker persuaded or compelled Malory to try to have Buckingham filled full of arrows,[100] but the political situation in 1450 gave none of the magnates reason to want Buckingham dead or even seriously damaged, whatever they may have come to feel five years later; and in regional politics Warwick had an occupation in his family's longstanding feud with the Percys on the Scottish border. Even great men have non-political motives or make mistakes in calculating political interest, but if Warwick had been behind the ambush, one would have expected Malory to be harder to catch eighteen months later. The best explanation for the facts at present known seems to be that Malory's attempt on Buckingham was caused by a private motive, whether 'personal' or 'political', that he had to change sides to find someone to protect him, but that even then the party he changed to was not that of the

---

[97] I am grateful to Dr Rawcliffe for this information.

[98] See P.J.C. Field, 'Four Functions of Malory's Minor Characters', *Medium Aevum* 37 (1968) 37–45; and Elizabeth Archibald, 'Malory's Ideal of Fellowship', *R.E.S.* n.s. 43 (1992) 311–28.

[99] Storey, p. 94.

[100] Matthews, pp. 16, 24; Carpenter, 'Warwickshire', p. 197.

Nevilles. Although he may have been involved with Warwick before, his first certain contact with a Neville comes, as we shall see, in 1457, when Warwick's uncle Lord Fauconberg bailed him out of prison, some three years after the Nevilles had formed their alliance with York. That leaves open at least the possibility that Malory may have been recommended to Warwick by York rather than vice versa.

Difficulties remain, but Malory's parliamentary career fills in a good deal of the most surprising part of his story, and lets us rule out some possibilities as to the kind of person he might have been. Much of the picture remains obscure, but there may still be discoveries to be made in the life of the honourable and gallant member.

VII

Prison

The outline of Malory's life for the next eight years is clear. He spent most of them in London prisons, but the authorities were unable or (much more likely) unwilling to assemble the necessary jury of Warwickshiremen to try him. The legal process against him is suspect from the beginning, although that does not mean that he was innocent.

When he was arrested, Malory should have been imprisoned in Warwick gaol and indicted before the sessions of the peace at Warwick.[1] What actually happened was an abuse and a novelty: the sheriff to whom Buckingham handed him over, and who had become (perhaps very recently) one of Buckingham's supporters, imprisoned him in his own house, and he was indicted at Nuneaton, where Buckingham's power was at its strongest. This and the indictment for theft at the same sessions of John Hathwick of Harbury, who was involved in a quarrel with Sir William Peyto, now another of Buckingham's supporters, suggest, as Dr Carpenter has pointed out, that the duke expected to find his process opposed in Warwick, most probably by the Earl of Warwick himself, and was taking steps to circumvent that.[2] The same is suggested by the writ of certiorari that called the proceedings against Malory into the King's Bench at Westminster. But for that writ, Malory's case would have gone from the sessions of the peace to trial at the assizes in Warwick. It is reasonable to assume that Buckingham procured the writ to avoid opposition in Warwick, and presumably by the earl.

There seems to be very little evidence that either Malory or Hathwick was a supporter of Warwick before this time, but even if Warwick's only interest in either matter were an objection to the flagrant hijacking of the legal process in 'his' county, the victims of that process would almost inevitably have looked to him for protection, and it would have been strange if he had denied it to them. The fact that Malory was never brought to trial suggests Buckingham had doubts about the outcome of a trial even in the King's Bench, and that he chose to make an example of Malory by

[1] Carpenter, 'Warwickshire', pp. 198, 293.
[2] Carpenter, pp. 198–9.

preventing that trial from taking place. Whether he feared that even at a trial in the King's Bench Warwick would succeed in tampering with jurors and witnesses or that he himself would fail in the same, the process achieved very satisfactorily what he wanted: the trial was repeatedly deferred, and Malory remained in prison.

Trials do not always bring the truth to light now, and did not in the fifteenth century, but the absence of one makes it harder to estimate the truth of the charges against Malory. The number of people involved, the variety of the allegations, and (as was argued in the previous chapter) their timing suggests that they were not wholly invented; but their comprehensiveness makes it plain that someone looked for people with grievances against Malory and organised them into court, and presumably encouraged them to make the most of their grievances. Although the rape charges plainly involve rape in the modern sense rather than (as some have wanted to believe) abduction or assault, when one charge came up in the King's Bench, it was pressed not by the alleged victim but by her husband, and under the statute of 6 Richard II, a statute whose purpose was to make elopement into rape despite the woman's consent.[3] Again, when an arable farmer is accused of extorting a modest sum on a single occasion from someone whose surname means Miller, we may guess not at a mediaeval protection racket but at a disagreement over a bill for grinding corn, in which the farmer may not have been wholly in the wrong.[4] If there had been no ambush for Buckingham in Combe Abbey woods, the normal legal procedures might not have been so blatantly disregarded; but it is hard to believe that Buckingham would have waited so long to put Malory out of circulation if he had thought the ambush was seriously meant to kill him. The damage alleged at Caludon is beyond belief, but the charges of breaking and entering at Combe are more credible, partly because of the detail – each item is valued – and partly because the stiff legal Latin conjures up an intrinsically plausible picture of a mob of looters intoxicated by the occasion. The Combe business may be what in the end did Malory most harm. Whether the court of King's Bench also found these charges plausible, or whether it found sacrilegious robbery a particularly convenient pretext for doing what the government's most powerful supporter wanted, one careful investigator was persuaded that these charges were what remained

---

[3] Printed in Baugh, p. 6; and see J.B. Post, 'Sir Thomas West and the Statute of Rapes, 1382', *B.I.H.R.* 53 (1980) 24–30 at pp. 26, 30n.

[4] Twenty years later, a local brewer apparently owed Sir Thomas's widow a larger sum, and, if her executor is-to be believed, the man used legalized intimidation to avoid payment: P.R.O. C1/60/102. On *Milner* see P.H. Reaney, *The Origin of English Surnames* (London 1967) pp. 162, 354 and p. 94 n. 49 supra.

uppermost in the mind of the court throughout Malory's years of confine-
ment.[5]

The legal process in London and Westminster began with the greatest
propriety. Malory was brought to the King's Bench in Westminster on 27
January 1452 by the Sheriffs of London (and therefore from their prison,
Ludgate) and when he had been charged he was returned to them.[6] The
court issued a writ of *venire facias* for twenty-four jurors to be present to try
him on the octave of the Purification (9 February). He was brought back to
the court on that day, and the sheriffs reported that no jurors had appeared.
The case was therefore deferred and Malory returned to Ludgate until the
quindene of Easter (26 April 1452). He was then produced in court, again
no jurors appeared, but this time he was committed not to the Sheriffs of
London but to the marshal of the court, and therefore to its marshalsea.
This prison, officially the Marshalsea of the Marshal of the King's Bench,
but even at this period usually called the King's Bench Prison,[7] must be
distinguished from 'the' Marshalsea, the Marshalsea of the Marshal of the
King's Household. The two prisons were distinct institutions, although
they were side-by-side in what is now Borough High Street in Southwark.

For security reasons if for no others, Malory would have presumably
have travelled between the King's Bench in Westminster Hall and his
prison in Southwark by boat along the Thames, boarding the boat at the
pier that was then called Westminster Bridge. ('Bridge' was used in an
obsolete sense: there was to be no bridge across the Thames at Westminster
until the eighteenth century.) His journeys were frequent enough to fix the
landscape in his imagination, so that when he later retold the story of the
abduction of Queen Guenivere, one of the details he invented was that Sir
Lancelot in his haste to rescue the queen rode into the Thames at the
'bridge' and swam his horse across to the south bank, before disappearing
into the Surrey countryside.[8] That Arthurian picture would have given
Malory something to dream about as he travelled back and forth to hear his
case deferred successively to the quindene of Easter 1452, the octave of
Michaelmas 1452, the octave of Hilary 1453, the quindene of Easter 1453,
the octave of Michaelmas 1453, the octave of Hilary 1454, and the quindene
of Easter 1454.[9]

In prison, some things necessarily passed Malory by, as when Eustace
and Thomas Burneby and others on 26 February 1452 at Saddington in

5   Baugh, pp. 14, 28–9.
6   Hicks, p. 97; Baugh, p. 8.
7   See *A Middle English Dictionary*, ed. H. Kurath et al. (Ann Arbor, Michigan, 1953–), *s.v.*
    kinges bench.
8   *Works*, p. 1125.16; P.J.C. Field, 'Malory's Place-Names: Westminster Bridge and Virvyn',
    Notes & Queries 232 (1987) 292–5.
9   Baugh, p. 9.

Leicestershire granted property in that place to John Pulteney and others: they specified it as that which they together with Thomas Malory knight and Robert Langham esquire now dead had had by enfeoffment of William Malory of Saddington.[10] Although it is only Langham who is dead ('defuncto'), the other survivors necessarily treated Malory as if he were dead too. Some of his alleged accomplices obtained pardons during 1452 and others later, but he remained in prison.[11]

His life, however, was not confined to prison walls and periodic boat trips to Westminster Hall. On 20 May 1452, he made a step towards freedom by agreeing to abide by the arbitration of Thomas Bourchier Bishop of Ely in unspecified quarrels between himself and John Duke of Norfolk.[12] We may assume that he was trying to make his peace over the illicit deer hunt at Caludon. Since Bourchier was Norfolk's brother-in-law, Malory was putting a certain amount of trust in his integrity, but we may also notice that the condition on Bourchier's award, the sum Malory would have lost if he had refused to accept the award, was a mere 200 marks. That sum might have been several times his annual income but it was hardly more than a quarter of the value of the damage he was originally said to have committed. Since for obvious reasons it was customary for an arbitration penalty to be much greater than the value of what was disputed, it seems that Norfolk had accepted before the arbitration began that the initial claims about damage had been greatly exaggerated.

Whatever sum Bishop Bourchier awarded, Malory may have been hard pressed to pay it. Prison in the Middle Ages was expensive both in itself and because it made it difficult to keep one's income coming in smoothly. This makes it plausible that on 26 May 1452, Malory should (although he later denied it) have borrowed £3 from Robert Overton, a London mercer who acted as a sort of moneylender to the London prisons.[13] On 21 October 1452, however, he achieved something rather more important: the court granted him bail on his own surety and those of Sir John Baskerville of Eardisley, Herefordshire, William Cecil of London, Thomas Ince of Stanford Rivers, Essex, and John Leventhorpe of Southwark, Surrey, esquires until 3 February 1453, whereupon the marshal was to keep him safe under the huge penalty of £2000.[14] The key figure in this may have been Leventhorpe, who had been a neighbour of Malory's in his childhood (the Leventhorpes lived at Newnham Paddox until 1433), who as Marshal

---

10 Leicester C.R.O., DE 2242/6/64: Eustace Burneby and Thomas Burneby esquires, John Slauston clerk, and John Marchaunt of Kibworth grant John Pulteney and Thomas Cotes of Honingham esquires and Simon Broke clerk lands in Saddington, Smeeton, and Westerby.

11 Baugh, pp. 15–19. Richard Malory was among those pardoned.

12 P.R.O. KB27/764, m. between 52d and 54d.

13 Baugh, p. 26.

14 P.R.O. KB27/766, m. 45d Rex.

of 'the' Marshalsea lived next door to Malory's prison, and who at this time was associated with both Buckingham and Norfolk.[15] Baskerville is recorded as a retainer of Buckingham's in 1451,[16] so it is possible that Malory, having made his peace with Norfolk, was being given an opportunity to make his peace more generally in Warwickshire. Four days later, Malory entered into a bond for £200 that he and Philip Burgh and Thomas Barton, presumably his servants, should keep the peace toward William Venner, hereditary keeper of the Fleet Prison.[17] He may have been trying to arrange that when his bail ended he should change prison to the Fleet. The Fleet, the prison for the king's debtors, although expensive and in summer smelly and diseased, was much the freest and most comfortable prison in London, and prisoners elsewhere competed for transfers, pretending to owe the king money. His period of freedom, however, was to end very differently.

Others in Warwickshire may also have been concerned to try to reconcile factions at this time, since apparently, when Malory arrived home, Monks Kirby Priory, which had a deed for completion, asked him and a number of other east Warwickshire landowners of various political leanings to witness it. The deed survives only in a copy in the register of Reginald Boulers, who became bishop of Coventry and Lichfield in 1453.[18] This register copy is dated 13 October 1453,[19] but the date must be wrong, since the witnesses include not only Malory, who if he had not been back in the King's Bench Prison would by then have been a fugitive, but Sir William Mountford, who died on 6 December 1452.[20] Any deed executed much before October 1452 ought to have appeared in the register of a previous bishop – Bishop

---

15 For Leventhorpe's life, see Wedgwood, *s.v.*, for his father as the Malorys' neighbour, Chapter III supra, and more generally P.W. Kerr, 'The Leventhorpes of Sawbridgeworth', *Trans. E. Herts. Archaeol. Soc.* 9 (1935) 129–51 and pedigree. Wedgwood felt unable to identify the man associated with Buckingham and Norfolk with the marshal, but the domicile of the John Leventhorpe who bailed Malory on this occasion establishes him as the marshal, and, as we shall see, in 1454 Malory was again bailed by a John Leventhorpe and a Thomas Ince in company that associates them with Norfolk.

16 Carpenter, 'Sir Thomas Malory and Fifteenth-Century Politics', *B.I.H.R.* 53 (1980) 31–43, at p. 38.

17 *C.C.R.* (1447–54) p. 396; cf. Margery Bassett, 'The Fleet Prison in the Middle Ages', *Univ. of Toronto Law Jnl* 5 (1943–44) 383–402.

18 Lichfield Joint Record Office, MS B/A/11, fol. 54^{r-v}. I am grateful to Mrs J. Hampartumian of the Record Office for an account of this entry. The copy in Bodl. MS. Dugdale 9, p. 335, has of course no independent authority. For Bishop Boulers's dates, see F.M. Powicke et al., *Handbook of British Chronology* (London 1961) pp. 251, 254. For background see Carpenter, *Locality*, p. 473.

19 The form of the date is '13 October 1453, 32 Henry VI'. The text of the deed follows the bishop's note of his part in the transaction, dated 'the penultimate day of August 1454'. The error cannot therefore have come about simply by the bishop's clerk writing the date on which he was working in place of the date in his original.

20 Wedgwood, *s.v.*

Close, who died about the end of that month, or one of his predecessors. That assumption is not unquestionable, since the entire transaction had proceeded at a very leisurely pace.[21] If, however, we take that as a working assumption, the deed will have been executed in the period from late October to early December 1452, although the priory will have had to wait until Bishop Boulers had been translated from his previous diocese (on 7 February 1453) before they had an episcopal register to have it copied into.

Whatever intentions of peace and good will to all men it began with, Malory's Christmas at home would seem to have been a disaster. On the day before he was due to surrender to his bail, the King's Bench is said to have ordered the distraint of all his goods.[22] Whether the court had heard that he had broken the law or simply that he was not going to return is not recorded, but the next record to name him is a commission issued to Buckingham, Edward Lord Grey of Groby, and the Sheriff of Warwickshire and Leicestershire on 26 March 1453 instructing them to arrest him.[23] That the Earl of Warwick was not included in such a commission is surprising, and suggests that he may have been suspected of favouring the wanted man. Dr Carpenter suggests the authorities might have been regarded east Warwickshire as in effect Buckingham and Grey's sphere of influence,[24] but two years before, the previous commission to arrest Malory had included Warwick, and the authorities are more likely to have suspected a lessening in Warwick's reliability than in his power.

The order for Malory's arrest might have been a response to the process seven weeks before in the King's Bench or to a quite different stimulus. As we saw in the previous chapter, this is the most likely period for Malory to have raided Lady Peyto's manor of Sibbertoft, and there is clearly a possibility that the order was a reaction to her petition to Chancery.

That raises the question of Malory's involvement with the Earl of Warwick. Warwickshire, like the rest of the country, was polarising towards civil war, and this would have put a new pressure on Malory to become a supporter of Warwick, and so to be at odds with those who, like the Peytos, supported Buckingham. As we have seen, John Hathwick of Harbury had been indicted with Malory at Nuneaton. By 1453, Hathwick had become a supporter of Warwick,[25] and Sir William Peyto was certainly at odds with him: Peyto and one of his men beat Hathwick up in London in 1451. During Malory's period of freedom on bail, Peyto was awaiting a trial

21 It had first been licenced by the king in 1399, then relicenced in 1445: *V.C.H., Warwicks.*, vi 251; Bodl. MS. Dugd. 9, loc. cit. Cf. also T. Madox, *Formulare Anglicanum* (London 1702) pp. 351–2.

22 Hicks, p. 107, giving no reference. No later scholar has found it, but the next item makes it plausible.

23 *C.P.R.* (1452–69) p. 61.

24 Carpenter, *Locality*, p. 453.

25 Carpenter, 'Warwickshire', p. 199.

for that assault, which later in 1453 found him guilty and fined him £60, which he did not pay, which eventually earned him three years in prison.[26] Malory was certainly later both an associate of John Hathwick and a supporter of Warwick, but with one complicated exception the clearest evidence as to whether or not he supported Warwick as early as 1453 is the absence of the earl's name from the commission to arrest him, which is a long way from conclusive.

The exception is an inference that can be drawn from one interpretation of the Sibbertoft petition. The events alleged at Sibbertoft could have happened if there had been no earl of Warwick at all. They could been provoked by some local circumstance such as Lady Peyto's origins – she was a Gresley of Drakelow,[27] and her family had been robbing Malory's wife's family for years – and then compounded by Malory's and Peyto's relationship to Buckingham. However, *if* the Sibbertoft raid was at this time, Lady Peyto's petition implies that Malory was thought of in Warwickshire as a member of Warwick's affinity. It speaks of an unsuccessful appeal Lady Peyto had made to 'my lord of Warwick'. If she appealed to the earl at this time, it would not have been as her lord and her husband's, so it must have been as Malory's.

If the Sibbertoft raid was at this time, Buckingham will have had the stimulus of an injury to one of his supporters to encourage him to catch Malory quickly, but even if he did not, there is no reason to suppose he took any longer to make his arrest on this occasion than on the previous one. We may assume that Malory was back in prison in the late summer and autumn of 1453 when a number of momentous events took place, all in one way or another pushing the country towards civil war. In August King Henry had a mental breakdown that was to last for seventeen months, and a few weeks later there was a skirmish between the Percys and the Nevilles near York that has been taken to be the first battle of the Wars of the Roses. In October, the birth of a son to King Henry and Queen Margaret after nine childless years made much more difficult one peace-making expedient that some had canvassed, making the Duke of York the king's heir; and later in the same month the final surrender of Bordeaux brought the Hundred Years War to an inglorious end, and reminded patriots how much they had lost in France since the heady days of the king's father.

In the midst of these great events, the legal process fastened its grip on Malory again. On the octave of Michaelmas (6 October), the marshal brought him back once more to the King's Bench, no jurors appeared, and he was again returned to the marshal, this time until the octave of Hilary, when the case was again deferred, no doubt for the same reason, until the

26 Baugh, p. 20. Peyto was in the King's Bench prison 15 June 1456 – 10 May 1459.
27 F. Madan, *The Gresleys of Drakelowe* (Oxford 1899) pp. 57–61.

quindene of Easter (8 May 1454).[28] On the 4 February 1454, the court ordered the marshal under the reduced penalty of £1000 to keep Malory securely and not allow him out on bail or otherwise without the written permission of the court.[29] When Malory appeared before it on 8 May, however, the court gave that permission, granting him bail until a month after Michaelmas (29 October) on his own surety and those of Sir Roger Chamberlain of Queenborough, Kent, John Leventhorpe of London, Edward Fitzwilliam of Framlingham, Suffolk, Thomas Boughton of Lawford, Warwickshire, William Worsop of Framlingham, John Valens of Framlingham, and Thomas Ince of Essex, esquires, and Ralph Worthington of Framlingham, Edmund Whateley of London, and John Hathwick of Harbury, Warwickshire, gentlemen.[30]

Of Malory's ten sureties, Chamberlain, Leventhorpe, and the four men from Framlingham (Norfolk's principal residence) were Norfolk's men, although Leventhorpe was apparently acceptable to Buckingham as well; Boughton was Lord Grey of Groby's man, and Hathwick, as we have seen, Warwick's; Ince's Essex origins suggest a connection with Norfolk, and Ralph Worthington is an unknown quantity. The balance of the group suggests that Norfolk had persuaded the other leading figures in Warwickshire to let Malory have another chance. Since Malory is next heard of in East Anglia, the duke perhaps wanted to see Malory for himself. He might have been thinking of taking Malory into his own affinity, either in Warwickshire or in East Anglia. With the probability increasing that at some time soon one of the little local skirmishes was going to turn into a real battle, a sensible magnate would think twice before rejecting a man who had perhaps fought in the wars in France and who had shown himself able to raise large numbers of armed men at short notice, even if he was something of a rough diamond.

The duke, however, was in for a disappointment. Even in the neighbourhood of a well-disposed magnate, Malory behaved in a way that suggested that even if he could raise men, he could not control them or himself. On October 29, he once again failed to appear in the King's Bench when his bail expired. The prosecution sought execution of the penalties against him and his sureties, but Leventhorpe and Ince appeared to say that Malory

---

[28] Baugh, p. 9. For Michaelmas as the octave and the quindene of Easter as 17 not 14 days after Easter Sunday, see C.R. Cheney, *Handbook of Dates* (London 1961) pp. 67–8. A scrutiny of the dates in this chapter will show that the quindene of Easter may not have been the only date that the King's Bench deemed to occur a few days later than the rest of the world, but I have only adjusted those for which I had Cheney's authority. The possible differences would not as far as I can see have any consequences for the story related here.

[29] Baugh, pp. 9–10.

[30] Baugh, loc. cit. For Chamberlain and Leventhorpe see Wedgwood, for Boughton, Carpenter, 'Warwickshire', p. 210.

was in prison at Colchester in Essex on suspicion of various felonies.[31] In these, however, the principal was for once said to be not Malory but his 'servant' John Aleyn alias Addelsey, who had undertaken a criminal spree of his own through the cloth towns of East Anglia.[32] Unless the men of Essex had misheard his name, it would seem that Malory's steward John Appleby had found it convenient since his outlawry in Warwickshire to go about under an alias. An Essex inquisition said that 'Aleyn' had stolen two horses, a bay and a grey, from the Abbot of Tilty at Great Easton in Essex on 21 May, a white horse from Richard Scott, vicar of Gosfield, on 27 June, and a sorrel and another bay from Thomas Bykenen and Thomas Strete of Gosfield on 2 July. It said too that Malory and Aleyn had ridden from Waltham Cross in Hertfordshire to Thaxted in Essex on 9 July, and from Thaxted to Braintree on 10 July, and Malory, knowing what Aleyn had done, had feloniously harboured and comforted him, that Malory, Aleyn, and others unspecified had plotted to rob William Green and William Algore, and that on 21 July while everyone in Gosfield was at mass, Aleyn and others with Malory's advice and consent went to John Green's house where William Green and his wife kept their goods and chattels, forced an entry using wire instruments, and would have carried off various of William's chests and coffers if they had not been interrupted. A second inquisition said Aleyn had also broken into John Green's house on the previous day: although it did not say Malory was involved, it described Aleyn as his servant.

The court, having heard this on 29 October, responded the following day with a writ of habeas corpus to John Hampton, governor of Colchester prison,[33] requiring him to produce Malory and to transfer proceedings against him into the King's Bench on the octave of St Martin (18 November). Malory, however, promptly became unavailable. He had been arrested in Essex and on 16 October handed over by Sir Thomas Cobham, the Sheriff of Essex, to Hampton; but on the very day the writ was sent he escaped, using (it was said) swords, daggers, and langue-de-boeufs.[34] Despite the fearsome array of weapons, however, he was recaptured and Hampton duly handed him over in the King's Bench on the appointed day, whereupon he was again committed to the marshal on penalty of £1000.[35]

The court rolls blandly record that Malory could not be tried on 29 October because there were no jurors and that his case was therefore

[31] Baugh, pp. 10–12.
[32] Baugh, pp. 22–6.
[33] See Wedgwood, s.n. For his annuity from Buckingham, see Rawcliffe, The Staffords, p. 234.
[34] Baugh, pp. 25–6.
[35] Baugh, p. 12.

deferred to the quindene of Hilary (27 January 1455).[36] There being no jurors then either, it was deferred again until the quindene of Easter (23 April), when it was deferred yet again until the octave of Trinity (8 June).

In the interim, however, Malory's circumstances changed as a result of events outside the prison walls. In early April, parliament, faced with the king's incapacity, had made the Duke of York Lord Protector during the king's pleasure or until the Prince of Wales came of age. On 30 December, however, the king recovered his faculties, and in February and March 1455 dismissed York's officers of state and replaced them with the Duke of Somerset's men. Tension built up in the country, and York and Warwick gathered an army and made their way to London to petition the king to dismiss Somerset. On 19 May, the day before they reached Royston, Malory was moved from the King's Bench Prison to the Tower of London.[37]

It has been suggested that the transfer was made to prevent the Duke of Norfolk, who the king himself at this time had said to be a committed Yorkist, from using his post as Earl Marshal (which made him responsible to the king for both marshalseas) to have Malory released to join the Yorkist army.[38] There is no doubt about Norfolk's responsibility for the marshalseas: an escape of prisoners some years later made the then duke so apprehensive that he procured an act of indemnity in parliament to protect himself; and he certainly in the last resort had the power to dismiss marshals and their deputies.[39] However, marshals were normally appointed for life and once appointed presumably developed a certain independence in the day-to-day exercise of their office. Had the Earl Marshal tried to intervene, against the customs of the office and the orders of the court of King's Bench, the marshal would have had to keep in mind that the king also could dismiss a marshal and take over his office.[40] The marshal would then have had to weigh up which master he would serve.

We can guess what decision would have been taken by the marshal who took Malory into the King's Bench Prison. Unlike his counterpart in the Marshalsea of the King's Household next door, John Gargrave was a thorough-paced Lancastrian: he was a king's esquire in 1435, one of thirty-two Lancastrians indicted before the lord chancellor at Rochester in 1450, and one of three Lancastrians whom York, returning from Ireland about that time, captured and detained in Ludlow Castle.[41] He is recorded as marshal from 1444 to January 1453, on the last occasion as John Gargrave

[36] Baugh, p. 9.
[37] Baugh, p. 13.
[38] Carpenter, 'Sir Thomas Malory', p. 40.
[39] R.B. Pugh, *Imprisonment in Medieval England* (Cambridge 1968) esp. pp. 118, 159. The earl marshal's right had been established in law in 1423: *C.P.R.* (1422–29) pp. 83–4.
[40] Pugh, pp. 158, 241.
[41] Wedgwood, *s.v.*; C.L. Kingsford, *English Historical Literature in the Fifteenth Century*, pp. 359, 365, 297.

senior, but was probably removed later that year.[42] If Norfolk had asked to
have Malory released in suspicious circumstances, there can be little doubt
that Gargrave would have returned him a dusty answer. By 1457, however,
there was a different marshal, William Brandon esquire of Framlingham,
who is recorded in office in 1457, 1458, and 1460.[43] Brandon is much more
likely to have paid attention to Norfolk's wishes, unless things were the
other way round: it was said that he could twist the duke round his little
finger. That however did not stop Norfolk from dismissing him in
Michaelmas Term 1460 for allowing prisoners to go about at large, and
appointing Thomas Bourchier in his place. (Brandon contested his dismiss-
al in the King's Bench, and lost.)[44] However, although Brandon called
himself 'keeper of the prison of the marshalsea' in a pardon he took out in
1458, he did not in a pardon in October 1455, which suggests that in May
1455 he was not yet in office.

It seems likely therefore that when Malory was moved from the King's
Bench Prison to the Tower, the day-to-day running of the former was in
charge of an unknown temporary or acting marshal whose political inclinations we cannot know. Those inclinations, however, need not have been
the reason for moving Malory. The south bank of the Thames was obviously insecure in times of unrest: both marshalseas had been broken
open and had their prisoners released in Cade's rebellion only five years
before, and in the Peasants' Revolt before that.[45] It is plain that Malory was
in some kind of special category: the court did not transfer all the prisoners
in its marshalsea to the Tower. Nevertheless, the fact that he was later
returned to the King's Bench Prison for two further periods suggests that
what the court feared was not treachery inside the marshalsea but rebels
outside it.

Three days after Malory was moved, the two parties in national politics
fought what came to be called the first battle of St Albans. York won,
Somerset and other lords were killed and Buckingham wounded, and York
took over the government. His victory does not appear to have had any
immediate effect on Malory's life. Malory was due to reappear in the
King's Bench on the octave of Trinity (8 June), but the Constable of the
Tower actually produced him on the quindene (15 June), whereupon he
had his trial set for the quindene of Michaelmas (13 October) and was
returned to the constable, who was to keep him safe under a penalty of

---

42 *C.P.R.* (1441–46) pp. 216, 408; (1452–61) pp. 7, 129, evidence in Wedgwood *s.v.* (despite
   Wedgwood's conclusions).
43 Wedgwood *s.v.*; *C.C.R.* (1454–61) p. 490.
44 Year Book 39 Hen. VI, pp. 32–4, in *Les reports des cases en ley*, 11 vols (London 1679–80).
   He was later apparently reappointed, perhaps in 1462, when Bourchier was pardoned
   as *late* Marshal of the Marshalsea of the King's Bench: Wedgwood, *s.v.*
45 Pugh, pp. 222–4.

£2000.[46] He was produced in court, presumably by the constable, on 13 October, his case was deferred for lack of jurors until the quindene of Hilary (27 January 1456), and, although the roll does not make it explicit, he was no doubt returned to the constable again for safekeeping, since it was the constable who produced him in the King's Bench in Hilary Term 1456.[47]

In the mean time, on 12 November the king's incapacity had overtaken him again, and on 19 November the parliament then sitting made York Lord Protector once more, an office he held until the king recovered, on 25 January 1456. On 24 November, perhaps hoping for better luck under the new government, Malory took out a general pardon effective for crimes committed before 9 July 1455.[48] When Thomas Gower, lieutenant of the Constable of the Tower, produced Malory in the King's Bench, not (as it had been arranged) on the quindene of Hilary itself but on the following Wednesday (30 January), Malory produced his pardon and offered sureties for his good behaviour.[49] His sureties were Roger Malory of Ruyton, Warwickshire, gentleman, and five London men: John Benford and William Cliff, gentlemen, Walter Boys, saddler, and Thomas Pulton and David John, tailors. The court declined to recognise either the pardon or the sufficiency of Malory's sureties, and returned him to the custody of the marshal to be taken back to the King's Bench Prison. Its grounds for rejecting the pardon are unknown, but even apart from Malory's record his sureties on this occasion are distinctly unimpressive. All six are obscure; Roger Malory was presumably a cousin, but what brought the others to Sir Thomas's aid is unknown.[50]

That day's proceedings also broke a pattern that had been maintained for three years. For the first time, despite the fact that a deputy sheriff of Warwickshire and Leicestershire, William Coton, was in court for the proceedings, there is no record of any arrangement or pretended arrangement for a trial in a subsequent term. The court seems at this point to have given up attempting to try the prisoner. Although it is possible that up to now it

46 Baugh, pp. 12–14.
47 Baugh, p. 9.
48 P.R.O. C67/41, m. 15.
49 Hicks, pp. 99–100. For Gower, see Wedgwood, *s.v.*, R.A. Griffiths, *The Reign of Henry VI* (London 1981) pp. 518, 521, K.B. MacFarlane, *England in the Fifteenth Century* (London 1981) pp. 167, 169.
50 Roger Malory of Ruyton-on-Dunsmore is recorded in a Warwickshire land deal in 1453: Stratford-upon-Avon, Shakespeare's Birthplace Trust, MS. DR 37/Box 40. Walter Boys was a witness at St-Dunstan-in-the-West in 1457 and enfeoffed William Venour and Thomas Poulton of his all in 1461: *C.C.R.* (1454–61) pp. 252, 482. If Venour was the keeper of the Fleet Prison, did he supplement his income by providing men of straw? Thomas Pulton of Desborough, Northants., was in business with Simon Malory, Sir Thomas's uncle, in London in 1434: P.R.O. KB27/692 rot. 67d. David John of London, cordwainer, is recorded in the following decade: *C.C.R.* (1461–8) p. 378.

had merely been putting on an appearance of attempting to try him, there is some reason to suspect a real change. Whereas previous King's Bench records are compatible with the court doing its duty, later ones are not. It may be that the subversion of legal process had taken place in Warwickshire up to now, but was to occur in Westminster from now on.

That fits in well enough with events nationally. It must have been obvious that Malory was a very special prisoner. The determination of the authorities to keep him inside, as expressed in penalties on his gaolers for keeping him safe, reached a record for mediaeval England.[51] Such interest by Lancastrian authorities cannot but have stimulated interest in the Yorkist lords, and even though, as we have seen, they may have found Malory not quite what they wanted when they had him, their interest must in turn have reminded the authorities to take no chances, and so, for instance, to move Malory to the Tower while other prisoners remained where they were. The government's supporters included the Lord Chief Justice of the King's Bench, Sir John Fortescue, who was sufficiently committed to Lancaster to go into exile after the Yorkists' eventual victory, and the aftermath of First St Albans, with the government changed by force of arms, is the very moment when even a lawyer normally committed to due process might be tempted give the law a helping hand. It is presumably only a coincidence, although it looks like yet another disaster for Malory, that these things happened just before his brother-in-law Thomas Walsh became Sheriff of Warwickshire and Leicestershire.[52] Walsh would no doubt have wished to see Malory free, and as a Leicestershire man need not have taken much account of Warwickshire magnates when picking his panel for the jury. He probably inclined to Lancaster in politics,[53] but despite any strains created by that or by having a particularly troublesome brother-in-law, the two of them got on well enough, as we shall see, for Walsh to become one of Malory's feoffees in 1462. That aside, however, we may reasonably be very suspicious of the legality of the rejection of Malory's pardon and of the cessation of attempts to assemble a jury to try him.

All in all, 1456 seems to have been a bad year for Malory. To add to his other troubles, he was sued in the King's Bench for debt. On 28 June,

---

51 Pugh, p. 240.

52 C.F.R. (1452–61) p. 175.

53 The family seem to have had a hereditary involvement in the Duchy of Lancaster's Honour of Leicester. Thomas's grandfather and namesake was steward of the honour in 1392–3, and Thomas himself was appointed receiver in 1458/63, 'presumably by Queen Margaret when she had the Duchy': Robert Somerville, The History of the Duchy of Lancaster (London 1953) pp. 375, 566, and cf. R.L. Storey in The Reign of Richard II, ed. F. Du Boulay (London 1971) p. 149n, and C.A. Robertson, 'Local Government and the King's Affinity in Fifteenth-Century Warwickshire and Leicestershire', Trans. Leics. Arch. & Hist. Soc. 52 (1976) 37–45, at p. 42.

Robert Overton alleged that Malory had lent him £3 on 26 May 1452 that he should have repaid on 8 September 1452, and he produced what he said was a promissory note of Malory's to prove it.[54] Malory denied it, and the court ordered a trial on the Saturday after eighteenth day of Michaelmas Term (18 September 1456), but no jurors appeared and the case was deferred until the Monday after the eighteenth day of Hilary Term (31 January 1457). It was then found that the sheriffs had not sent the writ, and the case was deferred again, until the Wednesday three weeks after Easter (11 May 1457), when it was further postponed for lack of a jury, with no date specified.

Malory may also have found it a burden that during this year he was again taken from the relatively familiar surroundings of the King's Bench Prison, this time to the custody of the Sheriff of Middlesex, which meant to Newgate Prison.[55] This is evident from a writ of January 1457 recited in an entry on the Controlment Roll for the following Michaelmas Term. The writ orders the Sheriffs of London to take custody of Malory, who had been committed to the *late* Sheriff of Middlesex on penalty of £1000 for more secure custody.[56] Malory therefore must have been committed to Newgate at least when the sheriffs changed over in November 1456, and perhaps very shortly after he left the King's Bench on 30 January 1456.

If 'more secure custody' is more than a formula, the reason for it is unknown. It might be political: Dr Carpenter has suggested that both Malory's pardon and his return to the King's Bench Prison were consequences of York's second protectorate,[57] and it is at least possible that his removal from the King's Bench Prison to Newgate was a consequence of the ending of York's protectorate, on 25 February 1456. The King's Bench might have come to distrust its marshal and his staff. Lord Chief Justice Fortescue was, as we shall see, involved in Malory's case in 1457, and William Brandon, who was marshal in the same year, was, as we have seen, Norfolk's man. Fortescue might already have been interested in Malory, and if Brandon was already marshal, he might have shown that interest by sending Malory to a different prison once York's protectorate was over. There is, however, no proof, and the fact that the court later sent Malory back to the King's Bench Prison for eighteen months is a reminder of how many non-political explanations are possible. Perhaps when Sir William Peyto was committed to the Marshalsea on 15 June, the two well-born trouble-makers between them made even a prison impossible to run in a sufficiently orderly way to allow the staff to do what they wanted, which

[54] Baugh, pp. 26–7.
[55] See Margery Bassett, 'Newgate Prison in the Middle Ages', *Speculum* 18 (1943) 233–46.
[56] Hicks, pp. 100–1.
[57] Carpenter, 'Sir Thomas Malory', p. 40.

was to extract the most money from the most prisoners in the shortest possible time.[58]

There was something of an irony in Malory being moved to Newgate for 'more secure custody' early in 1456, for on the night of 13 November that prison was to see a spectacular gaol-break: Lord Egremont and his brother, sons of the Earl of Northumberland, escaped and released a good many other prisoners on their way out, who got out on to the prison roof and fought off attempts to recapture them.[59] Perhaps Malory, who must have been one of the more experienced escapers in the place, was among them. Perhaps the damage they did had something to do with Malory's next change of abode: on 24 January 1457, Lord Chief Justice Fortescue ordered the Sheriffs of London to take custody of Malory, which meant a move from Newgate to Ludgate.[60] Fortescue also transferred to the new gaolers the £1000 penalty for keeping Malory secure.

It would therefore have been from Ludgate that Malory was brought on 12 May 1457, the day after Overton's case was last postponed in the King's Bench, to be sued for the same reason in the same court by a different man. Thomas Greswold asserted that on 3 July 1456 he had lent Malory £4 9s 8d, which was due to be repaid at Christmas and which Malory had not repaid despite frequent requests to do so.[61] Greswold asserted that Malory was in the Marshalsea at the time, but this is likely to be a legal fiction.[62] It is one of the oddities of Malory's life that the lender, a Warwickshire lawyer, was among the justices who presided over the Nuneaton inquisition, and also practised in the King's Bench: he was the prosecutor who demanded the forfeitures of Malory's sureties when Malory failed to surrender to his bail in October 1454. This time Malory admitted the debt, and judgement was given against him with damages of 3s 4d, leaving him, as the record notes, with a total indebtedness of £4 13s 0d.

This was potentially a serious matter. Other prosecutions may have been given up because they were simply too much trouble – perhaps in the end, no-one in Essex cared enough to spend the time in London necessary to pursue Malory for harbouring a horse-thief and planning a burglary that failed. Perhaps even Overton found the constant drain of fees in the King's Bench was costing him more than Malory owed him, while making it more

---

58 For Peyto, see Baugh, p. 20, for money-making, Pugh, p. 191 and passim.
59 R.L. Storey, *The End of the House of Lancaster* (London 1966) p. 149.
60 Dr Carpenter has him move from Ludgate to Newgate: 'Sir Thomas Malory', loc. cit.; but see Hicks, pp. 100–1.
61 Baugh, pp. 27–8.
62 Greswold sued as an attorney *iuxta libertates et privilegia a tempore que non est memoria usitata et approbata*: these immemorial privileges might have been more open to dispute in the case of prisoners not in the court's own prison.

likely that the defendant would have nothing to pay with in the end.[63] Greswold, however, as an officer of the court, knew how to work the system: he had got the fact of his debt on the court rolls in one move, he was ideally placed to make sure it did not drop out of the court's official memory, and the court was unlikely finally to set Malory free until the debt was paid. The sum involved might seem one that someone of his rank ought to have been able to take in his stride, but five years in prison could do lasting damage to a family's finances, and his financial record would not make it easy to borrow to get himself out of prison to get himself out of debt.

Greswold's advantages are clearly illustrated in the next record of Malory, when, on an unspecified day in Michaelmas Term 1457 he was brought back into the King's Bench, apparently for the sole purpose of being transferred from the custody of the Sheriffs of London to that of the marshal.[64] The roll formally recites that Malory is in prison because of matters unspecified pending before the lord king and because he stands condemned in respect of Thomas Greswold.

Within a fortnight, however, on 19 October, Malory was bailed until the morrow of St John (28 December) to William Neville Lord Fauconberg, and William Brigham of Brigham, Yorkshire, and John Clerkson of Arundel, Sussex, esquires.[65] Fauconberg was Warwick's uncle and principal lieutenant, and later became Earl of Kent and Lord Admiral of England; Brigham may be the man, probably a member of the Calais garrison, who drew an annuity from a village near Calais in 1461.[66] There is no direct evidence of what Fauconberg wanted with Malory, but at some time, as we shall see in the next chapter, a number of senior members of Warwick's affinity became feoffees for Malory, and this is the most likely time for it to have happened. What Malory was expected to do in return is unknown, but it presumably included putting whatever influence he might have in Warwickshire and elsewhere behind the Yorkist cause. It may have included better behaviour: this is the only known occasion when Malory left prison legally and returned on time. On 28 December, the day his bail expired, he duly surrendered himself in the King's Bench.

We know little of how Malory felt about his imprisonment, beyond the natural dislike shown by his repeated escapes and his request at the end of the *Morte Darthur* that his readers should pray for his release. Many readers of the *Morte Darthur*, however, have felt that one passage in the

---

63 For the fees, see Marjorie Blatcher, *The Court of King's Bench 1450–1550: A Study in Self-Help* (London 1978) ch. iii.

64 Hicks, pp. 100–1.

65 Hicks, loc. cit.; 'within a fortnight' because the law term began on the octave of Michaelmas: *Handbook of Dates*, p. 67.

66 *Complete Peerage, s.v.* Fauconberg; Matthews, p. 30. This man is presumably not the John Brigham from Devon recorded by Wedgwood.

book reflects Malory's prison experience. He says, speaking of an imprisoned knight:

> So sir Trystram endured there grete payne, for sykness had undirtake hym, and that ys the grettist payne a presoner may have. For all the whyle a presonere may have hys helth of body, he may endure undir the mercy of God and in hope of good delyveraunce; but when syknes towchith a presoners body, than may a presonere say all welth ys hym berauffte, and than hath he cause to wayle and wepe. Ryght so ded sir Trystram whan syknes had undirtake hym, for than he toke such sorow that he had allmoste slayne hymselff.[67]

Malory's period on bail to Fauconberg, however, may have included something even more distressing. In the accounts of Monks Kirby priory for the year 36 Henry VI (1 September 1457–31 August 1458) are three references to the Malory family. The first is a payment of sixpence in the name of Sir Thomas himself for the use of a watermill called Hubbock Mill, the second, eight shillings rental for pasture from Elizabeth Lady Malory and Thomas Roche, and the third, twopence for the obsequies of a Thomas Malory junior.[68] He was presumably Sir Thomas's son – perhaps, if he followed the common naming custom, his second son. As usual in the period, we can only guess at what Sir Thomas and Lady Malory felt about their son's death.

If these events fell in 1457, Malory's life in 1458 is a complete blank. We must assume he spent it and the early part of 1459 in the King's Bench Prison. In the course of Easter Term 1459, however, the King's Bench was informed that Malory had been illicitly at large in Warwickshire since Easter.[69] When Malory was returned by the Sheriffs of London to the marshal in 1457, the court had apparently not imposed any penalty for keeping the prisoner safe; it now rectified this with a penalty, rather surprisingly, of £100. Why it should have reduced the sum by an order of magnitude is unknown.

It has been assumed that Malory's appearance in Warwickshire means that he had again escaped from prison, perhaps even, one scholar suggested, with the connivance of the Duke of Norfolk.[70] This seems unlikely. One of the privileges of the Fleet Prison was the ancient custom, much prized by prisoners and gaolers alike, of prisoners going about free during the day provided they paid a fee to the Keeper and the wages of a *baston* – a tipstaff or warder – hired as escort. That the marshals of the King's Bench Prison admired this humane custom appears from the court's mandate of

[67] *Works*, p. 540.
[68] P.R.O. S.C.6/1107/7 respectively m. 5, 3, and 4.
[69] Hicks, p 101.
[70] Carpenter, 'Sir Thomas Malory', p. 40.

February 1454 requiring Malory to be kept secure. It specifically prohibits the marshal from allowing the prisoner to go free *pro bastonem seu aliquo alio modo*.[71] William Brandon, the marshal in 1459, was particularly liberal in this respect: as we have seen, in 1460 he was dismissed for allowing prisoners to go about at large. On 10 May 1459, six weeks after Malory went free, he released Sir William Peyto in circumstances so improper that an injured party succeeded in obtaining a judgement against him for Peyto's debts.[72] If the enterprising marshal was willing to release a Lancastrian like Peyto, it seems safest to assume that he put money above politics and that Malory simply paid on the way out.

When the court ordered Malory's return, the national political situation was not obviously worse than it had been for much of the previous five years. However, during the summer both sides gathered forces, which began to move in September. The Yorkists won a small battle at Blore Heath on 23 September, but were routed at Ludlow on 12 October.[73] The Yorkist leaders fled the country, York himself to Ireland and Warwick to Calais. In November, a parliament from which Yorkist sympathisers were excluded met at Coventry and attainted the principal Yorkists.

This was the beginning of the most turbulent eighteen months in fifteenth-century English history. It is a pity that there is no evidence of where Malory was during the early part of this period. He may have responded to the marshal's summons and been in the King's Bench Prison all the time, or he may have turned up very late with armour stains on his clothing and implausible excuses about getting lost coming down Watling Street. By Hilary Term 1460, however, he was back in the King's Bench Prison: on an unknown day in that term he was once more transferred to Newgate. The transfer is so plausible as a security precaution that it gives no grounds for suspecting that the court was suspicious of the loyalty of its marshal. Despite the Lancastrian victory at Ludlow, the government had been unable to gain a decisive advantage over the Yorkists. They failed to cut off supplies and reinforcements to Calais, and the Yorkists were able to recruit even in London itself: a man was executed for that in February.[74] With even London insecure, Kent and Surrey, which had gone up in Cade's rebellion, must have been still more suspect. In that situation, a prisoner with Malory's record was safer on the north bank of the Thames.

The authorities presumably feared what actually came to pass: the Yorkists mounted an invasion of England from Calais. They landed at Sandwich on 26 June, and passed through London on 2–5 July, leaving a

---

71 Baugh, p. 10.
72 Baugh, p. 20.
73 For the campaigns, see Anthony Goodman, *The Wars of the Roses* (London 1981).
74 Sir James Ramsay, *Lancaster and York*, 2 vols (Oxford 1892) p. 222; Cora L. Scofield, *The Life and Reign of Edward the Fourth*, 2 vols (London 1923) i 47–9, 55–6.

force to besiege the Tower.[75] The besiegers attacked using both artillery and infantry, but were unable to take the Tower or to prevent reinforcements to and forays by the garrison, which also used artillery, killing several people in the city. On 16 July, however, a decisive battle was fought at Northampton, which the Yorkists won, killing Buckingham and other Lancastrian peers and capturing King Henry. When the main Yorkist force returned to London with the king as a prisoner, the Tower, which was said to be running short of food, negotiated a surrender.

It is very probable that while these things were going on Malory was freed, either from Newgate when the Yorkists arrived in London, or – if someone had had the presence of mind to move him again – from the Tower when it surrendered. Freeing prisoners of one's own party was (and indeed is) standard practice after a revolution, and such an event fits in with the fact that the King's Bench records, a single postscript aside, break off abruptly at this point. The postscript is a marginal note saying succinctly 'Letters Patent allowed'.[76] Malory, in other words, by pleading a pardon which the court accepted, finally disposed of the charges brought against him in the King's Bench in January 1452 and of the others that had accumulated later. This last appearance of his in the King's Bench, however, was most probably in the autumn of 1462, and so may be considered in the next chapter.

Ten years later, when Malory was writing the *Morte Darthur*, the events of this period seem still to have been alive in his memory. Some have suggested that the *Morte Darthur* is in effect a *roman a clef* giving Malory's view of the politics of the times. This is not the place for a full account of the issues, but it seems to me demonstrable that that is not so, that Malory's main concern was to retell the received Arthurian story as he understood it, although events from his own time may occasionally combine with and reshape the legendary events of his story.[77] Which historical events might be involved has been much disputed, however, and even when they can be guessed at, it may be unclear whether Malory alluded to an event out of sympathy for the people concerned, or just because the event was strikingly memorable.

His source, for instance, gives him a seige of the Tower of London, and with fine disregard for the supposed chronology of the Arthurian legend he replaced its mangonels with modern guns such as he probably saw and

---

[75] Scofield, i 76, 80–96; Goodman, pp. 35–7, 125, 184–5, 204.

[76] Hicks, p. 107.

[77] For a fuller account of what follows see P.J.C. Field, 'Fifteenth-Century History in Malory's "Morte Darthur" ' in *Cultural Intermediaries in Medieval Britain*, ed. Françoise Le Saux (forthcoming).

heard, from one side or the other, firing at the real Tower in mid-July 1460.[78]
We cannot infer from this that, when the historical seige came to his mind
ten years later, he identified the garrison even momentarily with the (relatively) virtuous defender, Queen Guenivere, and the beseigers with the
ungrateful incestuous usurper Mordred. The account of the seige comes
from his sources, where it forms such an important part of the received
Arthurian story that he could hardly have changed it much if he wanted to,
and the guns may simply be there to add a touch of vividness.

One of the major difficulties with the view that the *Morte Darthur* em-
bodies either a Lancastrian or a Yorkist viewpoint is that those apparent
allusions that suggest sympathy with contemporaries seem to point in
different directions. When one of Malory's sources, for instance, has King
Arthur's enemies on the verge of defeat, Malory gives their leader a speech
suggesting abandoning their infantry because 'noble kynge Arthure woll
nat tarry on the footemen',[79] which may echo the Yorkist proclamation
before Northampton that lords and knights were to be killed but the commons spared. Another source has Queen Guenivere abducted and her
escort wounded, and Malory modifies that escort in ways that make it
resemble Queen Margaret's knights, 'the queen's gallants' who were
slaughtered at Blore Heath.[80] It is easier and more compatible with the
generosity of spirit that informs the *Morte Darthur* to suppose that Malory's
sympathies were aroused less by causes than by individuals behaving
chivalrously in difficult circumstances.

It is perhaps not surprising that most of the apparent contemporary
allusions are sympathetic: Malory as author is a notably uncensorious
person. One exception, however, seems to point particularly to the years
we are now considering. When Arthur is first chosen as king, Malory's
source has this brought about by conscientious though sometimes mis-
guided barons. Malory's barons are more selfish: they seem prepared to
procrastinate indefinitely, and in the end it is the commons (who have no
part in the source) who force them to accept Arthur as king. The end of that
scene may partly recall the acclamation of Edward IV as king in St John's
Fields in March 1461, but it begins with a sentence apparently original to
Malory that probably reflects his memories of England drifting into civil
war:

> Thenne stood the reame in grete jeopardy long whyle, for every lord
> that was myghty of men maade hym stronge, and many wende to
> have ben kyng.[81]

[78] *Works*, p. 1227.18–21.
[79] *Works*, p. 35.16–17.
[80] *Works*, p. 1121.14–29.
[81] *Works*, p. 12.11–13.

This sentence reads like a criticism of the English magnates of Malory's time as a class, but it reads still more like a criticism of the overweening ambition of one in particular whose wish to be king had for years put England in jeopardy, Richard Duke of York, who persuaded parliament to accept him as heir to the throne in October 1460, and whose head three months later was on a spike over the gates at York.

It would be natural to take a condemnation of the Duke of York written in a Yorkist prison as the utterance of a Lancastrian partisan, but *partisan* generally implies a wholehearted enthusiasm for a cause, and the passages in the *Morte Darthur* where Malory seems to be remembering Yorkist achievements with pleasure make it difficult to see him as a partisan in the full sense of the word. It would be easier to imagine him a partisan for the other side in the ten years and more when he was in serious trouble with the Lancastrian authorities, and as a result apparently sought protection from Yorkist 'lords that were mighty of men'. That, however, does not necessarily imply enthusiasm for the Yorkist cause, and it would be understandable if he did not feel any great enthusiasm for it, since more often than not, whether through his own fault or otherwise, the Yorkists proved unable to protect him. Indeed, the very fact that powerful men valued his service may have been what made his enemies so determined to keep him, and so have produced in the 1450s the colossal penalties on his gaolers and in the 1460s the imprisonment in which he wrote *Morte Darthur*, which is the principal subject of the next chapter.

VIII

Reversals

Once Malory is no longer the object of the attentions of the Court of King's Bench, it is much harder to discover what is happening to him. The year after his apparent release was the most active and bloody of the Wars of the Roses. The battles include alternate successes by Lancastrians and Yorkists at Wakefield in December 1460, Mortimer's Cross in February 1461, Second St Albans later in the same month, and Towton in March 1461. Since one of the warring parties had repeatedly tried to free him, and the other had shown itself determined to keep him in prison, Malory had reason to be in the thick of things. If he was, however, there is no reliable evidence of it.

Almost at the end of the *Morte Darthur*, Malory describes Arthur's last battle, a battle that like Towton, concludes a campaign at the cost of horrific casualties. He tells how one of the survivors heard a noise on the battle-field, and

> saw and harkened by the moonelyght how that pyllours and robbers
> were com into the fylde to pylle and to robbe many a full noble knyght
> of brochys and bees and of many a good rynge and many a ryche juell.
> And who that were nat dede all oute, there they slewe them for their
> harneys and their ryches.[1]

We might wonder if this passage gives an view of the aftermath of the Yorkist victory at Towton. The casualties and most of what is said about the pillaging, however, come from Malory's major sources, and although the last sentence does not, it could have been prompted by a different battle or by Malory's imagination alone.[2]

The evidence for what Malory was doing when things settled down after Towton is not much better, and what there is therefore needs to be used to

---

1 *Works*, pp. 1237–38. *pyllours* 'pillagers'; *harneys* 'harness', 'armour and arms'.
2 *Le Morte Arthur*, ed. J.D. Bruce (London 1903) lines 3416–19. The pillaging is not in *La Mort le roi Artu*, ed. Jean Frappier (Geneva 1964) §191. For a battle to have prompted the final sentence, many of its casualties would have had to have been left untended on a following moonlit night. With Towton, the first is made plausible by the number of casualties, and the second by the battle having been fought on Palm Sunday.

the full. One item, however, has generally been neglected: the *Morte Darthur* as a whole. Although it is in every way the largest surviving piece of evidence, something – perhaps its importance as literature – has prevented scholars from considering it as a historical object. However, when put with other records of its author's life, it can throw new light on Malory's life and times, some of which is reflected back on to the book itself.

This is best demonstrated in two stages, beginning with a group of records dating from after the death of Sir Thomas's son Robert. Robert presumably died shortly before 4 November 1479, when a special commission was appointed to investigate the lands held by Robert Malory esquire, deceased tenant-in-chief, in the counties of Warwick, Leicester and Northampton.[3] Three days later, writs of *diem clausit extremum* for Robert Malory were sent out to Warwickshire and Northamptonshire only.[4] No return to either writ is known, and in June of the following year writs for Elizabeth Lady Malory were sent to all three counties.[5] The consequent inquisitions post mortem, in July and August, said she had died on 30 September or 1 October 1479, holding for life the manors of Newbold Revel in Warwickshire, Swinford in Leicestershire, and Winwick in Northamptonshire, and various associated properties; that she had held Newbold Revel of a ward of the king and one property in Winwick of the king in chief; and that her heir was Nicholas, son of Robert, son of Sir Thomas and herself, aged thirteen (one jury said fourteen). Nicholas's wardship and marriage accordingly fell to the king, and in October 1480 they were granted to a certain Margaret Kelem, not in one of the routine transactions made for a specified sum and recorded in the Fine Rolls, but by enrolled letter patent in return for unspecified services 'to the king and Elizabeth his consort Queen of England'.[6]

However, in February 1486, six months after Henry VII came to the throne, one Ralph Wolseley appeared in Chancery to claim that the Leicestershire inquisition had unjustly deprived him of Swinford and its associated lands.[7] He said that Sir Thomas had long ago conveyed the properties to four (named) feoffees, who had reconveyed them to eight others including Wolseley, who, as sole survivor, was seized of them at the

---

3 *C.P.R.* (1476–85) p. 183. The commissioners, Sir Walter Mauntell of Heyford, John Hulcote esquire of Bradden, and Richard Middleton esquire of Greensnorton, were all Northants. men, and Hulcote and Middleton were members of the king's household. For Mauntell see Baker, *Northants.*, i 183 and *Cal. I.P.M. Hen. VII*, i 55; for the others, Wedgwood, *s.vv.*

4 *C.F.R.* (1471–1485) p. 175.

5 These writs were not enrolled, but the originals survive with the inquisitions in P.R.O. C140/75/46.

6 *C.P.R.* (1476–85) p. 220.

7 Nichols, *Leicestershire*, iv 362, from P.R.O. KB 27/900 Rex rot. 5–7.

time of the inquisition. Margaret Kelem had by then married Thomas Kingston of Childrey in Berkshire,[8] and neither she nor her husband appeared to answer Wolseley's case. A further inquisition at Leicester found for Wolseley, and stated that the profits had gone to Margaret Kelem until the accession of Edward V, to William Catesby until the accession of Henry VII, and to Wolseley thereafter. In Michaelmas Term 1487, the manor and lands and their profits retrospectively to the 1480 inquisition were awarded to Wolseley. A final writ of *diem clausit extremum* for Robert Malory sent to Leicestershire in May 1488 was presumably to formalize the return of the disputed properties to Nicholas, who would have come of age about then.[9] He certainly held them when he died, on 22 January 1513.[10]

This lawsuit, and especially Wolseley's circumstantial testimony, provide a key to part of Malory's later life. First and foremost, the proceedings reveal a pattern of political malversion whose origins lie thirty years earlier. In those days, as we have seen, Malory's importance in the struggle between York and Lancaster had been quite out of proportion to the social status suggested by the surviving evidence of his property, income, and family connections. His importance may have been a function of his ability to cause trouble: when he was first imprisoned in 1451, the charges against him alleged that in many of his alleged crimes he had had the help of scores of armed men, raised at very short notice. If his imprisonment was not political at first, it soon became so. He spent the rest of the decade in prison without being brought to trial, the Duke of York as Protector granted him a pardon that was dismissed under suspicious circumstances, his gaolers were threatened with extraordinary fines if he should escape, he was twice bailed out by leading Yorkist lords, he was moved for what look like security reasons from prison to prison, and he was freed after the Yorkists seized power. He looks, however we may have to qualify this in the light of his book and his later career, like not merely a man of consequence, but a Yorkist one.

In particular he looks like a follower of York's principal ally, Richard Neville, Earl of Warwick. A connection might have begun at any time after Warwick acquired his earldom in 1449, and, as we have seen, there is some evidence to suggest that it did. To the evidence already mentioned it may

---

8 Nichols, loc. cit., *V.C.H., Berks.*, iv 350, and *Cal. I.P.M., Hen. VII*, iii 69, 537, 559 together show that this Thomas Kingston was Margaret Kelem's husband, that they were married by 1487, and that he died in 1506. The Margaret who was widow first of Edward Kelem and then of Richard Churchyard who died (six months after Churchyard) in Nov. 1498, must therefore be a different woman: see *Cal. I.P.M., Hen. VII*, ii 128, C. Kingsford, *The Greyfriars of London* (London 1915) p. 121. In fact, Kingston's wife Margaret probably died shortly before he did, since he bequeathed her best clothes as well as his own in his will, made in August 1505: P.R.O. Prob 11/15, fol. 19.

9 *C.F.R.* (1485–1509) p. 72.

10 P.R.O. C142/27/115.

be added that at some time Warwick's Clerk to the Kitchens was Malory's brother-in-law, Robert Vincent,[11] the man from whom, also (apparently) in 1449, Malory acquired part of the disputed Swinford property,[12] and that Malory's main accomplice in 1451 seems to have been a man from Carlisle, one of the centres of Neville power: Richard Neville certainly brought some northerners into Warwickshire and settled them at strategic points.[13] Most significantly however, the man who bailed Malory out of prison in 1457 was Lord Fauconberg, Warwick's uncle and, until his death in 1463, his principal lieutenant.[14] Wolseley's evidence clinches the matter: his co-feoffees included Walter Blount, esquire (Wolseley's brother-in-law), and Walter Wrottesley, who were among Warwick's half-dozen ablest and most valued supporters.[15] Since both men were knighted at Towton on 25 March 1461 and Wolseley's evidence did not call them knights, their enfeoffment will have taken place before Towton, perhaps when Malory was on bail to Fauconberg in 1457; but whenever it did, Malory must then at least have been a political supporter of Warwick.[16]

Most of the rest of the evidence for the 1460s points in the same direction. King Edward offered a general pardon in New Year 1462, and in the autumn Malory took advantage of it.[17] He then apparently took it to the court of King's Bench, which accepted that it wiped the slate clean of the charges against him.[18] In Michaelmas Term 1462, he conveyed part of his Northamptonshire property to his son Robert and Robert's wife Elizabeth in what was presumably a marriage settlement, and shortly afterwards followed the king, Warwick and Fauconberg north to beseige three castles that the Lancastrians had captured, Alnwick, Bamburgh, and Dunstanborough.[19] The leisureliness with which Malory took out his pardon, like

---

11 *The Visitations of Northamptonshire 1564 and 1618–19*, ed. W.C. Metcalfe (London 1887) pp. 149–50.

12 Nichols, iv 361; E. Vinaver, *Malory* (Oxford 1929) pp. 117, 121.

13 Wedgwood, *s.v.* John Appleby; Carpenter, 'Warwickshire', pp. 165–6.

14 Hicks, p. 101; Baugh, p. 29; Matthews, p. 30.

15 Nichols, iv 362; Wedgwood gives biographies of all three men.

16 It may be more than a coincidence that in July 1458 Blount retained for life a Richard Malory esquire with a fee assigned on a Derbyshire manor, and that he and Richard Malory esquire were dealing in land in Derby in or before 1473 (*Ancient Deeds*, vi 391, P.R.O. C146/10341). This must be the Richard Malory of Radcliffe-on-the-Wreake, Leicestershire, who was accused of complicity with Sir Thomas in his second raid on Combe Abbey, on whom see pp. 60–1 above.

17 P.R.O. C67/45, and cf. Scofield, i 230. The first pardon (m. 47) is dated 9 January; Sir Thomas's (m. 14), 24 October 1462.

18 Hicks, p. 107. This record is only dated as after the previous entry (of Hilary Term 1460), but if Malory had successfully re-presented his 1455 pardon, there would have been no need for him to take out another.

19 G. Farnham, *Leicester Medieval Pedigrees* (Leicester 1925) p. 140 from P.R.O. CP40/806, m. 62 Northants.; 'Brief Notes', pp. 157–8.

his taking part in the Alnwick campaign, again points to his being a Yorkist.

One other point should be noticed. It is unlikely that he would have put his Leicestershire lands alone into the hands of feoffees when they were the least valuable of the three divisions of his property, and when they were held of the Hospitallers, an order with which he had family connections. Indeed, they were held specifically of the preceptory of Dingley in Northamptonshire,[20] the incumbent of which (from January 1468 for at least two years and perhaps much longer) was his kinsman Sir John Malory.[21] Malory had stronger reason to provide the protection of enfeoffment for his more valuable properties in Warwickshire, held of the Duke of Norfolk, and in Northamptonshire, held of Coventry Priory and the king.[22] The proceedings over Winwick in 1462 show that he had feoffees in Northamptonshire too: the property was conveyed by Malory himself, Thomas Walsh esquire of Wanlip in Leicestershire, and Philip Dand. Walsh and Dand will be Malory's feoffees. Thomas Walsh, along with John Walsh (his brother),[23] and William Walsh, was a Swinford feoffee: Dand was not. It was common to use partly overlapping groups of feoffees for lands in different counties, and it can be assumed that Malory did the same in Warwickshire.

In September 1464 Malory witnessed the marriage settlement of John, son of William Feilding of Newnham Paddox in Warwickshire, and Helen, daughter and co-heiress of Thomas Walsh, esquire.[24] However, although Helen was a minor, there were no Walshes among the witnesses. It is therefore probable that all the adult male Walshes were dead. Her father certainly was: he had died a year or so earlier.[25] Taking all the records together with the appearance of the Walsh coat of arms in the armorial window at Newbold Revel,[26] it is a reasonable assumption that Malory was Helen's uncle – there is no direct evidence of his wife's maiden name – and that he was witnessing the marriage settlement as in some sense her guardian. The witness list conjures up a picture of integrated county society of a kind from which Malory had been excluded by his imprisonment in the 1450s, but to which, with his son married to a Pulteney and his niece to a Feilding, he could now feel that he had been readmitted.

One unexpected aspect of the marriage settlement, however, is that William Feilding, the bridegroom's father, was a committed Lancastrian

---

20 P.R.O. C142/27/115.

21 See pp. 79–80 above.

22 P.R.O. C140/75/46; C142/27/116; C142/28/41.

23 Farnham, p. 141.

24 Nichols, iv 368.

25 A writ of *diem clausit extremum* survives, dated 24 Oct. 1463 (P.R.O. C140/11/41) but both copies of the inquisition are now lost.

26 Illustrated in Dugdale, *Warwickshire*, p. 83.

who was to die fighting at Tewkesbury in 1471.[27] This may not be as surprising as it seems at first sight. The Malorys and the Feildings were neighbours in two counties: Newbold Revel and Newnham Paddox were adjacent manor houses in the parish of Monks' Kirby in Warwickshire, and the Feilding lands that were being settled on the young couple were in Stormsworth (modern Starmore), where part of Malory's Leicestershire lands also lay. On its own this marriage might suggest no more than that as long as there was no personal grievance, in a non-ideological struggle like that between Lancaster and York, normal neighbourly relations could resume very quickly after the fighting stopped.

The remaining records from the 1460s, however, show that before the end of that decade something had gone very much awry in Malory's Yorkist allegiance. On 14 July 1468 King Edward offered a second general pardon, and among the fifteen people excluded from it by name was Sir Thomas Malory.[28] He was excluded again from Edward's third pardon, on 22 February 1470.[29] Repeated scholarly searches of the legal records have found no trace of arrest, charge, trial, or verdict, but the *Morte Darthur* shows that he was in prison at about this time: it was finished in prison at some time during King Edward's ninth regnal year (4 March 1469 to 3 March 1470).[30] It looks as if the Yorkists learned from their predecessors' difficulties with Malory, and simply put him in prison without formal charge.

This is not all the book can tell us about its author's imprisonment. Since there are references to that imprisonment scattered throughout, the whole of it must have been written in prison, and since it was written to a coherent plan and with the help of a splendid library of Arthurian sources unlikely to have been available both in Malory's earlier Lancastrian imprisonment and in his later Yorkist one, it may be assumed that the whole book was written during the Yorkist imprisonment in which it was certainly completed. Even if it was written without serious interruptions, it could hardly have taken much less than two years to write. Malory may also have written a verse romance, *The Wedding of Sir Gawain and Dame Ragnell*, during the same imprisonment, in which case the estimate would have to be increased to allow for the composition of 850 or so lines of not very good verse – and bad verse does not always come more easily than good.[31] Since, however, it could have been written without a library of sources, it might have composed (if he wrote it at all) during it his Lancastrian imprisonment in the 1450s. It is therefore best left out of account here.

27 Wedgwood, *s.v.*
28 P.R.O. C67/46, m. 39; cf. Scofield, i 461.
29 P.R.O. C67/47, m. 9; cf. Scofield, i 506.
30 *Works*, p. 1260.25.
31 For *The Wedding*, see p. 2 and n. supra.

From the other factors, we might guess at the *Morte Darthur*, and perhaps Malory's Yorkist imprisonment, having been begun some time in 1467 or 1468.

It is natural to assume that Malory was imprisoned and excluded from pardon because of something he had done as a follower of Warwick, whose estrangement from Edward became serious in July 1467, and deepened until it reached outright rebellion in July 1469.[32] The dates chime neatly, and they raise the question of when Malory was released from prison. If he was first imprisoned (say) in the summer of 1467, he might have completed the *Morte Darthur* very soon after Edward's ninth regnal year began, and before Warwick rebelled. In the first fortnight of that rebellion, Warwick's troops marched through London, but did not take the Tower, in which (since he had been sent there at a similar earlier moment of danger) Malory is likely to have been held.[33] However, after their victory at Edgecote on 26 July, Warwick's forces captured Edward and held him prisoner, governing in his name until about the middle of September.[34] During these two months, an order for Malory's release might have been issued, and if issued might have been obeyed. By the end of September, however, a Lancastrian rising had compelled Warwick to release the king, since men would not come in to fight for a king whom they knew to be a prisoner. The rising was put down, and Edward returned to London as king in October. The Lancastrian danger forced Edward and Warwick into a winter of uneasy truce, during which the three factions manoeuvred for power. Malory's second exclusion from pardon, in February 1470, shows that the king's party still thought of him as an enemy, and so that, if he had still been in the Tower when Edward returned to London, he would have remained there throughout Warwick's second and even less successful rebellion in April and his subsequent flight to France. He would only have been freed when Warwick and the Lancastrians together drove Edward into exile in October 1470. About that time, prisoners of Warwick's party are known to have been released from various London gaols.[35]

Malory must have prospered during the Lancastrian readeption, since when he died he was buried in Greyfriars, Newgate, the most fashionable church in London, under a marble tombstone with an epitaph describing him as

---

[32] Scofield, i 429–95.
[33] Scofield, i 496. There was, at least in Henry VII's time, a library in the Tower 'next the waterside': H.M. Colvin et al., *The King's Works*, iii (London 1975) 264–6. I am grateful to Mr Colvin for drawing my attention to this.
[34] Scofield, i 497–503.
[35] Robert Fabyan, *The New Chronicles of England and France* (London 1811) pp. 658–9.

Thomas Mallere valens miles qui obiit 14 die mensis marcii anno domini 1470 de parochia de monkenkyrkby in comitatu warwici.[36]

(The epitaph says *1470* because in the fifteenth century the year began on 25 March.)[37] On the day Malory died, 14 March 1471 by our reckoning, Edward landed again at Ravenspur; and in the following June, a month after Edward's victory at Tewkesbury, a writ of *diem clausit extremum* for Sir Thomas Malory was sent to Northamptonshire only. In November the consequent inquisition post mortem said he had died on 12 March holding no land in the county.[38]

Scholars have been much exercised by this inquisition. The problem is not the two-day difference in dates between the epitaph and the inquisition: that, if it was not casual error, may have been an attempt to discourage treason charges against Sir Thomas by making appear that he died before King Edward landed. Nor is it the assertion that Malory held no lands in Northamptonshire – from the later inquisitions on his widow it would be natural to assume that he had conveyed all his rights to her, either directly or through feoffees. The problem is the absence of inquisitions in Warwickshire and Leicestershire. As a solution it has even been suggested that the subject of this writ and inquisition was Thomas Malory of Papworth, who was not a knight and who died eighteen months earlier.[39] Everything falls into place, however, if we suppose that in addition to Wolseley, Wrottesley, and Blount among Malory's Leicestershire feoffees, at least one of his unknown Warwickshire feoffees was still alive, but that Philip Dand, his last Northamptonshire feoffee, had died. If the authorities knew this, they would have known that his Warwickshire and Leicestershire properties were protected, but his Northamptonshire lands and his heir were potentially vulnerable to the king. When the inquisition met, however, the family was able to show not only that Sir Thomas's son and heir Robert was of age, but that Sir Thomas had not held the

---

[36] B.L. Cotton Vitellius F.xii, fol. 284^r; Matthews, pp. 32–3. I take the MS.'s *sub lapide* to refer to one of the 'seavenscore gravestones of Marble' sold in 1545, for which see J.G. N[ichols] 'Register of the Sepulchral Inscriptions existing temp. Hen. VIII in the Church of the Grey Friars, London', *Collectanea topographica et genealogica* v (1838) 274–90, at p. 275. Nichols prints the epitaph, without the *sub lapide*, at p. 287.

[37] Howard Maynadier, *The Arthur of the English Poets* (London 1907) p. 264.

[38] P.R.O. C140/36/12.

[39] Martin, p. 173; Matthews, p. 158; R.R. Griffith, 'The Authorship Question Reconsidered' in *Aspects of Malory*, ed. T. Takamiya et al. (Cambridge 1981) pp. 159–77, 218–22. For Thomas of Papworth St Agnes's rank and death-date, see pp. 8–10 supra. The disputed I.P.M., like the Northants. I.P.M. on Sir Thomas of Newbold's widow and one of the two Northants. I.P.M.s on his grandson Nicholas, was held at Northampton, near to the Newbold Revel family lands at Winwick, whereas the undisputed I.P.M. on Thomas of Papworth was held at Thrapston, near his family's lands at Sudborough: P.R.O. C140/31/16.

Northamptonshire lands either, presumably because they had passed from Dand to Lady Malory.

In 1471 King Edward was in no position to persecute the widow and the orphan of a dead enemy. He had more than enough living enemies to occupy him, among them Wrottesley who, although Edward had made him a Knight of the Garter, had actively supported the readeption government. Edward felt strongly about his sworn brotherhood, and had Wrottesley imprisoned until he died. But if Edward's exile had strained his habitual clemency in some respects, it would also have reminded him of his need for friends, old and new. Among Edward's old friends who had refused to support the readeption government, despite their connections with Warwick, were Blount and Wolseley. Blount, already a peer, was rewarded for his loyalty with the Garter. Edward set about making new friends partly by offering a fourth general pardon, in November 1471, containing no named exceptions.[40]

The Northamptonshire inquisition of 1471 should have shown Lady Malory and her son the desirability of finding new feoffees to replace the ones who had died. One later record, however, suggests that the family was politically isolated. In 1480/81, Lady Malory's executor – apparently, from the wording of his bill, her only executor – an obscure Leicestershire clerk about to begin a baccalaureate in canon law at Cambridge, had to seek redress in Chancery because he had been intimidated by a Coventry brewer to whom he said Lady Malory had sold 'certeyn merchaundises' without written security, and who refused to pay the £7 19s 0d owing, which the executor needed for bequests under Lady Malory's will.[41]

If the Malorys were defenceless against a local tradesman, they would certainly have been defenceless against aggressors in positions of real power; and in 1480, with an heir who was a minor, they were highly vulnerable. However, Wolseley, even as a sole feoffee, should have been able to protect their Leicestershire lands. He did not have the political weight of his late brother-in-law, but he was a loyal Yorkist and a powerful and litigious man. Among the few who could have overborne him, much the most likely to have done so are the queen's family, the Wydevilles. The natural reading of Margaret Kelem's grant is that her services, whether they were genuine or a cash payment, had been mainly or wholly to the queen. Her future husband Thomas Kingston was also persona grata to the Wydevilles: he was summoned to be knighted at the coronation of Edward

---

40 P.R.O. C67/48; cf. Scofield, ii 21.

41 P.R.O. C1/60/102; A.B. Emden, *A Biographical Register of the University of Cambridge to 1500* (Cambridge 1963), *s.v.* Mansfield. The P.R.O. list dates this group of Chancery petitions only 20 Edw. IV, but since this one is addressed to Thomas Rotherham as Archbishop of York, a see to which he was provided on 7 July 1480, it can be dated 7 July 1480 / 3 March 1481.

V.[42] He was not enough of a Wydeville partisan for Richard of Gloucester to refuse to continue him as sheriff of Berkshire and Oxfordshire in 1483, but although he lived until 1506, neither Richard as king nor Henry VII knighted him or gave him any further recorded employment.[43] Moreover, the Wydevilles had strong local connections – their family seat was at Grafton Regis in Northamptonshire, and the queen before her marriage to King Edward had been Lady Ferrers of Groby in Leicestershire. The Wydevilles were ideally placed to initiate and influence special commissions, letters patent, inquisitions post mortem, and grants of wardship, and by 1480 they had had nine years of stability in which to forget the possible political consequences of a reputation for greed.[44]

Even the speed with which William Catesby acted suggests Wydeville involvement. He was perhaps even greedier than they were – he confessed in his will to having acquired a good deal of other people's land 'by wrongful purchase'[45] – and since he was a Northamptonshire man too, he was also well placed to know what was going on just over the county boundary at Swinford. In this case, however, evidence of his victim's weak points was thrust into his hands by circumstances not of his devising. In February 1481, at King Edward's command, he collected evidences of the Malorys' title to their lands for Margaret Kelem; there were four boxes of them, plus the fine that had settled Nicholas's mother's jointure. He delivered most of these documents to another man to take to Margaret Kelem, and for their own protection, the two of them made an indenture listing the deeds they had handled. Catesby's copy, signed by the other man, survives.[46] No doubt, given Catesby's habits, he scrutinized the Malorys' muniments for flawed title while he had them, but information found or claimed to have been found in 1481 does not explain his seizure of Swinford two years later, at the very beginning of Richard of Gloucester's tenure of power. That suggests that he was very sure of himself, which in turn suggests he was acting against Gloucester's particular enemies, the Wydevilles, or a client of theirs. The legal pretext he used is unknown, but his confidence that he would be able to remain in possession is shown by the appearance of his coat of arms in Swinford church.[47]

This background provides a plausible explanation for the surprising sequence of records in 1479 and 1480. When Robert Malory died, presumably in day-to-day charge of the family estates, the Wydevilles expected to

---

42 *Grants &c. from the Crown during the Reign of Edward IV*, ed. J.G. Nichols, Camden Soc. Pubs 60 (1854) pp. 69–71.

43 *C.F.R.* (1471–85) pp. 246, 257, 268.

44 For their greed, see M.A. Hicks, 'The Changing Role of the Wydevilles in Yorkist Politics to 1483' in *Patronage, Pedigree, and Power*, ed. Charles Ross (Gloucester 1979) pp. 60–86.

45 J.S. Roskell, 'William Catesby, Counsellor to Richard III', *B.J.R.L.* 42 (1959) 145–74.

46 P.R.O. E40/14705.

47 Nichols, Pl. 54 (facing iv 365), no. 6.

find that he held the family lands in Warwickshire and Northamptonshire, but that Wolseley held the Leicestershire ones. They therefore had the escheators act in the first place only in Warwickshire and Northampton- shire, but as a check procured a royal commission to enquire into the whole of the Malorys' estates. Despite the anticipatory wording of their com- mission, the commissioners found that the feudal tenant had been Lady Malory, not Robert, and that she had held of Wolseley in Leicestershire and of the chief lords of the fees in the other counties. While the commissioners were disentangling this, the Wydevilles thought of a way – presumably by intimidating the jury – in which they could include the Leicestershire lands too in an otherwise legitimate catch. Hence the inquisitions on Lady Malory's holdings in all three counties, which transferred the Malory lands entire to a Wydeville client, who, when they fell was promptly robbed by a more powerful predator. It cannot have been hard, even for a man with a Yorkist past like Wolseley, to have persuaded Henry VII's courts to redress what were in effect the wrongs of a Lancastrian heir oppressed by Edward IV's wife and Richard III's minister.[48]

All in all, Nicholas Malory had reason to be pleased with the way things turned out. The powerful aid of Ralph Wolseley, whatever undiscovered price he had to pay for it, had at the very least recovered his lost estate from the Catesbys, saved it from being swallowed up in Catesby's attain- der, and re-established the Malorys' title in the king's courts. Margaret Kelem presumably did not exploit him as some medieval wards were exploited, since he married her new husband's daughter, Katherine King- ston.[49] He may even have been pleased with his marriage. Someone at Newbold Revel in his generation was: one of the parlour windows was embellished with stained-glass versions of all the coats of arms to which either family was entitled.[50] On a more practical level, Nicholas became a feoffee for his father-in-law, and seems to have been his most active execu- tor.[51] Nevertheless, Nicholas learned from his narrow escape: when he died, he had got rid of the small part of the Winwick property that the

48 Dr Carpenter appears to say (*Locality*, p. 527) that being robbed by Catesby made Nicholas an associate of Catesby's boss, Lord Hastings, but a predator and his victim are hardly associates in any ordinary sense of the word.
49 See *V.C.H., Berks.*, iv 350.
50 Dugdale, *Warwickshire*, p. 83. The seven coats of arms, of which Dugdale identified the last three, are Kingston, Kingston impaling an imperfect version of Childrey (Thomas Kingston's paternal grandmother was a Childrey), Childrey likewise impaling King- ston, Walsh, Pulteney, Revell, and Malory. Taken with the record evidence of Sir Thomas's connections with the Walshes given above, this makes it probable that Sir Thomas's wife was a Walsh, which in turn makes it probable that their son Robert's wife was a Pulteney.
51 *C.P.R.* (1494–1509) p. 132; *Cal. I.P.M., Hen. VII*, iii 69–70; P.R.O. Prob 11/15, f. 19. There were three executors, but administration was granted to Nicholas.

Malorys had held of the king in chief, and everything else that he had inherited from his grandparents was safely in the hands of numerous feoffees.[52]

No doubt the Swinford affair had its own momentum, with each party acting mainly in its own financial interest against its immediate predecessor, but it is hard to believe that it could have begun in 1479 or continued through all its phases had there not been a lasting awareness that, at some time during the 1460s, the previously Yorkist Sir Thomas Malory of Newbold Revel had become to some degree a supporter of the defeated house of Lancaster. This same awareness may even have had a posthumous effect on his book: Caxton, printing the first edition of the *Morte Darthur* under the last Yorkist king, apparently took pains to reduce the number of times that Malory's name was mentioned in it.[53]

The investigation, however, can be taken a stage further. Although the records suggest that Malory became a Lancastrian, close consideration of them casts doubt on the assumption he did so by following the Earl of Warwick. In July 1468 Warwick was not (yet) a Lancastrian, and Edward had recently had proof that he was not.[54] This was convincing enough for Edward to put him on the commission that tried Lancastrian suspects in June and July 1468. The immediate future was to confirm Edward's assumption. Neither of Warwick's two rebellions, in the summer of 1469 and the spring of 1470, was pro-Lancastrian – indeed, he sacrificed the first one to defeat a Lancastrian uprising. He fled from the second to his stronghold of Calais, and it was only when the garrison there refused to let him in that he took refuge in France, and only then that, under intense pressure from King Louis, he and the Lancastrian exiles reluctantly formed the alliance that defeated Edward three months later.

Those excluded from pardon two years before Warwick's reluctant conversion, however, all appear to be Lancastrians. In such dangerous times general pardons were naturally used to isolate the irreconcilable. People at large were encouraged to take out pardons to obliterate past offences; and, as his danger increased, King Edward even had it proclaimed that anyone who could not afford to pay should have a pardon for nothing (an

---

52 P.R.O. C142/27/115, 116; C142/28/41; C142/30/85. One of his nine feoffees was his nephew Nicholas Kingston.

53 Vinaver suggested (*Works*, p. xxxviii) that Caxton's motives were partly literary, to make a collection of eight tales look more like one coherent book, but that does not explain his apparently removing a reference in the middle of one tale (*Works*, p. 683.4). Norman Blake attributed the reduction in references to Sir Thomas to his being in moral rather than political bad odour: 'Caxton Prepares His Edition of "Le Morte Darthur" ', *J.L.* 8 (1976) 272–85.

54 Scofield, i 434–5; Ross, pp. 120–2, 128, and for the rest of this paragraph Scofield, i 457, 520–30.

expedient to which the Lancastrians had also been driven at a critical moment during Cade's rebellion).[55] Those excluded, therefore, should only have been people the king thought presented a real and present threat to him; and the list at the head of the pardon shows that that meant active and committed Lancastrians.

Apart from those excluded in groups (which included those with Queen Margaret in France, and the Lancastrian garrison of Harlech), fifteen people were excepted by name in July 1468. They were Henry VI, Queen Margaret, Prince Edward, Humphrey Neville, knight, Thomas Malory, knight, Robin Marshall late of Culham, Oxfordshire, esquire, Hugh Mill late of London, gentleman, Gervase Clifton late of London, knight, William Verdon late of London, scrivener, Peter House late of London, esquire, Morgan ap Thomas ap Griffith late of Carmarthen, gentleman, Henry ap Thomas ap Griffith late of the same, gentleman, Owen ap Griffith ap Nicolas late of the same, esquire, Maurice ap Owen ap Griffith late of the same, gentleman, and Thomas Philip late of Rea, Gloucestershire, yeoman. Of these fifteen, eleven had long records of fighting or plotting to restore the Lancastrians to the throne or both, and nine were certainly in action against the government in one way or another at the moment when the pardon was issued. A tenth – King Henry – presumably would have been if he had not been a prisoner in the Tower since 1465.[56] It is reasonable to assume that the others were similarly, although perhaps more recently, engaged in the Lancastrian cause, and there is some little evidence to strengthen this assumption in each case. It will throw some light on Malory if the others excluded with him are examined individually.

The exclusions of King Henry in the Tower and Queen Margaret and Prince Edward in France need no explanation. Sir Humphrey Neville was the senior (and perhaps only) legitimate sane adult male of the elder branch of the Nevilles of Raby, and a natural rival to the leading members of the younger branch of that family, Warwick and King Edward, who were his first cousins of the half blood once removed.[57] The two sets of Nevilles and their supporters had been killing each other since before Sir Humphrey was born, and he himself had been raising rebellions when he could and making peace when he had to ever since Edward and Warwick had seized power in 1461. The summer of 1468 was one of his active periods: the commander of the forces in the field against him was paid £200 two weeks after he was excluded from pardon.[58] The descendants of

55 Scofield, i 510–11; I.M.W. Harvey, *Jack Cade's Rebellion* (Oxford 1991) p. 97.
56 His imprisonment began on 24 July 1465: Scofield, ii 382–3.
57 *Complete Peerage, s.vv.* Westmorland, Nevill, and Deincourt; W. Worcestre *Itineraries,* ed. J.H. Harvey (Oxford 1969) pp. 344–5; H.J. Swallow, *De Nova Villa* (Newcastle-upon-Tyne 1885) pp. 50, 137; J.R. Lander, *Crown and Nobility 1450–1509* (London 1976) p. 134n.; Matthews, pp. 132–5. There are some notable errors in this last.
58 Scofield, i 423.

Griffith ap Nicholas had followed a similar course in south-west Wales, where they had for some years been the principal supporters of Jasper Tudor, Earl of Pembroke.[59] They were also active at this time, leaving their usual area of operations to join Jasper Tudor's attempt to relieve Harlech in late June, and burning Denbigh before being repelled by Yorkist forces. There had been five of them, but Owen's elder brother Thomas had been killed in a skirmish near Machynlleth, probably shortly before July 1468 and possibly on their journey north. The absence of his name shows that the authorities were acting on up-to-date information about present dangers.

King Edward had lived with trouble in the far north and west for years. It had always been contained in the past, and it was to be contained in 1468. At least three of the remaining six men excluded from pardon, however, and a good many more who were not, were involved in something much more novel and alarming: a conspiracy in the home counties. The affair had come to light on 14 June, when Edward's agents in Kent had arrested a Lancastrian courier called John Cornelius with letters from the Lancastrian exiles to sympathizers in England.[60] The government promptly had Cornelius tortured. This in itself suggests official panic: the leading authority says that this is the only case in which torture is known to have been officially authorised in England before the time of Henry VIII.[61] The letters and Cornelius's testimony led to a wave of arrests and trials. Clifton and Mill were certainly implicated: indeed Mill seems to have been one of the most active in drawing others into the plot.[62] House may have been drawn in by Mill – he came originally from Gloucester, and Mill from Harescombe, two miles away – or by his wife and her circle.[63] He had married the widow of John Hampden of Great Hampden in Buckingham-

---

59 *Dictionary of Welsh Biography* (London 1959), *s.vv.* Gryffydd ap Nicolas and Rhys ap Thomas; Howell T. Evans, *Wales and the Wars of the Roses* (Cambridge 1915) pp. 93–4; Scofield, i 458–9; Sir John Lloyd, *A History of Caermarthenshire* (Cardiff 1935–9) i 257–62; Matthews, p. 250; G. Whitteridge, 'The Identity of Sir Thomas Malory, Knight-Prisoner', *R.E.S.* n.s. 24 (1973) 257–62.

60 Scofield, i 454.

61 John Bellamy, *Crime and Public Order in England in the Later Middle Ages* (London 1973) p. 140. Bellamy excludes the torture of the Templars in 1310, where the government reluctantly gave way to ecclesiastical pressure from abroad.

62 Wedgwood, *s.vv.*; the account of Mill is confused by his arrest and trial being dated 1466, before the pardon that freed him at his trial was granted. See also M.A. Hicks, 'The Case of Sir Thomas Cook, 1468', *E.H.R.* 93 (1978) 82–96.

63 He was granted a general pardon as late of Gloucester, gentleman, in January 1460; commissioned to arrest disturbers of the peace in Buckinghamshire in June 1462; sheriff of Bedfordshire and Buckinghamshire 1463–4; pardoned as esquire and late sheriff March 1465; excluded from pardon July 1468; and died before his wife, who died 19 Jan 1469, having previously been the wife of John Hampden of Great Hampden: *C.P.R.* (1452–61) p. 549; ibid. (1461–67) pp. 204, 439; *C.F.R.* (1461–71) pp. 122, 159, 216; P.R.O. C67/46 m. 39, C140/27/3; Wedgwood, *s.v.* Hampden; G. Lipscomb, *The History of*

shire. The Hampdens were irreconcilable Lancastrians, and four of their feoffees, although not excluded from pardon, were involved in the plot: Thomas Danvers of Waterstock, Oxfordshire, Richard Danvers of Prescott, Oxfordshire, his half-brother, John, Lord Wenlock, husband of Richard's sister Agnes, and Sir John Plummer, alderman of London, husband of Agnes's daughter Margaret.[64] Given these connections, it looks as if House was excluded from pardon because he was involved in the Cornelius plot.

The precise threat represented by the other three and by Malory himself is less easy to identify with certainty, but much the most plausible explanation for their exclusion must be that they too were involved in one or other of the three disturbances that were occupying the authorities at the time. William Verdon or Vernon became (as Vernon) a member of the Scriveners Company of London in 1464,[65] and (as Verdon) was excepted from pardon again in 1470, with Marshall, Philip, and Malory. Nothing else is known of him, but since the first, second, and fourth of those called 'late of London' seem to have been involved in the Cornelius plot, he probably was too. Marshall, despite his rank, is even more obscure. Since an esquire's family is unlikely to go entirely unrecorded, and there is no trace of any Marshalls in or near Culham before the seventeenth century,[66] he may have been at Culham as a sanctuaryman. He might have come to Culham from further north: a Robert Marshall of Southwell, Nottinghamshire, gentleman, escaped from Nottingham gaol in 1465.[67] Since Culham is only ten miles from Thomas Danvers's home at Waterstock, he too, is more likely to have been involved in the Cornelius plot than in rebellions in the far north and west. Thomas Philip (or Philips or Phelps) is rather better recorded. In the winter of 1463–64 he started riots in and around Gloucester serious enough to bring the king and his court down from Coventry in a hurry, and to keep the judges so busy in Gloucester that the next law term at Westminster had to be put back by eighteen days.[68] Some of the rioters were executed, but

---

Buckinghamshire (London 1748) ii 232–3.

    A second Peter House, who must be assumed to be the son of the first, surprisingly appears in King Edward's household immediately after the readeption, took out a leisurely general pardon in April 1472 as late of Great Hampden esquire, alias late of London esquire, and was still in the king's household in 1479: *C.P.R.* (1467–77) pp. 263, 439; ibid. (1477–85) p. 159; P.R.O. C67/49 m. 34.

64 I owe this information to Dr Michael Hicks.

65 *Scriveners' Company Common Paper*, London Rec. Soc. Pubs 4 (1968) 22. I owe this reference to Miss Betty Masters of the Corporation of London Records Office.

66 I owe this information to Miss S.J. Barnes of the Oxfordshire County Record Office.

67 *C.P.R.* (1461–67) p. 296.

68 C.L. Kingsford, *English Historical Literature in the Fifteenth Century* (Oxford 1913) pp. 355–6; Scofield, i 318; Judith Avrutick, 'Commissioners of Oyer and Terminer in Fifteenth-Century England', M.Phil. thesis (London 1967) pp. 145–7; *C.P.R.* (1461–67) pp. 131, 474, 525; *Rot. Parl.*, v 511. He has been confused with a namesake from Dartington, Devon, attainted at the same time (names in same column of *Rot. Parl.*).

Philip escaped to Queen Margaret in France. He was attainted, but pardoned in 1466, having earned his living in the mean time as a chapman. It was an ideal occupation for a courier, and he may have been taking advantage of it again. Since Rea is two and a half miles from Harescombe and two miles from Gloucester, he seems likely to have been associated with Mill or House or both, and therefore with the Cornelius plot rather than with the northern or western insurrections.

In Malory's case, geography is unhelpful, but there are other and better clues. Richard Danvers of Prescott had a brother, Sir Robert Danvers of Culworth in Northamptonshire. When Sir Robert died in 1467, his executors were his brother Richard, his sister Agnes, Lady Wenlock, and his son-in-law George Burnaby of Watford, Northamptonshire.[69] George Burnaby's father Eustace Burnaby of Watford (died December 1463) was the husband of Malory's sister Philippa, his partner in his earliest alleged crime in 1443, and one of that first set of feoffees who later transferred Malory's Leicestershire lands to Wolseley and the others.[70] Malory, therefore, had in his nephew a strong link with the Danvers family and Wenlock, who were involved in the Cornelius plot. He had a second link with Wenlock through Warwick. Surprisingly for someone involved in the Cornelius plot, Wenlock was one of Warwick's closest associates.

In the 1450s, Wenlock had been Queen Margaret's chamberlain, but at the end of the decade had thrown in his lot with the Yorkists, where he proved himself a capable soldier and an outstanding diplomat.[71] His abilities brought him a peerage and a place in the royal council from Edward, and made him one of Warwick's most trusted advisers. It seems likely that he came into contact again with the exiled Lancastrians during the course of his many foreign embassies, or through the independent diplomatic connections that Warwick kept up with the King of France, who was giving the exiles refuge and support. In January 1468 the French ambassador in London reported having had discussions about Warwick's affairs with the earl's council, and with Wenlock in particular.[72] By that time, Wenlock, like Warwick, had been alienated by King Edward's preference in foreign policy for Burgundy rather than France, and at home for the Wydevilles rather than the men who had won him his kingdom. He had the motive and opportunity for listening to Lancastrian overtures, and to such an agile politician it may have been second nature to look for political reinsurance

---

69 F.N. Macnamara, *Memorials of the Danvers Family* (London 1895) p. 113.
70 *C.C.R.* (1422–29) pp. 424, 442, taken with *The Visitation of the County of Warwick in the Year 1619*, Harleian Soc. Pubs 12 (1877) 79; G.L. Kitteridge, *Sir Thomas Malory* (Barnstaple, Mass., 1925) p. 8; and Nichols, iv 362. Malory (with others) as a feoffee sold land in Saddington, Leics., to Burnaby and others at some time before Feb. 1452, perhaps about 1441: Leicester C.R.O., MS. DE 2242/6/64.
71 Roskell, 'John Lord Wenlock of Someries', *Pubs of Beds. Hist. Rec. Soc.* 38 (1957) 12–48.
72 *Patronage, Pedigree, and Power*, p. 98.

for himself, and perhaps for Warwick too. However, even listening would have had to have been kept secret from the king, and anything more serious from Warwick as well, who still believed that he could find a way to control his royal cousin. What Wenlock did has remained secret. It can only be guessed at from the fact that Cornelius under torture implicated Wenlock's servant John Hawkins in the plot, that Hawkins was also tortured, and under torture threw out unspecified allegations against his master, and that Hawkins was executed.[73] Wenlock was not touched. Quite apart from the difficulty of getting a conviction out of the Lords, he was just about to leave England in charge of the escort that would take Edward's sister to Burgundy, to marry the duke and clinch the vital alliance that would strengthen England against France and York against Lancaster. To have arrested Wenlock would have shattered confidence at home and abroad. King Edward may have had suspicions, but except in so far as the execution of Hawkins was a warning, he must have suppressed them.

Malory and Wenlock may well have met for the first time in July 1460, when, as we saw in the previous chapter, Malory seems to have been finally released from Lancastrian imprisonment. It was then that the Yorkist earls passed through London on their march to Northampton, leaving behind a force under Wenlock and others to besiege the Tower.[74] They would certainly have freed their sympathizers from London gaols, and, once free, Malory probably watched or even took part in the siege. His fictional siege of the Tower in the *Morte Darthur* contains what seems to be a reminiscence of the real siege in his substitution of guns for the older siege-artillery of his sources.[75] He and Wenlock no doubt met again in 1462, when they both took part in the sieges of the northern castles, sieges that have also left their mark on Malory's book, in his suggestion that Lancelot's castle of Joyous Garde was either Alnwick or Bamburgh.[76] In addition, of course, their common connection with Warwick, and the marriage of Malory's nephew to Wenlock's niece, may have brought them together at many other times.

Since Malory had these connections with the Cornelius plot, and no discoverable ones with anyone else actively disaffected in 1468, we must assume that he was in some way involved in the plot, and that that was why he was excluded from pardon. It is tempting to speculate that he was drawn into the plot by Wenlock's diplomatic skill and betrayed under torture by Hawkins. However, intriguing as it is that Wenlock and Malory were apparently the only supporters of Warwick's to have been involved in

73 Scofield, i 454, 460–1.
74 Scofield, i 80–96.
75 *Works*, p. 1227.25 and note. This is the only time guns are mentioned in the *Morte*.
76 *Works*, p. 1257.27 and note.

the Lancastrian cause in 1468, we have at present no grounds for going further – for suggesting, for instance, that Malory was in some way Wenlock's agent, or that his imprisonment, like Hawkins's execution, might have been partly a warning to Wenlock. We can only say that further investigation of the relationship between them is very much called for. It might shed light not only on national politics at the end of the 1460s but also on why, so surprisingly for someone of his rank and politics, Malory did not hold local office in Warwickshire or witness more than (as far as we know) one of his neighbours' charters in the early years of that decade. It may yet be found that he was frequently abroad on foreign embassies with Wenlock.[77]

Be that as it may, if Malory was imprisoned for involvement in the Cornelius plot, he cannot have been imprisoned until after the plot was discovered, on 14 June 1468. It is of course possible that he was already in prison then for some other offence, but it is unlikely. Only two of the other fourteen people excepted from pardon are known to have been in prison at the time: King Henry was in the Tower, and Hugh Mill was in the Fleet, presumably enduring (if that is the word) the lax régime provided for the king's debtors. When Mill's involvement in the plot came to light he was promptly transferred to the greater security of the Tower. Most and perhaps all of the remaining twelve people excepted, despite their Lancastrian records, seem to have been free (although Marshall's freedom may have been something of a technicality – he might have had less real liberty than Mill). Probability therefore compels us to assume until other evidence appears that Malory too was free until the plot was discovered. In that case, given the length of the *Morte Darthur*, we must assume that he was arrested and imprisoned almost immediately after the discovery of the plot, that he began writing soon after he was imprisoned, and that he was still writing and still a prisoner until some time close to the latest possible completion date for his book, 3 March 1470.

It follows from this that Warwick cannot have succeeded in freeing Malory from prison in 1469. We can presume that, despite Malory's involvement in a Lancastrian plot, Warwick, who was very short of men, would have preferred to see him free. During his second rebellion, in the

---

[77] Dr Carpenter, drawing attention to the infrequency with which Sir Thomas Malory of Newbold Revel's name occurs in the records of the 1460s, suggested that he had become senile or unhinged or was almost continuously in prison: 'Warwickshire', p. 305, 'Sir Thomas Malory', p. 41. She exaggerated the silence, since she incautiously followed William Matthews in assigning the *Morte Darthur* and perhaps other records to another Thomas Malory, and missed the Swinford enfeoffment, the Feilding charter, and the implications of the Winwick enfeoffment: that Malory was able to act freely in law and had feoffees able and willing to act with him at least once in the early 1460s. Nevertheless, the small number of these records and the complete lack of local offices during the decade still demand explanation.

spring of 1470, he gave the vital command of his base in Calais to none other than Wenlock,[78] and his followers were a politically motley lot including a number of irreconcilable Lancastrians.[79] Nevertheless, much as both Warwick and Malory may have wished to see Malory free, it is a safe assumption that King Edward succeeded in keeping him in prison until the Lancastrian victory of October 1470.

Malory's long imprisonment without trial was unusual, but not unique. Sir Thomas Tresham, an ex-Speaker of the House of Commons, who was involved in another Lancastrian plot in November 1468, was also arrested and held without trial until October 1470.[80] Presumably, Malory and Tresham were not tried because their local influence was such that juries could not have been relied on to convict. However, there is reason to believe them guilty, even though we do not know precisely what they were suspected of. Like Warwick, Edward needed the active support of every influential man he could get. He must have been sure of their guilt before having them imprisoned. He reconsidered such cases from time to time: Sir John Marney, who was arrested with Tresham, was released and pardoned after six months, but Malory and Tresham were not.[81]

It is unlikely that we will ever discover exactly what Malory had done. His career does not provide the grounds for speculation given, for instance, by that of a consistently political animal like Wenlock. However, the existence of the *Morte Darthur* shows that what he was suspected of was not a crime of the gravest kind. Without the book, it could be argued that it was only because King Edward was in the middle of a civil war that he did not take the time to go to Warwickshire and have Malory tried in the presence of himself and a retinue large enough to make the jury see things from the royal point of view. By those means, after the November 1468 plot, he was able to have the heirs to two peerages convicted and executed.[82] The *Morte Darthur* however shows that Malory's long imprisonment was honourable and even comfortable. He was given conditions in which he could write a substantial and demanding book, and these conditions included ready access to one of the most remarkable libraries in the country.

It has even been suggested that this library might have been that of the king's brother-in-law, Anthony Wydeville, Lord Scales (who became Earl

---

[78] That this appointment was a disaster at first is hardly grounds for questioning Wenlock's loyalty to Warwick: see Roskell, 'John Lord Wenlock'. Warwick appeared in flight at the harbour mouth before Wenlock had had time to gain the garrison's confidence; six months later, he brought them round for Warwick and Lancaster.

[79] Ross, *Edward IV*, p. 143.

[80] Ross, p. 123; Roskell, *The Commons and Their Speakers in English Parliaments 1376–1523* (Manchester 1965) pp. 282–3.

[81] Ross, loc. cit. If released, they would surely have been pardoned as Marney was, and they were not.

[82] Scofield, i 480–2.

Rivers when his father met a violent end during Malory's imprisonment).[83] Any such suggestion must be very tentative, but even if it were untrue, we might owe Anthony Wydeville something no less important. He may have played a part in bringing the *Morte* into being in print. He was of course Caxton's most important patron, and may have suggested the printed edition to him and have provided the manuscripts for it. The surviving manuscript was in Caxton's printing house from at least 1483 until perhaps 1498, and although Caxton, surprisingly enough, printed from a different manuscript, Anthony Wydeville may have provided that too.[84] Wydeville morality could easily encompass promoting Malory's book while defrauding his heir.

We may even guess not merely at the degree of crime that Malory committed, but at its kind. Unlike the rebels in the north and west, most of those involved in the Cornelius plot had been guilty of little more than words. They had given the Lancastrian agents shelter and perhaps a little money, had expressed regret, sympathy, and perhaps hopes for the future, and had not told the authorities of the approaches made to them. In the eyes of the law, they had harboured and comforted the king's enemies, and had concealed what they had done, thereby committing misprision of treason.[85] Malory's feelings may well have included feelings of guilt at disloyalty to King Henry, who had probably knighted him – the *Morte Darthur* makes a great deal of loyalty in general, and this bond in particular.

Much of what Malory was saying at that time may be echoed more discreetly in his lament for English political fickleness near the end of the *Morte Darthur*:

> Lo ye all Englysshemen, se ye nat what a myschyff here was? For he that was the moste kynge and nobelyst knyght of the worlde, and moste loved the felyshyp of noble knyghtes, and by hym they all were upholdyn, and yet myght nat thes Englyshemen holde them contente with hym. Lo thus was the olde custom and usayges of thys londe, and men say that we of thys londe have nat yet loste that custom. Alas! thys ys a greate defaughte of us Englysshemen, for there may no thynge us please no terme.[86]

---

83 Griffith, 'The Authorship Question', esp. p. 172; more fully but without references in his 'Arthur's Author', *Ventures in Research*, Series 1 (Greenvale, N.Y., 1973) pp. 7–43, esp. 17–20. For a critique, see Carole Meale, 'Manuscripts, Readers and Patrons in Fifteenth-Century England', *Arthurian Literature* IV (1985) 93–126. Professor Griffith also argues that Anthony Wydeville may have been the patron of the *Morte Darthur*, that it may have been shaped to his tastes, and that the lost first gathering of the only surviving MS. may have contained a dedication to him: 'Arthur's Author', pp. 20–6 et seq.

84 For the surviving MS. see p. 4 supra, and for Caxton printing from a different one, *Works*, pp. c–civ.

85 Hicks, 'Sir Thomas Cook.'

86 *Works*, p. 1229.6 and note.

This is the only passage in which Malory gives anything approaching a direct political comment on his times, and on its own it is very opaque. In early 1470, a Yorkist might have found a good many similarities between King Edward and King Arthur: Edward's fighting qualities would make it much easier to see him rather than the unwarlike Henry as a 'great king and noble knight', and, like Arthur at this point in the story, he had recently been deserted by some who had followed him for years, whom he had 'upheld' with gifts of titles and offices. His generosity to the queen's family, which Warwick and his followers so much resented, a Yorkist partisan (particularly if that generosity had not deprived him of anything) might have felt to be simply natural and proper part of this. A Lancastrian partisan on the other hand, aware of the way King Henry's support had melted away a decade before, might have felt the legitimate Henry was the modern-day Arthur. He might have seen Henry's extravagance (particularly if he himself had benefitted from it) as no more than a proper regal generosity, necessary for 'upholding' the royal affinity the king needed if he was to govern the country. Nor are these the only possibilities: a patriot might have seen either king as good enough, both as a disaster, and feared that between them they would destroy the country. Nor can we invoke the ambiguity of the passage to help us interpret it: there would obviously be circumstances in which it would be unwise for a Lancastrian partisan or a detached observer to make explicit his reservations about the government in power, but a Yorkist partisan might have subtler reasons for being reluctant to spell out even to himself an impending disaster for his cause.

A view, even a very tentative view, of what Malory thought can only be attempted by invoking the political and verbal context. We must assume from his exclusions from pardon and his imprisonment by the Yorkists that he was a Lancastrian supporter. In that context the first-person-plural pronouns of this passage imply a national guilt in which he shares. He and his country had deserted Lancaster, and he at least, driven in part no doubt by that sense of guilt, wants now to return to his former allegiance. His sense of guilt will no doubt have been accentuated while he was writing by King Henry being imprisoned in the same building. Allegiance, however, need not be unqualified, and it seems unlikely that Malory was a Lancastrian partisan, if a Lancastrian partisan means someone with the kind of blinkered vision that would have identified Henry completely with the sympathetic Arthur, and the Yorkists collectively with the villainous Mordred. The generous width of sympathy apparently implied by the totality of the contemporary allusions in the *Morte Darthur* suggests this, as does Malory's double imprisonment. When he was writing, he could look back on a Yorkist imprisonment something short of two years in length, and a Lancastrian imprisonment of almost ten years, in poverty, sickness, and suicidal depression. The most natural reading of the passage is that it does not imply any detailed correspondence between Henry and Arthur, and still less between the Yorkists and Mordred, but simply that Henry was, like Arthur, on the whole a good king whose people (and particularly Sir Thomas Malory) ought to have been faithful to him.

Even so much helps to confirm that King Edward, when he imprisoned Malory, had identified a real enemy. The Yorkist kings, however, unlike their Tudor successors, were given to mercy, and King Edward was especially generous to those who had once fought for him, as Malory had in 1462. One of Warwick's senior lieutenants, Sir Geoffrey Gate, who had also been on the 1462 expedition, was captured after Warwick's unsuccessful rebellion in 1470. All those who were caught with him suffered the full rigour of the law, but Gate was allowed to take sanctuary, and soon afterwards pardoned.[87] Similarly, it appears, Malory was imprisoned, but under circumstances in which he had access to the best collection of vernacular literature in the country, and could use it. To this royal generosity, when King Edward was fighting for his life, we owe the existence of the *Morte Darthur*.

---

[87] Scofield, i 521–2.

IX

Kinsmen

Another set of fifteenth-century events so far unconsidered may shed indirect light on Sir Thomas Malory's life. We must begin with one of the officers of his most famous prison, the Tower of London. Whatever its uses as prison, royal palace, menagerie, arsenal, shipyard, mint, and record office, for any fifteenth-century English government, the Tower was important primarily as the fortress straddling the walls of the country's capital. Any government would remember that during the Peasants' Revolt in 1381, whether by treachery or failure of nerve in the garrison, the rebels had gained access to the Tower, where they had insulted the king's mother, murdered his chief minister, and put themselves in what might have been, had they been better organised, a position of impregnable power. Those events were a potent reminder that the government should keep the Tower under a competent commander with strong nerves and impeccable loyalty, who had the respect of the garrison, and whose rank and income could 'carry' his office if the government itself were in trouble.

With that encouragement, successive fifteenth-century governments seem to have taken some trouble to find the right man for the job. A list of fifteenth-century Constables of the Tower, however, shows that an ideal candidate was not always available.[1] Governments can be seen making compromises that reflect in little the twists and turns of national politics. We see the difficulties created for Henry IV and Richard III by the limited support each had among the aristocracy when he came to the throne, Edward IV's reliance in his later years on men he had promoted into or within the peerage, and particularly on his wife's family, the Wydevilles, and Henry IV's political skill and Henry VI's lack of it. The former, while Richard II was still nominally king, manoeuvred him into appointing a constable who must have been in effect Richard's gaoler. The latter, having granted the reversion of the constableship to the seventeen-year-old Henry Holland, later the same year allowed a royal favourite, Lord Saye and Sele,

---

[1] See Appendix IV for a list of Constables. It may be the more useful in that a surprising number of distinguished historians have confused the post with that of Deputy Constable or Lieutenant-Constable of the Tower, or Constable of England.

to exploit the office regardless of security considerations at a time of national unrest. Saye paid a heavy price for his greed: three years later, the garrison his other interests cannot have left him time to get to know handed him over to the threats of Jack Cade's rebels, who put him through a travesty of a trial before an intimidated bench of justices and executed him at the Standard in Cheapside.[2]

The list also shows that governments thought it important that when the office of constable fell vacant, it should be filled as quickly as possible. When Sir Thomas Rempston, for instance, died unexpectedly in 1406, drowned in a boat trying to shoot London Bridge against the tide, a new and daring permanent appointment was made the very next day. Despite the many political reversals of the century, there appears to be only one occasion on which constableship was left vacant for more than a month: the ten months between Edward IV's accession and his grant of the constableship to the Earl of Worcester on 2 December 1461.

The delay was not for practical reasons. When the Yorkist forces, with Henry VI as their prisoner, arrived in London in July 1460 after the Battle of Northampton, the Lancastrian garrison abandoned the Tower in a mass escape to sanctuary,[3] and the Yorkists retained control of it through all the vicissitudes of national politics of the following year. By March 1461, they controlled not only the Tower but also the machinery of government, through which King Edward could have issued a grant of office in the usual form. Nor was the delay caused by a sense of administrative propriety. Had Edward been more scrupulous than his brother Richard in respecting appointments made by his predecessor, he would have waited another few weeks: the Act of Attainder against the Duke of Exeter and other Lancastrians completed its progress through the Commons on 21 December.

The main reason for delay seems to be that the man Edward wanted was not immediately available. The Earl of Worcester had prudently removed himself to Italy in 1460, and in the course of his return journey only reached Canterbury on 1 September 1461. Even then, however, Edward waited another three months to appoint him. The reason must surely have been that England's most important fortress was already being looked after by someone else.

Since he was prepared to ignore Exeter's rights, Edward could have appointed a temporary Constable, but no grant 'during pleasure' is recorded. Alternatively, he could have superseded the incumbent with a Keeper, as the Lancastrians did in 1413, 1425, 1450, and 1460. On the first occasion, Henry V effectively suspended the Constable for allowing an

2 I.M.W. Harvey, *Jack Cade's Rebellion* (Oxford 1991) pp. 92–3.
3 R.A. Griffiths, *The Reign of King Henry VI* (London 1981) p. 863.

escape; and on the second, when the then Constable seemed to be about to provoke a civil war, Henry VI's council appointed Richard Wydeville esquire, chamberlain to the Duke of Bedford, as Keeper for eight months.[4] On the other two occasions, during Cade's revolt and the campaign leading up to Northampton, Thomas Lord Scales superseded Saye and Exeter respectively.[5] There is no record of Edward appointing a Keeper either. However, in an emergency he might have appointed a temporary officer in some informal way that left no record, and in fact he seems to have done so for at least part of the time, since on 13 August 1461, Henry Bourchier Earl of Essex was paid as Constable of the Tower of London.[6]

Like his predecessors, however, Essex would have been expected to delegate most of the work to his official deputy, the Lieutenant, leaving him free to put his political weight at the king's service in other ways. Although the Lieutenant's title is often 'the king's lieutenant of the Tower', he seems normally to have been appointed by the Constable. On the only occasion on which the lieutenancy is granted by enrolled letter patent, the grant specifies that it is made with the permission of the then Constable, the Duke of York.[7] On this occasion, however, since the new king was prepared to make an irregular appointment to the constableship, he may have done the same to the lieutenancy, and appointed directly himself. The Yorkists would of course have given command of the Tower to someone they had confidence in from the moment the Lancastrians abandoned it. That person need not have been appointed to any official post, but, three weeks after Edward became king, someone held at least one of the two official senior posts, since on 25 March 1461 a commission was issued to deliver a prisoner 'to the Constable of the Tower or his Lieutenant'.[8] Although many rules can be broken in a national emergency, the routine nature of this transaction and the lieutenant's customary particular responsibility for prisoners suggests that if only one post was filled, it was more likely to be the lieutenancy. The commission does not name the lieutenant, but he could have been the man known to be Lieutenant of the Tower on 28 October 1461, five weeks before Worcester became Constable. That man was called Robert Malory, and it is with him that the remainder of this chapter will be concerned.

---

4 Edward Powell, *Kingship, Law, and Society* (Oxford 1989) pp. 137–8; *Proc. & Ord. P.C.*, iii 167; Griffiths, p. 90, n. 45; and cf. pp. 72–81. Robert Morley, appointed Keeper in 1413, was succeeded in 1414 by John Dabridgecourt: see James Wylie and W.T. Waugh, *The Reign of Henry V*, 3 vols (Cambridge 1914–29) i 250, 36, 261; *C.P.R.* (1413–16) p. 103.

5 P.R.O. E403/779 m. 8, 9; Anthony Goodman, *The Wars of the Roses* (London 1981) pp. 35–7, 125, 184–5. This admirable book calls Scales 'Lieutenant' of the Tower, but he is not so called in e.g. P.R.O. E403/779 m. 8, 9.

6 He was paid £23. 6s. 8d: P.R.O. E403/822.

7 *C.P.R.* (1408–13) p. 303.

8 *C.P.R.* (1461–7) p. 31.

Robert Malory, Lieutenant of the Tower of London, is apparently the subject of something over a dozen records spanning the eleven years 1461–71. The first of them suggests he was a compassionate man: one of its two components is a letter to the king from a prisoner complaining that during nearly a year's imprisonment he has had nothing to eat except what Robert Malory 'your lieutenant', out of charity and not as part of his duty, paid for out of his own pocket. Other conclusions may emerge if the whole group of records is set against the major political events of the time.

Edward IV proclaimed king 4 March 1461

1. 28 October 1461 to 11 July 1464   Robert Mallore esquire is Lieutenant of the Earl of Worcester, Constable of the Tower of London; Master Robert Mallory is Lieutenant of the King's Tower of London.[9]
2. 1 May 1462   Robert Malory is granted by mainprise of William Preston of London gentleman and William Pulton of the parish of St Anthony in London draper the farm of the subsidy and alnages of cloth for Norfolk, Suffolk, and Essex for seven years from Easter last past.[10]
3. 7 April 1463   The Mayor of York, Brother John Langstrother, Sir James Strangways, Geoffrey Middleton, and Robert Malory are commissioned to arrest Humphrey Neville and bring him before the king in council.[11]

Edward begins to be estranged from Warwick September 1464

4. 3 February 1466   Robert Malore esquire is granted a personal general pardon.[12]
5. Easter 1469   Robert Malory's appointment as alnager expires; no replacement until December.

Warwick defeats and captures Edward 26 July 1469

6. 12 August 1469   Robert Malory esquire of London is allegedly implicated in the death of Earl Rivers.[13]
7. 30 August 1469   Robert Malorry is appointed searcher of ships in London and adjacent ports.[14]

---

[9] Scofield, i 273n, ii 400–1. The former reference is to a payment of 11 July 1464 on the Issue Roll for Easter Term 4 Edward IV. It was authorised by P.R.O. Warrant for Issues E404/72/3/85, dated 23 July 1463, but if Malory had left his post in the interim the Issue Roll would have called him 'late lieutenant'.

[10] C.F.R. (1461–71) p. 74.

[11] C.P.R. (1461–67) p. 279.

[12] C.P.R. (1461–67) p. 476.

[13] P.R.O. KB 27/836, m. 61d.

[14] C.F.R. (1461–71) p. 251.

Edward regains his freedom

8. 15 December 1469 Robert Malory's successor as alnager is appointed.[15]
9. 9 May 1470 Robert Malorry of London esquire alias Robert Mallorre late of London esquire alias Robert Mallory gentilman alias Robert Malurre gentilman alias Robert Malore is granted a general pardon at New Sarum.[16]

Readeption of Henry VI

10. 25 October 1470 Robert Malorry is replaced in the London customs.[17]
11. 5 November 1470 Robert Malory is made escheator for Cambridgeshire and Huntingdonshire.[18]
12. 17 December 1470 Sir John Say, Sir Edmund Gray, Robert Mallere, and eight others are commissioned to arrest 44 men for robberies, murders, and other crimes committed at Ware, Hertfordshire.[19]
13. 30 January 1471 Robert Malory and Geoffrey Downes are granted by mainprise of John Clopton and John Dorset of London the subsidy and alnages of cloth for Norfolk, Suffolk, Essex, Cambridgeshire, and Huntingdonshire for seven years from Michaelmas last past.[20]

Edward returns 14 March, victor at Tewkesbury 4 May 1471

14. 18 June 1471 Robert Malory is replaced as escheator, his successor eventually accounting for both of them.[21]
15. 27 July 1471 Robert Malory is replaced as alnager.[22]
16. 12 December 1471 Robert Mallory of London esquire alias Robert Malorre late of London esquire alias Robert Mallory gentilman alias Robert Mallure gentilman is granted a general pardon at Westminster.[23]

The fifteenth-century use of social ranks for individuation was discussed in Chapter I. That usage is more difficult to apply to social ranks below that of knight: lower rank means geographically restricted consequence, so a subject can more easily go unrecorded, and it is harder to be sure that

15 *C.F.R.* (1461–71) p. 252.
16 P.R.O. C67/47, m. 4.
17 *C.F.R.* (1461–71) p. 277.
18 *C.F.R.* (1461–71) p. 271.
19 *C.P.R.* (1467–77) p. 250. For Say, see Wedgwood *s.v.* and Harvey, pp. 179–81.
20 *C.F.R.* (1461–71) p. 277.
21 *C.F.R.* (1471–85) pp. 18–19.
22 *C.F.R.* (1471–85) p. 17.
23 P.R.O. C67/48, m. 24.

records even from nearby places do not record different people. Nevertheless, these records may be taken to imply that in London in the years from
1461 to 1471 there was only one Robert Malory who could be called esquire
or gentleman. Even in London, one man of either of those ranks would
hardly be unknown to another, and once they knew of each other's existence, they would have made sure that they were distinguished by additional appellations. It would be unreasonable to assume that these
documents record (say) one Robert Malory involved in high politics and
another pursuing an inoffensive career collecting wool taxes and customs
dues, both of whom by coincidence finished their active careers in midsummer 1471.

Three of the records, however, have no obvious London connections
(except in that each is a government act), and need to be considered individually to establish whether they involve the same Robert Malory as the
others. This is easily demonstrated with the commission to arrest
Humphrey Neville. As we saw in the last chapter, Neville was a cousin of
King Edward and the Earl of Warwick. In the previous year, after being
pardoned attainder on condition that he live in the Tower of London, he
had absconded to his native northern England (where he was later pardoned again).[24] Given fifteenth-century views of the personal responsibility of gaolers for the safekeeping of prisoners,[25] it would have been
strange if any commission to recapture him had not included the Lieutenant of the Tower.

The other two documents, however, are a different matter. The commission to arrest troublemakers in Ware could easily involve a second
Robert Malory. Ware may now be a commuter suburb of London, but in
the fifteenth century, the almost twenty miles of countryside separating the
two places might have been thought sufficient on its own to distinguish
two namesakes. That alone, however, would not prove there were two
namesakes: it would remain possible that the insecure readeption government was fortifying a local group with a reliable man of its own, whom it
expected to find time in the intervals of work in the capital to keep the
Hertfordshire gentry on their toes. To identify the man named in this
record and as the escheator, we may have to look to the evidential context,
which, as we shall see, suggests that there may have been a suitable Robert
Malory alive at the right time in Hertford, but that there was not one in
Cambridgeshire or Huntingdonshire. It will be best to defer further consideration of the two records until we have considered that evidence.

Robert Malory's *curriculum vitae* suggests a man of outstanding energy

[24] *Rot. Parl.*, v 478, 511; *C.P.R.* (1461–7) pp. 122, 267, 279.
[25] An earlier Lieutenant of the Tower was fined a thousand marks for an escape, and only
pardoned at the request of parliament: *C.P.R.* (1413–16) p. 191.

and administrative capacity. Collecting King Edward's taxes, as well as running the Tower of London, would have required those talents. Edward, from the beginning of his reign, and without waiting for due parliamentary approval, spent a great deal of time ensuring that all available sources of revenue brought in as much money as possible, and systems and men that did not produce results were changed.[26] The records also show that Robert Malory's loyalties were primarily to the Earl of Warwick rather than to King Edward. This is implied by the whole pattern of events and spectacularly in the accusation that he was implicated in the deaths of Richard Wydeville Earl Rivers and Sir John Wydeville, King Edward's father-in-law and brother-in-law.

According to the Burgundian chronicler Waurin, during Warwick's rebellion in the summer of 1469, Rivers and his son took refuge in Chepstow Castle, but reports of their whereabouts reached Warwick, who threatened that if the people of Chepstow did not hand them over he would destroy the place.[27] Warwick's emissaries took them to Kenilworth near Coventry, where they were beheaded on Warwick's orders. A short but circumstantial note in the *Coventry Leet Book* says that Lord Rivers, Treasurer of England, and Sir John Wydeville his son, both of whom had been captured at Chepstow, were beheaded at Gosford Green, just outside Coventry, on 12 August 1469.[28] The two sources could be reconciled by positing what would anyway be a plausible sequence of events: an initial imprisonment at Kenilworth for maximum security, followed by execution at Coventry for maximum publicity.

That is almost all that has been known about this startling occurrence, but a little more can be added from an accusation laid in the court of King's Bench when King Edward's party were back in power. The king's mother-in-law, Jacquetta Duchess of Bedford, accused those she thought responsible for the deaths of her husband and son. Since the case did not come to trial, because (not surprisingly) none of the defendants were available, there are no further documents, but the accusation at least gives a list of the men the Duchess believed to have been responsible. The list gives thirty-five names in sufficient detail to inspire some confidence. It begins with Richard Neville Earl of Warwick and Salisbury and John Langstrother Prior of the Hospital of St John of Jerusalem in England 'of St John's Street in the county of Middlesex knight',[29] and works its way down the social ladder by way of another Knight Hospitaller, three more knights, eleven

---

[26] Charles Ross, *Edward IV* (London 1974) pp. 373–5; J.R. Lander, *Crown and Nobility* (London 1976) pp. 38–41, 163–70.

[27] Jehan de Waurin, *Recueil des chroniques*, R.S., v 580–1.

[28] *Coventry Leet Book*, ed. Mary Dormer Harris, E.E.T.S., ii (1908) 346. Gosford Green was where Bolingbroke and Mowbray were to have had their trial by combat in Richard II's reign: *V.C.H., Warwicks.*, viii 121.

[29] Cf record no. 3 above.

esquires, and two gentlemen, and ends with a groom from Coventry. The twelfth name is Robert Malory esquire. The indictment does not go into detail about the part any individual played in what happened, but the Lieutenant of the Tower of London might have known more than most of those present about how to organise an execution. Everyone present must have been a close adherent of Warwick's, since no amount of precedent for summary execution of political opponents captured in arms could be expected to reconcile the king to what they were doing. It was a moment when those whose loyalty or nerves were weak would have found urgent business elsewhere.

Loyalty to Warwick looks like the keynote of Robert Malory's career: he gains and loses employment, and particularly politically sensitive employment, as Warwick's fortunes wax and wane. The office of alnager was politically least important, and could plainly be carried out by deputy in absentia, since the alnager appointed (for Yorkshire) immediately before Malory's second appointment for East Anglia was Warwick's brother John Neville, Marquis Montagu. The lieutenancy of the Tower was much more important in every way, and although there is no direct evidence for the end of Malory's term of office,[30] his general pardon of February 1466 may have been an inducement to go quietly at a time when the rift between Warwick and Edward was deepening. It may be noticed that a compassionate man might have found himself uncomfortable if he had responsibility for the safe-keeping of Henry VI, who was imprisoned in the Tower on 24 July 1465,[31] although we should not infer a causal connection between the two possibilities. Conversely, in May 1470, a month after Warwick had fled to France (and nine months after the death of Earl Rivers), Malory felt the need for a pardon urgently enough to pursue the court to Wiltshire to get one. When Warwick was was politically on top, however precariously, after he had defeated and captured King Edward, Malory was appointed to a useful post dealing with shipping in and around the capital; when Warwick came to the top again in the readeption, Malory resigned that post to help with local government in the Fens; and of course after Warwick's death, although he had survived the slaughter, as his third pardon shows, he disappears from political life altogether. There is, as we shall see, reason to suppose that he lived on for some years, in peace although naturally without employment. If so, it may be inferred that he had done nothing unforgivable and that he was not thought of as dangerous once Warwick was dead.

---

[30] Richard Haute esquire of Ightham Kent and Danbury Essex was lieutenant on 29 May 1471: Wedgwood, s.v.

[31] Scofield, ii 382–3. Henry had his own gaoler, Thomas Grey of Cawdon, esquire of the body to King Edward: Wedgwood, s.v.

Who then was this Robert Malory who helped to kill King Edward's father-in-law? Although the men who became Lieutenants of the Tower were not always socially prominent, it would be surprising if no trace of his origins could be found at all. Of the ten men of the right name known from fifteenth-century Britain, three appear to have lived too early and four too late. We may rule out Robert Malory of Walton-on-the-Wold in Leicestershire, last recorded in 1411;[32] Sir Robert Malory, Prior of St John, who died in 1439 or 1440;[33] and Robert Malory of Hutton Conyers in Yorkshire, who seems to have died as a child, probably by 1462.[34] At the other end of the century, Robert Malory of Papworth St Agnes in Cambridgeshire was born, according to his proof of age, on 4 November 1457;[35] and Sir Robert Malory of Litchborough in Northamptonshire had an elder brother who was born in 1455.[36] Proofs of age are not always reliable, but what other evidence there is for the families is consistent with the ages given in these two. Robert Malory of Saddington in Leicestershire is recorded only from 1493 to 1508,[37] and a Scottish Robert Malory is known from a single record of 1488 – an accusation of cattle theft.[38]

These set aside, there are three Robert Malorys apparently of the right generation. Of these, the most obscure is an uncle and namesake of Sir Robert Malory of Litchborough, a man known from only four records. At some time between 1467 and 1473 he was accused by a man who may have been his stepfather of withholding Litchborough estate records; he held the manor of Litchborough in 1471/72; he was involved in a small Northamptonshire land deal in 1477; and he died in 1487, when he was succeeded by his son John.[39] The first two records give him no rank, but the third and fourth call both him 'gentleman'. The paucity of records and the low ranks are typical of the Litchborough Malorys in the fifteenth century. At one point there seems to be a complete break in the records for a generation, when even the name of the head of that branch of the Malory family is unknown; and they made no mark in national or local politics until this Robert's son John and three of his first cousins were attainted for fighting

---

32 Pardoned as brother of William Malory of Tachbrook Mallory and Walton-on-the-Wolds in 1388, party to a Bramcote fine in 1411: P.R.O., typescript 'Index to Pardon Rolls 1377–99', p. 183; *Warwickshire Feet of Fines*, ed. Ethel Stokes et al., 3 vols, Dugdale Soc. (1932–43) iii, no. 2463.

33 See Chapter V supra.

34 See p. 15 supra.

35 See p. 179.

36 See pp. 19–20 supra and 193 infra.

37 B.M. Add. Ch. 21508; *The Court Rolls of the Manor of Bromsgrove and Kingsnorton 1494–1504*, ed. A.F.C. Baber, Worcester Historical Soc. n.s. 3 (1963) pp. 14, 140; Farnham, *Village Notes*, iv 15; B.M. Add. Ch. 22304.

38 *The Acts of the Lords of Council in Civil Causes 1478–95* (London 1839) p. 114.

39 P.R.O. C1/38/254; Baker, *Northants.*, pp. 406–7; P.R.O. E210/2741; *Cal. I.P.M., Hen. VII,* iii 507.

against Henry VII at Stoke-by-Newark in 1487.[40] It would been foolhardy to infer from their anti-Tudor politics at that time anything about their political inclinations in earlier decades, but the surviving records of this Robert Malory of Litchborough do not make him look like someone whose enemies would have called him esquire after he had ceased to be Lieutenant of the Tower of London.

The remaining two men were closely related, being first cousins once removed. They may have been nephew and great-nephew respectively of Sir Robert Malory, the Prior of St John who died in 1439/40, and since the name Robert was unusual in their branch of the Malorys in earlier generations, it is not unlikely that they were both named after him.

The elder was Sir Thomas Malory of Newbold Revel's first cousin, Robert son of Simon Malory of Clerkenwell in Middlesex. As we saw in Chapter V, Simon Malory followed Prior Robert from Warwickshire to the Hospitaller Priory at Clerkenwell, where he stayed on after Prior Robert's death and where he was eventually himself buried in the priory church. This is important because the Duchess of Bedford identified the man who had taken part in the killing of her husband and son as 'Robert Malory late of London esquire alias Robert Malory of St John's Street in the county of Middlesex esquire'. Two things should be noted about the man she named. The first is his rank: well after ceasing to be Lieutenant of the Tower, he is still called esquire. The second is that the extraordinary form of his domicile is identical with that given for the second man accused, Sir John Langstrother, Prior of St John. It means the Hospitaller priory at Clerkenwell, and it strongly suggests that the Lieutenant of the Tower was the son of Simon Malory.

However, there are difficulties. Robert son of Simon is known from at most five records, all from the London area in the years 1438–60. They begin at very much the time one might expect from a first cousin of Sir Thomas of Newbold Revel. The five records make their subject executor of a William Malory in 1438, legatee to his own father in 1443, party to an Essex land deal in 1446, a fairly prosperous householder in Hertford – said to have had an annual income of £10 – at an unspecified time in the reign of Henry VI, and a salter in London in 1460.[41] Although income was not the only factor affecting social rank, an income of £10 was the very lowest level at which a man could normally call himself a gentleman: for the possessor of such an income to call himself an esquire would have invited ridicule,[42]

---

[40] See p. 193 infra.

[41] London, Guildhall Library, MS 9171/4, fols 3ᵛ–4ʳ; P.R.O. Prob. 11.1, fol. 117ᵛ; *Feet of Fines, Essex*, iv, Essex Archaeol. Soc. (1964) 36; *V.C.H., Herts.*, iii 491n, Thomas Chauncy, *Historical Antiquities of Hertfordshire* (London 1700) p. 16; *Calendar of the Plea and Memoranda Rolls of the City of London 1458–84*, ed. P.E. Jones (Cambridge 1961) p. 156.

[42] See H.L. Gray, 'Incomes from land in England in 1436', *E.H.R.* 49 (1934) 607–39.

and in fact the only designation of rank in any of these documents is 'salter', which suggests a status below, or at best outside, the gentry.

The five records, however, may not all refer to the same man. The record of the salter comes fourteen years after the previous one, and spells the family name *Maluery*. The only other known occurrences of this spelling are in records of a family of London salters later in the century who eventually abandon *Maluery* entirely for *Salter*: they will be descendents of the man recorded in 1460.[43] The change of spelling, consistently adhered to in descendants, and the fourteen-year gap in the records suggest different men. Any suggestion as to a relationship between them would have to be tentative in the extreme, but one possibility should be mentioned. We have noticed that No. 12 in the list of records of the Lieutenant of the Tower might not belong with the rest. If its subject were the salter, then, even if the salter were not the man recorded from 1438 to 1446, there would be a possible geographical connection between them. We might guess that they were father and son-and-heir, and that the son, having inherited the father's property in Hertford, had become the kind of substantial citizen the government would look to to deal with troublemakers in Ware, a mile away.

There are therefore two possibilities, both, despite the surprising Clerkenwell connection, unpromising. If the 1460 record stands alone, we have a London tradesman so obscure that he was recorded only once or twice in his life. If it represents the same man as the four earlier records, its subject was so obscure that he could remain unrecorded for more than a decade at a time, and, when he was recorded, he looks as if he would barely have counted as a member of the gentry. In either case, by the 1460s he had adopted a distinctive spelling of his name, a spelling never attributed to the Lieutenant of the Tower, not even in his 1470 and 1471 pardons, when he should have given every variant of his name that anyone had ever used. Those pardons do give several variant spellings, including the unusual *Mallure*, but not *Maluery*. Whichever permutation represents the Robert Malory of 1460(–70), neither has much about it to suggest that he ever became the Lieutenant of the Tower of London.

There remains Robert son of Sir Thomas Malory of Newbold Revel. He is first recorded in Michaelmas Term 1462, when Sir Thomas settled lands on his son Robert Malory esquire and Robert's wife Elizabeth.[44] Robert also held land at Market Harborough in Leicestershire in May 1462, June 1466,

---

43 E.g. *Calendar of the Plea and Memoranda Rolls*, p. 92; *C.P.R.* (1467–77) p. 545; Guildhall Library, MS 9171/8, fol. 37.
44 P.R.O. CP 40/806, m. 62.

and July 1471, and is recorded as having held land there in July 1478.[45] The first document calls him esquire, the others give him no rank, and the wording of the last suggests he was dead, although it might only mean that he had disposed of the property. In two documents of January 1473, the lord of Saddington, Leicestershire, is called Robert Malory esquire.[46] If more than one man were involved in these documents, they would surely have been distinguished by appellations of some kind. The Leicestershire county boundary would not have been a sufficient distinction between Robert Malory of the Newbold Revel and Robert Malory of Saddington or Market Harborough or both when the Malorys of Newbold Revel held land at Swinford and Starmore in Leicestershire, only eight miles from Saddington and ten from Market Harborough. Moreover, since Robert Malory of Newbold's mother was apparently a Walsh of Wanlip, a family with lands in Market Harborough, and his wife a Pulteney of Misterton, a family with lands in Saddington, it is particularly likely that he would have held property in those two places.[47]

These records make Robert Malory of Newbold Revel look a more plausible Lieutenant of the Tower than his namesakes from Litchborough and Clerkenwell. Where they look too low in rank, he is three times called esquire. Where neither of them has any discernible politics, he is at least, in an age when father and sons tended to take very much the same political line,[48] the son of a man who at the appropriate time was very closely allied to Warwick. He also had connections with Clerkenwell, not as obvious as those of his cousin, but nevertheless real, both through his cousin and through the Hospitaller knight Sir John Malory.[49] The Saddington connection suggests that the Robert Malory of Saddington mentioned above, who flourished from 1493 to 1508, might be this man's son, perhaps his second son.

One difficulty, however, stands in the way of this identification. When Sir Thomas died, his inquisition post mortem, taken on 6 November 1471, said that his heir, his son Robert, was twenty-three years old 'and more'.[50] That would make Robert at most fourteen when first recorded as Lieutenant of the Tower. A party that has just been successful in a *coup d'état* may well be short of distinguished loyalists for responsible posts, and the Yorkists had particular difficulties in 1460, since they needed every experienced soldier they could spare for actual fighting in the midlands and the north, but they would have had to be very short of men indeed to have

---

45 J.E. Stocks, *Market Harborough Parish Records*, 2 vols (London 1890–1926) i 177, 181–2, 184, 187–8.

46 Leics. C.R.O. DE 2242/6/65–7.

47 Stocks, i 180; Leics. C.R.O. DE 2242/6/64.

48 See K.B. MacFarlane, 'The Wars of the Roses', *P.B.A.* 50 (1964) 105.

49 See Chapter V supra.

50 P.R.O. C140/36/12.

given effective command of the country's most important fortress to a fourteen-year-old.

There are, however, reasons for doubting the age that Sir Thomas's inquisition post mortem gives for his heir. Robert Malory held land in Winwick and Market Harborough in 1462, when, if that inquisition is to be believed, he was about fourteen. Although it was legally possible for a minor to hold land, it would be very unusual. Furthermore, both documents describe him as an esquire, which would also have been improper before he came of age. If the age in the inquisition is wrong, it is difficult to be sure what age is right.[51] One possibility, however, could have produced the extant reading particularly easily by scribal error. An inquisition post mortem, unlike a proof of age, only gives the age of the heir once, and a single error of *viginti* (say) for *triginti* would have been easy to commit and would have involved no administrative error such as an erroneous grant of wardship that needed later correction. A birthdate of 1437/38 for Robert would be slightly more compatible with the birth of his father, probably between December 1414 and June 1418, and that of his son Nicholas, between 25 July 1465 and 1 August 1467. It would also fit more naturally with Robert's marriage (although child marriage was a fact, even an abuse, in the fifteenth century), and with his being named after Prior Robert Malory, who was alive at the earlier date and seven years dead at the later one. There would be nothing implausible about the appointment of a Lieutenant of the Tower aged (say) twenty-four at a time when the most experienced soldiers were desperately needed elsewhere. Indeed, Lieutenant Robert Malory's eventual superior, the Earl of Worcester, had been appointed Treasurer of England at the age of twenty-four, an office that was no sinecure.[52]

One other record of the Lieutenant of the Tower may help solve the problem of identification with as high a degree of certainty as the available evidence permits. When the readeption government appointed new officers to the counties, the ex-Lieutenant of the Tower was made escheator

---

[51] It is not even possible to define Robert's age relatively to the Thomas Malory junior who was buried at Monks Kirby in 1457/8, who was presumably the son of Sir Thomas of Newbold Revel, and the brother of Robert. Given the naming customs of the time, it is quite likely that he was Sir Thomas's second son, but even that does not establish which was the elder. If the family followed custom in naming the second son after the father, it might have done so too in naming the first son after the father's father. Sir Thomas's eldest son would then have been called John, and whether he died young or became a Hospitaller and renounced his inheritance on entering the order, Robert the eventual heir would have been younger than Thomas. However, for a particularly valued benefactor and patron, a family might set custom aside, so Robert might be a first-born son named after Prior Robert, and so older than Thomas.

[52] *Complete Peerage, s.v.*; MacFarlane, *The Nobility of Later Medieval England* (Oxford 1973) pp. 232–3.

for Cambridgeshire and Huntingdonshire. Whichever Robert Malory was the lieutenant, the government's choice seems surprising, because none of the three Robert Malorys we have been considering seems to have had any previous connection with either county. Robert Malory of Papworth St Agnes did – the boundary between them ran through Papworth – but the appointment was made the day after his thirteenth birthday. The identity of the sheriff nominated for the two counties at the same time may however go some way towards explaining the choice. The sheriff, also a stranger to both counties, was William Feilding, a determined Lancastrian later to be killed fighting at the Battle of Tewkesbury.[53] He came from Newnham Paddox in Warwickshire, the estate next to Newbold Revel, and in 1464, as we saw in the previous chapter, his son had married Sir Thomas Malory's niece. His presence in Cambridgeshire makes it most likely that the Robert Malory who was his administrative colleague was his neighbour from Newbold Revel.

Why the two of them took on these offices is unclear. It has been suggested that part of Feilding's motive was a wish to leave himself free to sit for Warwickshire in the Readeption Parliament.[54] Perhaps Robert Malory was appointed escheator so as to share control of the two counties as far as possible between the two uneasy allies who formed the readeption government, Feilding as a supporter of Lancaster being balanced by Robert Malory as a supporter of Warwick. Whatever the reason, their joint involvement must surely tip the balance of probability in favour of identifying the effective commander of the Tower of London and the man accused of involvement in the death of the queen's father and brother as Robert son of Sir Thomas Malory of Newbold Revel.

[53] Wedgwood, *s.v.*; *Paston Letters*, ed. Davis, ii 593.
[54] Wedgwood, *History of Parliament: Register*, p. 314.

X

Armorial

Malory wrote his *Morte Darthur* for 'gentlemen and gentlewomen', meaning of course the whole of the gentry, not just those in the lowest rank, below esquire.[1] Throughout the *Morte Darthur* the gentry and its symbolic centre, knighthood, are important largely because they imply a code of behaviour that sets standards in matters ranging from morals to fighting ability.[2] Malory touches on the most important parts of that code when he says of his favourite minor character:

> He ys a noble knyght and a myghty man and well-brethed; and yf he were well assayed . . . he were good inow for ony knyght that beryth the lyff. And he ys jantill, curteyse, and ryght bownteuous, meke and mylde, and in hym ys no maner of male engynne, but playne, faythfull an trew.[3]

However, what Malory expected of the gentry extends beyond these virtues, to other less predictable areas of behaviour. One scholar even suggested that they include hearty eating,[4] and a passage in the fifth tale points to others:

> As [Sir Tristram] growed in myght and strength, he laboured in huntynge and in hawkynge – never jantylman more that ever we herde rede of. And as the booke seyth, he began good mesures of blowynge of beestes of venery and beestes of chaace and all maner of vermaynes, and all the tearmys we have yet of hawkynge and huntynge. And therefore the booke of venery, of hawkynge and huntynge is called *The Booke of Sir Trystrams*.
>
> Wherefore, as me semyth, all jantyllmen that beryth olde armys ought of ryght to honoure Sir Trystrams for the goodly tearmys that jantylmen have and use and shall do unto the Day of Dome, that

1 *Works*, p. 1260.20.
2 For chivalry in the *Morte Darthur*, see recently Terence McCarthy, *Reading the Morte Darthur* (Woodbridge 1991) pp. 72–100.
3 *Works*, pp. 1088–89.
4 Felicity Riddy, *Sir Thomas Malory* (Leiden 1987) pp. 60–83, esp. p. 79.

thereby in a maner all men of worshyp may discever a jantylman
frome a yoman and a yoman frome a vylayne. For he that jantyll is
woll drawe hym to jantyll tacchis and to folow the noble customys of
jantylmen.[5]

The gentleman, then, 'labours' in hunting and hawking, and knows the
jargon of those pursuits. He should also, it appears, if he can manage it,
bear an ancient coat of arms.

Enthusiasm for hawking and hunting shows clearly enough in the *Morte
Darthur* and the *Wedding of Sir Gawain and Dame Ragnell*, although the only
historical evidence of Malory's feelings on those matters is the raid on
Caludon Park, which might have been precipitated more by dislike of the
Duke of Buckingham than by anything more positive. In contrast, heraldry
in his writings seems largely to be taken over from his sources.[6] There is,
however, evidence to suggest that his family at least were enthusiastic
about heraldry, and his remark about 'olde armys' implies that he shared
that enthusiasm.

It may seem fortunate, then, that we have an account of Malory's coat of
arms from this century's most distinguished student of English heraldry,
Sir Anthony Wagner, who blazons it as *quarterly 1 and 4 (Revell), ermine a
chevron gules and a border engrailed sable; 2 and 3 (Malory) or three lions passant
sable.*[7] It is with trepidation that I suggest that Sir Anthony's case is not
proved. Sir Thomas Malory had a right to both coats of arms, and someone
in his family – almost certainly his grandson Nicholas – quartered them,
but there is doubt whether Sir Thomas himself did so. There is also some
reason to doubt whether either coat of arms quartered is described quite
accurately. A brief look at the origins of the various Malory coats of arms
will put the problem in context.

The earliest known Malory device is pre-heraldic: in 1155/8 Richard
Malory of Kirkby Mallory displayed a simple fleur-de-lys on his seal.[8] At
about the same time, his brother Anschetil had a seal too, although no
impression of it has survived.[9] At some time during the following century,

5 *Works*, p. 375.15–29, slightly repunctuated.
6 One possible exception is the green shield 'wyth a maydyn whych semed in hit' that Sir
   Gareth borrows in the Great Tournament episode, which might be an allusion to a
   jousting association founded by the French Marshal Boucicaut: see *Works*, p. 1111.8, and
   P.J.C. Field, 'Fifteenth-Century History in Malory's *Morte Darthur*' in *Cultural Intermediaries in Medieval Britain*, ed. Françoise le Saux (Lampeter 1993), forthcoming. See also
   C.W. Scott-Giles, 'Some Arthurian Coats of Arms' in *The Coat of Arms* viii (Oct. 1965)
   332–39 and ix (Jan. 1966) 30–5.
7 Anthony R. Wagner, *Historic Heraldry of Britain: An Illustrated Series of British Historical
   Arms* (London 1939) p. 63 and Plate XIII.
8 B.L. Add. Ch. 47619.
9 B.L. Add. Ch. 53093. For the text of this charter, see *Documents Illustrative of the . . .
   History of the Danelaw*, ed. F.M. Stenton (London 1920) pp. 249–50.

however, the senior branch of the Malory family adopted a variant of the arms of the de Montfort earls of Leicester, from whom they held Kirkby Mallory. The earls' arms were *gules, a lion rampant a queue fourchée argent*, the Malorys' *or, a lion rampant a queue fourchée gules*.[10] Such a coat of arms must be read as a public declaration of loyalty to the earls, and could hardly have been adopted without prior permission. The Malory lion appeared in the church at Kirkby Mallory; Sir Anketil Malory III displayed it on his seal of arms; his widow Alice impaled it with her own arms in the church at Castle Bytham in Lincolnshire; and their son Sir William Malory of Papworth St Agnes used it on his seal.[11] The Malorys of Tachbrook Mallory also bore it, as did the Malorys of Hutton and Studley.[12] The lion is sometimes found with minor variants – a collar of a different tincture, for instance – but the Malorys of Welton sought greater variation: in 1230/80, the head of the Welton Malorys had on his seal a lion rampant to sinister *a queue fourchée*, and later heads of the family apparently settled on a demi-lion *a queue fourchée*, though the divided tail is not always apparent.[13] This is not surprising: the less expert could mistake the division of the tail for one of the flourishes lions' tails were often given to fill the heraldic shield, and the more expert sometimes disapproved of charges not found in nature.[14]

Given the troubles between Simon de Montfort and the king, Sir Anketil Malory I of Mowthorpe had reason to adopt a coat of arms that would not remind the king whom he served of the great earl, but the Mowthorpe coat of arms is unknown. The remaining two branches of the Malory family did in fact adopt coats of arms entirely different from the other branches and from one another. Why they chose the coats of arms they did is unknown. The Malorys of Draughton and Newbold might have done so partly to

10 *Complete Peerage*; Sir Bernard Burke, *The General Armory of England, Scotland, Ireland, and Wales* (London 1880); and James Doyle, *The Official Baronage of England* (London 1886) *s.vv.*; Charles Bémont, *Simon de Montfort* (Oxford 1930) Appendix C and Plates II–III; J.W. Papworth, *An Ordinary of British Armorials* (London 1874) i 77. *A queue fourchée*, 'with a divided tail'.

11 Nichols, *Leicestershire*, iv 771; Northampton C.R.O. Stopford Sackville, 175; P.R.O. E326/8817; *Gentleman's Magazine Library*, ed. G.L. Gomme, vii 84; Lincolnshire C.R.O. H.D. 92/77.

12 Nichols, iii 499–500, 234; Stratford-upon-Avon, Shakespeare's Birthplace Trust, MS. DR 37/2933; E. Reid-Smith, 'Provisional List of Warwickshire Coats of Arms', Birmingham Reference Library, typescript (1958) no. 443; T.D. Whitaker, *The History and Antiquities of Craven*, ed. A.W. Morant (Leeds 1878) p. 537; Thomas Tonge, *Heraldic Visitation of the Northern Counties*, Surtees Soc. Pubs 41 (1863) 51–2.

13 *Ancient Deeds*, iv 190, v 58, 448; E41/107; R.H. Ellis, *Catalogue of Seals in the P.R.O.*, Personal Seals I (1973) item P509; and cf. the arms of William Malory from the St George's Roll (c.1285) in Joseph Foster, *Some Feudal Coats of Arms* (Oxford 1902) p. 161.

14 E.g., apropos of this very device, John of Guildford, 'A Book of Arms' (c.1394), Bodl. MS. Lat. misc. e. 86, fol. 30r–v.

distance themselves from Simon de Montfort, whose defeat and disgrace were recent enough when their branch began to make it prudent for them to avoid any suggestion of involvement with his cause.

The Litchborough Malorys apparently bore *argent a cross lozengy sable and or*.[15] The arms of the Malorys of Draughton, Winwick, and Newbold are a more complicated matter. Their first known seal is that of Sir Roger Malory of Draughton in 1293 and is non-heraldic, as are those of Roger's brother Sir Peter and son Simon;[16] but Simon's son Sir Stephen had a heraldic seal bearing *a fess nebuly between three boars' heads couped, in the field the letters S.M.E.*, and Sir Stephen's son Sir John one bearing *a [simple] fess between three boars' heads couped*.[17] The five permutations on this in Monks Kirby church in Dugdale's time establish that the tinctures would have been *azure* for the field and *or* for the device, and also suggest a flourishing family with a keen interest in heraldry.[18] There was a sixth variant in the windows of the church at Swinford in Leicestershire.[19] It may be worth noting that *argent a fess between three boars' heads erased proper* has been attributed to the Mowbray family, although it was not their principal coat of arms,[20] but it would be improper to suggest a causal relationship when no feudal connection is known between the two families in the right period.

In 1366, John Malory of Winwick, not yet knighted, attempted to persuade seven of his neighbours to add their seals to his on one of his deeds 'because his seal was unknown to many'.[21] In the fulness of time, however, he inherited a better-known coat of arms for his seal. Coats of arms had by this time been recognised as real property,[22] and when his maternal grandfather's Revell inheritance was divided up in 1382/3,[23] he – his mother presumably having been her father's eldest daughter – acquired both the manor of Newbold Revel and the Revell coat of arms.

The Malorys now of Newbold Revel had the right to use the Revell arms if they chose, either alone or quartered with their previous coat of arms. They seem, however, not to have been interested in quarterings. There is some evidence, which we will return to, that Sir John wanted to replace the

---

15 Baker, *Northants.*, i 406–7, and cf. Robert Glover, 'An Ordinary of Arms', B.L. MS. Harl. 1392, p. 353.

16 B.L. Add. Ch. 21728; Detached Seals 123 and 149; Add. Ch. 21753.

17 B.L. Add. Ch. 21771, 22549, 21779. His seal as sheriff of Northamptonshire bore his monogram: Add. Ch. 6047.

18 Dugdale, *Warwickshire*, p. 79.

19 Nichols, Plate LIV, facing iv 365.

20 Papworth, *Ordinary*, *s.v.*

21 B.L. Add. Ch. 21779. Slots are cut for the other seals, but there is no sign they were ever affixed.

22 Wagner, p. 20.

23 Dugdale, p. 82 (where the names of both John's parents are wrong).

boars' heads with the coat of arms of his great-great-uncle Sir Peter, to which he also had a hereditary right; but the next solid evidence shows that the family had abandoned all other coats of arms for one or more versions of the Revell arms. In September 1422, John Malory made grants in Draughton and Monks Kirby, in each case using a seal bearing the Revell device.[24] In December 1433, he made a grant in Cosford using a new seal, with the Revell device modified by having the chevron between three trefoils.[25] The apparent change in his coat of arms (seals are normally the surest evidence of early arms)[26] is surprising, but it is also important to notice that each seal included only a single coat of arms.

Dugdale records that in the seventh year of King Henry V, the Duke of Gloucester as *custos Angliae* sent writs to the sheriffs commanding them to choose in each county

> a certain number . . . of Kts and Esquires, bearing arms from their ancestours, such as were most able and sufficient to serve the K. for defence of the Realm; all which were to attend the K. Councell at Westm. the Tuesday in the first week of Lent. For which purpose 13 being chosen in this County, this John Malory was one.[27]

That amounted to public recognition of both his qualifications, his bearing what his son was to call 'olde armys', as well as of his being 'able and sufficient' in the defence of the realm. In some periods, coats of arms have been prized largely for the number of their quarterings, but the Malorys of Newbold Revel did not apparently share that view. By the standards of their time, they had the right to quarter at least the Malory boars' heads and Sir Peter Malory's arms with the Revell chevron, but John chose not to do so. Nor did his brother Simon and his brother or cousin Prior Robert: despite what a later period might expect in the way of signs of cadency, the arms Simon displayed in Chilverscoton church and Prior Robert put on his seal under a chief of the arms of his order were exactly the arms of Revell as John had used them in 1422. There is no evidence that John's son Sir Thomas, or Sir Thomas's son Robert, felt any differently about this.

The Malorys do, however, seem to have varied the Revell arms in one respect. According to Sir Anthony Wagner, those arms are recorded in several fourteenth-century rolls of arms as *or a chevron gules, a border*

---

24 B.L. Add. Ch. 28647; Martin, p. 173. The Monks Kirby deed belonged to a Bristol solicitor, Thomas Webb Williams (fl.1891–1923), who lent it to Martin, who produced it before the Society of Antiquaries. I have not been able to trace it.

25 P.R.O. WARD/2/1/3/2. Glover's Ordinary (p. 388) includes for Malouree *ermine a chevron gules, a bordure engrailed sable, on the chevron a trefoil argent.* Hicks (p. 9) notices that Papworth's *Ordinary* includes for Malory *ermine a chevron gules between three trefoils slipped argent, a bordure engrailed sable.*

26 Wagner, p. 23.

27 Dugdale, p. 83.

engrailed sable.[28] The arms in Chilverscoton church give the field as *ermine*, not *or*. This is no sign of cadency, since the same tinctures were found in the churches at Monks Kirby and Swinford, in the Newbold Revel parlour window commissioned by John's great-grandson Nicholas, and as an element in the arms of Nicholas's descendants, the Andrewes family of Charwelton, Northamptonshire, in 1564.[29] Dugdale always identified this coat of arms as 'Revell', but even without the change of tincture, after the Revell line died out it might have been better called of 'Malory of Newbold Revel'. With the change of tincture, the change of name is surely unavoidable.

Three generations after John and Simon Malory, there was another significant change. Nicholas, as we have seen, had the coats of arms of his and his wife's families displayed in a parlour window at Newbold Revel.[30] The window was designed to make a statement about Nicholas's place in the world. Most of the coats of arms must be merely claims to kinship: given the number of living members of the Kingston, Pulteney, and Walsh families, they cannot have been intended to be taken as his own arms. Two, however, were his: one inherited from Revell, the other from Sir Peter Malory the judge, who had died some eight generations earlier. The intervening generations had handed on the knowledge of Sir Peter's coat of arms, and Sir John Malory is said to have used it on his seal in 1377,[31] but however strong the family's rights to that coat of arms, there no evidence that they ever wanted to quarter it with another. Nicholas, however, did. Although the two coats of arms appear separately in the Newbold Revel window, in another near-contemporary source, they appear, quartered precisely as Sir Anthony Wagner gives them, as the arms of 'Mal lere'. The source is Peter le Neve's Book, a painted book of arms made about 1490 and later.[32] The date establishes that the arms are Nicholas Malory's, even if (as we have no reason to assume) they were supplied later by one of his daughters.

It is worth noticing that the Malory arms as le Neve gives them put the chevron in the first and fourth quarters and the lions passant in the second and third. This suggests that Nicholas was quartering two Malory coats of arms, the chevron as principal and the lions as secondary. Had he been heraldically commemorating the union of the Malory and Revell families,

---

28 Wagner, p. 63.
29 Dugdale, pp. 79, 83, Nichols Plate LIV, facing p. 365, *The Visitations of Northamptonshire 1564 and 1618–19*, ed. W.C. Metcalfe (London 1887) p. 1.
30 See p. 136 and note supra.
31 Nichols, iv 368, without further reference. Nichols also says *or 3 lions passant guardant sable* was displayed in the church windows at Swinford, which was of course a Malory manor, and at Ratby, four miles north of Leicester: iv Plate LIV (facing p. 365); iv 377.
32 Wagner, p. 64, and cf. p. 30n. Le Neve's Book, now B.L. MS. Harl. 6163, was edited by Joseph Foster in *Two Tudor Books of Arms* (London 1904).

he would surely have put the lions, as the husband's arms, first and fourth, and the chevron, as the wife's, second and third. This again suggests that the chevron should here be called the arms not of Revell but of Malory of Newbold Revel.

There is, however, some uncertainty about what the Malorys thought to be Sir Peter's coat of arms. The Parliamentary Roll of Arms, an authoritative source contemporary with Sir Peter, gave him *or a iii lupars passaunz de sable*.[33] That of course is the royal arms of England with the tinctures changed, and the 'leopards passant' are what would now be called 'lions passant guardant in pale'. Sir Peter was proclaiming his loyalty to the king he served (no doubt with permission) just as his kinsmen had proclaimed theirs to the earls of Leicester. Over time, as increasing numbers of coats of arms came to be needed, it became necessary to differentiate similar devices, and the original leopard or lion passant, which looked directly at the viewer, came to be called a lion passant guardant, distinguished from the lion passant, which looked to its own front, and even from the lion passant *regardant*, which looked back towards its tail. There was a period in which different people understood *leopard* and related terms in different senses,[34] and this apparently had its effect on what was thought to be Sir Peter Malory's arms. The versions in the Newbold Revel parlour window and Peter le Neve's Book give lions passant in the strict sense; but versions in Monks Kirby church, one on its own, the other quartered with Malory of Newbold Revel, both give lions passant guardant.[35]

That presents us with a problem. We can hardly doubt that Sir Thomas Malory bore what he believed to be an ancient coat of arms and was proud of it, but we do not know what it was. He might have borne the Malory of Newbold Revel arms that his father bore, in cheerful awareness that his doing so was making them more ancient still. (If he did, we may at least guess that he did so without trefoils, which never appear later.) It would then have been Nicholas, who clearly had an interest in heraldry, or his father Robert, of whose interests we know nothing, who saw the possibilities of Sir Peter's arms and quartered them with those he inherited. On the other hand, it might have been Sir Thomas who decided to revive Sir Peter's arms; but if so, we do not know his version of them, and specifically what form the lion took. Artist's error and other unknowns loom too large for any confident explanation of the differences between the various versions of Sir Peter's arms, but one particularly economical possibility is that Sir Thomas and Nicholas used the same blazoned version of Sir

---

[33] *Parliamentary Writs and Writs of Military Summons*, ed. F. Palsgrave, 2 vols (London 1827–34) i 417.

[34] See G.J. Brault, *Early Blazon* (Oxford 1972) glossary, *s.v. liepart*.

[35] Dugdale, p. 79.

Peter's arms, Sir Thomas understood *passant* in the sense originally intended, but Nicholas, understanding it in a more modern sense, 'corrected' his grandfather's version. If so, the quartered coat of arms in le Neve's book would be Nicholas's, but Sir Thomas's would be the one in Monks Kirby church: *quarterly 1 and 4 (Malory of Newbold Revell), ermine a chevron gules and a border engrailed sable; 2 and 3 (Sir Peter Malory) or three lions passant guardant sable.*

XI

Conclusion

This study has attempted to identify the author of the *Morte Darthur*, outline his life, and gain such scattered insights into his personality as the evidence allows. The outline of his life shows, for instance, that John Bale was for once right when he guessed that Malory mixed writing and politics: *inter multiplices reipublicae curas, non intermisit literarum studia.*[1] Much, however, remains obscure. Our state of knowledge of Malory's coat of arms is one example: his coat of arms represented him to his peers, and was plainly important to him as such, yet we cannot say exactly what it was. And beyond the uncertain areas of Malory's life are others, including much of his public life, of which we know nothing at all. Some will be of more interest to most readers nowadays than Malory's coat of arms, but they are likely to remain a blank, sometimes because they were unimportant to Malory and his contemporaries, sometimes because their nature made them more private.

Somewhere near the boundary between the little known and the entirely unknown come Malory's motives. The most sensational part of his life is alleged the eighteen-month criminal spree, beginning with an attempt to murder the Duke of Buckingham, that he was said to have undertaken in 1450–51. We may hope to form some estimate of the truth of the accusations, and might even endorse, at least for this period, Dr Carpenter's phrase about a 'reckless career',[2] a phrase that is at least in part a judgement on motive. Any fuller judgement, however, is extraordinarily difficult. In contrast, a biographer in a more modern period would hope, having settled whether his subject was (as is not quite proved in Malory's case) the only son and the youngest child, to establish whether he was spoilt by his parents, by his elder sisters, and by the servants, whether he suffered from Great Expectations, whether he was unable (as we say) to 'adjust' to the loss one after another of three promising ways to respect and influence, and whether he turned to violence because he could not adjust,

---

[1] John Bale, *Illustrium Maioris Britanniae scriptorum summarium* (Ipswich 1548) fol. 208ᵛ.
[2] Carpenter, *Locality*, p. 612.

or out of an obstinate determination to surpass his father in local and national politics, or from some other motive altogether.

Again, almost ten years in Lancastrian prisons is likely to have had long-term effects on Malory and his family, both financially and psychologically. That imprisonment is the best-recorded part of his life, but although there is some evidence in the court records of short-term financial embarrassment, and one apparent echo in the *Morte Darthur* of an illness in prison, there is no solid evidence of long-term effects at all.

When it is so difficult to make out Malory's feelings in such relatively public matters as crime and punishment, it is depressing but hardly surprising that we should know next to nothing of his feelings about his family. He seems to have got on well with his brother-in-law Eustace Burneby, but it is hard to say anything about what he felt for his parents, his sisters, or his wife. He and his wife stayed together despite his tribulations, and she seems to have managed the estate while he was in prison, and to have held the family lands when he died: might we venture a guess that he trusted, even respected, her? Despite the death of one of his sons during the relatively well-recorded prison years, however, there is no evidence at all of his feelings – or hers for that matter – for their children.

There is one source, however, that can tell us a great deal about Malory's feelings, tastes, thoughts, and habits of mind. It is difficult to write a long book – even a long bad book – without revealing a great deal about oneself. (Malory may have written a short book as well, but we can leave *The Wedding of Sir Gawain and Dame Ragnell* out of account: it seems unlikely to tell us anything about him that we could not learn from *Le Morte Darthur*.) When we read the *Morte Darthur*, we see and feel and think with Malory, and because it is a great book, it may tell us more about his mind than we could know about the mind of any other English subject of the fifteenth century.

Unfortunately however, that 'more' is still far less than we might wish. There must be real doubts about how profoundly anyone can understand the mind of someone who is not alive to interact with the understander, and especially someone from a distant time, when thoughts and feelings were to some extent – the would-be understander must make his own estimate – systematically different from those today. Added to that, there is, as with the courtier Geoffrey Chaucer, the civil servant Edmund Spenser, and the London businessman William Shakespeare, a gap between life and writings. In Malory's case, anything the book tells us will only reveal Malory as he was at the end of the 1460s, when he may not have been quite the same person as (for instance) the man who aroused Buckingham's ire at the beginning of the 1450s. More important, however, the events of the *Morte Darthur* are neither close reflections of Malory's life nor wholly the product of the free play of imagination. He often writes as if he were obliged to retell the story in his sources and his only freedom lay in proportioning his narrative. Although his sense of constraint and the fact that he actually changes more than he admits are both of course elements in his character, any kind of constraint must make it more difficult to estimate his cast of mind from his writings.

Furthermore, although the *Morte Darthur* gives us a clear impression of an individual mind telling us the story (I have attempted a formal assessment of that impression elsewhere),[3] the emotions and perhaps even the opinions revealed in the story will have been influenced by the imaginative process. Even if the story provides a parallel to some event in Malory's life, it would be unsafe without corroborative evidence to assume that the author felt identical emotions and held identical opinions when he faced people rather than paper. Imaginative discrepancies may be particularly likely to be generated when an author immerses himself in a fictitious and emotionally powerful story set centuries before his own time.

These uncertainties suggest that any attempted full assessment of Malory's personality from his writings that took due account of the evidence of the historical records would require another book as long as this present one, and might still be doomed to failure. I would like instead to put forward an unsystematic group of three features of Malory's writing that may have implications for his life.

In the first place, Malory's style suggests his mind was strikingly unacademic.[4] The other great masters of late-mediaeval English literature, Chaucer, Langland, and the anonymous author of *Sir Gawain and the Green Knight*, are in various degrees aware of fashionable texts and relish fashionable intellectual issues, like reconciling freewill with divine foreknowledge, or the salvation of the virtuous pagan. In contrast, Malory's reading seems not to have extended much beyond Arthurian literature, and he relishes consensual opinions, both proverbs and generalizations resembling proverbs, such as 'oftetymes thorow envy grete hardynesse is shewed that hath bene the deth of many kyd knyghtes.'[5] Again in contrast with those authors, neither his words nor his thought offers much in the way of show or virtuosity of expression. He prefers straightforward expressive structures, and on the rare occasions when he embarks on elaborate ones he often seems to have trouble with them.[6] Given the background the historical records suggest, it would be surprising if he had had an academic training, but his style suggests neither training nor natural talent for the *avant-garde* academic issues or literary techniques of his day. Nor is

---

3   See P.J.C. Field, *Romance and Chronicle* (London 1971) pp. 142–59.
4   For his style, see *Romance and Chronicle* and Mark Lambert *Style and Vision in Malory's 'Le Morte Darthur'* (New Haven 1975).
5   *Works*, p. 223.9–11. *kyd* = 'famous'.
6   E.g. his stumbling exposition of love and summer: *Works*, pp. 1119–20.

anything about the way his mind works visibly analytic or introspective. This apparent cast of mind, with its occasional incoherences of expression and the underlying incoherences of thought they suggest, may have made it more difficult for Malory to avoid trouble in life as well as literature – and considering that his likely expositors in our own time are academics, it may still count among his misfortunes.

A second more restricted feature of Malory's mental landscape may also have contributed to his problems. Throughout the *Morte Darthur* he makes large claims for the dignity of knighthood: he regularly refers to it as 'The High Order of Knighthood'.[7] That phrasing must surely reflect his real feelings. A knight who felt so strongly about the importance of his rank would be particularly likely both to make large claims for himself and to feel a sense of responsibility towards others that he might often find difficult to make good.

A third notable feature is the historical allusiveness of the *Morte Darthur*. To the possible allusions reviewed during the course of this book, we may add that when the *Morte Darthur* as a whole is compared with its sources, it shows a greatly increased emphasis on the way in which the division of noble houses could ruin a kingdom.[8] Although this possibility was a political reality throughout the Middle Ages and after, and in consequence was a commonplace in the literature of the time – both Geoffrey of Monmouth and Shakespeare, for instance, see it as one of the implications of the King Lear story – it is hard to believe that Malory, writing in the midst of a civil war that had done immense damage to his country and put him in prison, was treating it as a mere literary commonplace. This may be the one point at which considering Malory's life and writings together may make it possible to guess his motives for an otherwise inexplicable act. It must be stressed that this is a complex inference, and if any one of its several parts, literary or historical, is unsound, the whole is invalid, but that if they are all sound it remains only a possibility suggested by possibilities. Nevertheless, if in the 1460s Malory deplored the way in which his country had been riven by faction, if he blamed the division on great lords of his time, but above all on the Duke of York, whose cause he had to some degree supported, and if he saw Henry VI as a good king destroyed by his subjects' fickleness, then what drove him to desert York for Lancaster, the winning side for the losing one, may have been a bad conscience.

Even as a possibility, this may not be a fashionable view. There is, however, this much to be said for it, that it fits in with the conclusion drawn by

7 For instances, see Tomomi Kato, *A Concordance to the Works of Sir Thomas Malory* (Tokyo 1974) *s.v.*
8 Cf. Charles Moorman, 'Lot and Pellinore: The Failure of Loyalty in Malory's "Morte Darthur" ', *M.S.* 25 (1963) 83–92.

Malory's most sympathetic modern critic when he considered the paradox presented by the contrast between Malory's life and his book:

> I find in it, sometimes implicit, sometimes explicit, an unforced reverence not only for courage (that of course) but for mercy, humility, graciousness, and good faith. . . . I cannot conceive that even the best of [earlier heroes] could ever have been made to understand why Sir Lancelot wept like a beaten child after he had healed Sir Urry. . . . In such passages, and indeed almost everywhere, we meet something which I chiefly hesitate to call 'morality' because it is so little like a code of rules. It is rather a civilization of the heart (by no means of the head), a fineness and sensitivity, a voluntary rejection of all the uglier and more vulgar impulses. . . . It makes the *Morte* a 'noble' as well as a 'joyous' book.[9]

Sir Launcelot of course wept because he had a bad conscience. That, however, brings us back to the gap between the book and the life: that Malory should have understood this (which he did not find in his French source) cannot prove that he himself felt it in any given situation.

That in turn is a reminder that what we are certainly left with is not what Malory himself or any member of his family did or felt, however sensational, but what he wrote. Since in his book his attention was so firmly on King Arthur and Sir Launcelot, rather than on King Henry or King Edward or Sir Thomas Malory, that is very likely what he wanted.

---

[9] C.S. Lewis, 'The English Prose *Morte*' in *Essays on Malory*, ed. J.A.W. Bennett (Oxford 1963) pp. 7–28, at p. 9.

APPENDIX I

The Malory Family in the Middle Ages

This appendix gives a summary account of the various heads of the eight principal branches of the Malory family in the Middle Ages to provide some sort of bearings for the identification of other Malorys. It is inevitably for the heads of the various branches that the best evidence survives, and often through them that the status of their branches can be assessed and the junior members of the family identified, insofar as those things can be done at all.

Kirkby Mallory and Papworth

Any account must begin in the twelfth century with Aschetil Malory, his son Robert, and Robert's sons Richard and Anschetil, noticed in Chapter III. The elder son, Richard, gave land in Swinford, Leicestershire, to the nuns of Nuneaton c.1155, but had other unspecified lands in the administratively joint counties of Warwick and Leicester in 1187–92.[1] There is no reason to doubt that those lands included Kirkby Mallory in Leicestershire, which his descendants were to hold for nearly two centuries, and which later records suggest was the senior Malory estate.[2] In 1246, for instance, another Richard Malory is recorded as lord of Kirkby Mallory and Walton-on-the-Wold in Leicestershire and Tachbrook Mallory and Botley in Warwickshire,[3] although all but Kirkby had for generations been held by the descendents of Anschetil brother of the elder Richard. In 1246 Kirkby was apparently held by a Richard Malory and Tachbrook certainly by a John Malory: the former then must be the feudal superior of the latter.[4] The later Richard also held lands in Welton in Northamptonshire, where

---

1 *Calendar of Documents preserved in France*, ed. J.H. Round (1899) i 376–7; *Pipe Roll for 1187–8*, p. 119, ibid. *1191–2*, p. 131.
2 For the most authoritative collection of information about the Malorys of Kirkby Mallory see Farnham, *Notes*, iii 147–60, but see also Nichols, *Leicestershire*, iv 761–6.
3 Nichols, iii 501.
4 Nichols, locc. citt.

another branch of the family lived who are later recorded as owing homage to Kirkby Mallory.[5]

A Welton deed witnessed by the first Richard Malory and an Anchetill Malory, presumably his brother, names Richard's heir as his son William, and a William Malory took over Richard's debts at the exchequer in 1193 and paid them off in 1204; he is recorded as a knight in 1216.[6] This William Malory 'of Kirkby' was succeeded by his son Richard also 'of Kirkby', who lived c.1210 and was succeeded by his son Thomas, who was eventually succeeded by his son Henry Malory also 'of Kirkby': a set of grants to Holy Trinity Hospital, Northampton, makes the descent explicit.[7] Richard held half a knight's fee in Leicestershire, apparently in Swinford and Bredon, of the Honour of Leicester in 1210/12; he died in Mountsorrel Castle during the Barons' Wars of 1215–17, and his widow was suing for dower in 1221.[8] Richard's son and heir Thomas became a ward of Henry de Segrave, no doubt through the offices of his brother Stephen de Segrave, a prominent judge later justiciar of England, who had been granted the administration of the Honour of Leicester in 1218.[9] Thomas married Christina de Segrave and was still alive in 1240: she survived him.[10]

This Thomas Malory seems to have been succeeded first by his son Richard, who, as has been said, apparently held the family estates in 1246.[11] Richard will have died childless, since he was succeeded by Henry, who witnessed a deed for Simon de Montfort about 1254, and with Matilda his wife went to law over land in Burton Overy in Leicestershire in 1261.[12] Henry was succeeded in turn by his son Thomas, who in 1275 quitclaimed some of the lands of Christina his grandmother.[13] He held Kirkby Mallory of the Earl of Leicester in 1284, 1296, and 1316, was knighted with the Prince of Wales in 1306, served in the Scottish campaign of 1311–12, and is last recorded in a lawsuit in 1317.[14] He was succeeded by his son Ralph,

---

5 Nichols, iv 762; cf. also Baker, *Northants.*, p. 458.
6 *Ancient Deeds*, iv 117–18; *Pipe Roll for 1193*, p. 105; *The Great Roll of the Pipe 1204*, p. 221; Nichols, iv 761.
7 *Ancient Deeds*, ii 461, 475, 468, 470.
8 *The Red Book of the Exchequer*, ed. Hubert Hall, 3 vols (R.S. 1896) ii 553; Nichols, iv 361; *Rolls of the Justices in Eyre 1221 and 1222*, ed. Doris Stenton, Selden Soc. Pubs 59 (1940) 573, 608, 650.
9 *Rolls of the Justices*, p. 608; F. West, *The Justiciarship in England* (London 1968) p. 264 and passim.
10 George Farnham, *Medieval Leicestershire Pedigrees* (Leicester 1925) p. 25; *Ancient Deeds*, ii 468.
11 Nichols, iii 501.
12 *Records of the Borough of Leicester*, ed. Mary Bateson, 3 vols (London 1899–1905) i 47–9; Farnham, *Notes*, i 271.
13 Henry of Pytchley, *Book of Fees*, ed. W.T. Mellows, Northants. Rec. Soc. 2 (1927) pp. xv, 46–7, 49 and n.
14 *Feudal Aids*, iii 97; Nichols, iv 761; *Feudal Aids*, v 183; William Shaw, *The Knights of*

who in 1320 was both lord of Kirkby Mallory and M.P. for Leicestershire.[15] He was suffering from paralysis in 1326, but still held Kirkby Mallory in 1330, and was still alive in 1337.[16] His will called him a knight.[17]

The next three heads of this branch of the family were all called Anketil Malory. Their careers overlap, but fortunately they can be distinguished by rank. It is natural to assume they were father, son, and grandson, but there is no known record of their relationship to each other or to Sir Ralph. Sir Anketil I held Kirkby Mallory in 1345 and 1361.[18] These are almost the only records of him, but his successor Anketil II made much more of a mark, partly by extensive land dealing and connections with the court, but first by marrying a la Zouch of Harringworth whose brother became Archbishop of York.[19] In 1345, the archbishop granted Anketil the manor of Sudborough in Northamptonshire, and by 1349 he was the archbishop's chief executor.[20] He granted Sudborough to his daughter Ala and her husband Thomas Greene of Isham in 1360, and sold Kirkby Mallory to the Abbot of Leicester in 1361, the appurtenances of the manor including the homage and service of Sir John Malory of Welton for Welton.[21] Sir Anketil was pensioned as an esquire of the Black Prince in 1368, and was king's knight to Richard II in 1378.[22] Since Ala's husband was the elder brother, and her sister Katherine's husband Ralph the son and heir of King Richard's favourite Sir Henry Greene,[23] Sir Anketil II must have been near to the centre of things at court. He is on many Lincolnshire (especially Kesteven) commissions from 1380, was sheriff of Lincolnshire in 1382 and 1388, and in 1389 exchanged his pension for the Keepership of Somerton Castle, the manor of Somerton and other lands in Lincolnshire; he also became a feoffee for William Malory of Tachbrook and Walton.[24] He was dead by December 1390.[25]

Sir Anketil III also began his career with an ambitious (and in his case

England, 2 vols (London 1906) i 117; Calendar of Documents relating to Scotland, ed. J. Bain, 4 vols (Edinburgh 1881–8) iii 428; Farnham, Pedigrees, p. 18.

15 Farnham, Notes, iii 154–5; Parliamentary Writs, II(3) 1136.

16 C.C.R. (1323–7) p. 445; Feudal Aids, vi 559; Nichols, iv 761.

17 Farnham, Notes, iii 155.

18 Farnham, Pedigrees, p. 24.

19 Northants. C.R.O., MSS. SS 2366–7, 1656, 2354; and cf. J.G. Hunt, 'The Origin of Two Bishops', Genealogists' Magazine 13 (1959–61) 172.

20 Northants. C.R.O. ut cit.; Testamenta Eboracensia I, ed. James Raine, Surtees Soc. Pubs 4 (1836) 55–6.

21 V.C.H., Northants., iii 245–7; A. Hamilton Thompson, The Abbey of St Mary of the Meadows, Leicester (Leicester 1949) p. 155; Nichols, iv 762 col. 1.

22 C.P.R. (1377–81) 172.

23 V.C.H., Northants., loc. cit.

24 List of Sheriffs, P.R.O. Lists and Indexes 9, s.v. Lincs.; C.P.R. (1385–89) p. 191; Nichols, iii 497–8.

25 C.F.R. (1383–91) p. 346.

illicit) marriage, to Alice Basset, Lady of Castle Bytham, daughter of Sir John Dryby and Anne Gaveston, widow of Ralph Lord Basset of Sapcote and previously of Sir Robert Tocket.[26] When he was pardoned for this, his mainpernors included Sir Henry Greene.[27] He often called 'Anthony' Malory. He too was extensively employed in Lincolnshire from 1380, where he was a J.P. and succeeded Sir Anketil II as Keeper of Somerton Castle; but he also picked up the manor of Shelton in Bedfordshire in 1387.[28] He was knighted, but perhaps very shortly before he died: all references to him as a knight seem to be posthumous.[29] When he died in March 1393, his heir was his son Thomas, aged twelve; but when Alice died in October 1412 Thomas was dead: her heir was Thomas's daughter Elizabeth aged eleven.[30]

Thomas's brief career as the head of this branch of the family and the only known fifteenth-century Sir Thomas Malory apart from Sir Thomas of Newbold Revel is described in Chapter IV. The direct line of the Malorys of Kirkby was continued by his younger brother William. William was born in 1386, and in 1391 Sir Anketil III prudently obtained a licence to acquire for his four-year-old younger son from his kinsman Sir William Papworth the reversion of the manor of Papworth St Agnes on the Huntingdonshire-Cambridgeshire border.[31] Sir William Papworth also acquired Sir Anketil's manor of Shelton in 1398, perhaps as part of some family arrangement, since, like Papworth, Shelton came to William Malory in the end: indeed, the first adult record of him, an accusation of violence at Shelton by Sir William Malory in 1411, suggests he may have been effectively in possession soon after he came of age.[32] Sir William inherited half his mother's

---

26 *Complete Peerage*, s.v. Basset of Sapcote; *C.C.R.* (1377–81) p. 159; *C.F.R.* (1405–13) pp. 454–6; *Register of Bishop Philip Repingdon 1405–19*, ed. Margaret Archer, Lincoln Rec. Soc. 57–8 (1963) ii 275–7 [Alice's will]; Farnham, *Notes*, i 6, v 76, 78. Tocket is sometimes given as Alice's second husband, apparently because Ralph Basset is named before him in Alice's will. The name order, however, will be a matter of etiquette: if Alice had remarried in the seven months between her swearing as Ralph's widow on 27 Sept. 1378 not to do so without the king's licence and being pardoned on 28 May 1379 for marrying Anketil without that licence, there would be some trace of it in the official record.

27 *C.F.R.* (1377–83) 135.

28 *C.P.R.* (1377–81) p. 514, (1391–96) p. 380, and passim; *V.C.H., Beds.*, iii 162.

29 E.g. Alice's will, and *C.P.R.* (1405–8) p. 452.

30 P.R.O. C136/75/19, C137/90/15. Elizabeth married a Yorkshireman, Robert Ever, by whom she had a son who died childless and three daughters: Farnham, *Notes*, v 78, *Heraldic Visitations of the North, Part III*, Surtees Soc. Pubs 144 (1930) 611.

31 P.R.O. C138/19/24; *C.P.R.* (1388–92) p. 503. The licence allowed reversions successively from Anketil and Alice to William, Thomas, and Sir William Papworth's 'right heir', and Sir William Papworth's 'right heir' was Elizabeth daughter of Thomas Malory knight: P.R.O. C138/12/28. That proves kinship, but the degree of it is uncertain.

32 *V.C.H., Beds.*, iii 162 (where the editor wrongly emends his source's 'Sir William Papworth' to 'Sir William Malory of Papworth'); *C.P.R.* (1408–13) p. 319.

estate in 1412, and Papworth in 1416, but imitated his ancestors by dealing in land too, acquiring the manor of North Stoke and half the manor of Careby in Lincolnshire in 1413, and holding properties in Shropshire in 1428; in 1429 he took part in a parliamentary election for Huntingdonshire, though disqualified by being a resident of Cambridgeshire.[33] He imitated them too in serving the king, which took him abroad in 1418 and 1430.[34] He sold his Lincolnshire manors by 1443; and died in June 1445 holding Papworth, Shelton, and part of Sudborough, the last seized from his Greene cousins, who promptly reoccupied it.[35]

Sir William's heir was his only known child, Thomas Malory of Papworth. As one of the candidates for the authorship of the *Morte Darthur*, Thomas's career has been described in Chapter I.

Thomas's death in late September or early October 1469 produced inquisitions in Cambridgeshire and Northamptonshire. Both, like his will, give his heir as his son John, but whereas the former says that John was seventeen, the latter says that he was only ten – an unlikely age for the eldest of ten children.[36] John's wardship and marriage were granted out in the usual way; but he died childless in July 1471, leaving his brother Robert, aged fifteen, as his heir.[37] Robert lived to take possession of the family estates but also died childless, in January 1492, when his heir was his brother Anthony (named fourth in Thomas's will) aged twenty-four.[38] Anthony in due course became a J.P. for Cambridgeshire and four times sheriff of that county; his will was proved in October 1539.[39] Richard Malory, who is said to have been his son, became a member of the Mercers' Company of London (as Thomas had intended for his third-named son William) and later Lord Mayor of London.[40]

---

33 Alice's will ut supra; P.R.O. C138/12/28, C138/19/24; Lincs. C.R.O. H101/28–9; *Feudal Aids*, iv 248, 252; J.S. Roskell, *The Commons in the Parliament of 1422* (Manchester 1954) pp. 18–19. Restrictions in MS H71/19 show that some or all of these lands were part of the Basset estate.

34 *Catalogue des rolles gascons*, ii 236, 269.

35 Lincs. C.R.O. H71/17–19, 71/15a, 92/75, 92/77; P.R.O. C139/117/10, 139/125/4, 139/144/41.

36 P.R.O. C140/31/16. Cambs. gives his birth as 13 Nov. 1451/11 Nov. 1452, Northants. as 13 Jan. 1462.

37 *C.F.R.* (1461–71) pp. 258, 261; P.R.O. C140/36/11. Robert's proof of age gives his birth as 4 Nov. 1457, a discrepancy of three weeks from John's I.P.M.: P.R.O. C140/68/57.

38 *C.C.R.* (1476–85) p. 103; *Cal. I.P.M., Hen. VII*, i 289, 307.

39 Martin, p. 171; P.R.O. List of Sheriffs; P.R.O. Prob 11/27/254. Sheila Mallory Smith infers that William, named third in Thomas's will, was his third son and therefore that he must have died before Robert (*History of the Malory Family*, pp. 65, 147), but Anthony willed his estate in succession to Alice his wife, Henry his son, William Malory, and Audrey Anthony's daughter, and Alice made a William Malory supervisor of her will (Prob 11/31/159ᵛ), so perhaps Thomas's will, which names Robert before John, did not give his other sons in order of age either.

40 Thomas Fuller, *Worthies of England*, ed. J. Nichols (London 1811) p. 167.

Tachbrook Mallory and Walton-on-the-Wold

The first major major branch of the Malory family to diverge from that of Kirkby Mallory is that of Walton-on-the-Wold in Leicestershire and Tachbrook Mallory in Warwickshire. The lands at Walton appear always to have been the more important – indeed the Tachbrook property was legally part of that at Walton[41] – but because Walton is confusable with Welton I will use Tachbrook as a short title for this branch.

The first known Tachbrook Malory is Anschetil, son of Robert Malory and seneschal to Robert third earl of Leicester.[42] As constable of Leicester Castle, Anschetil was Earl Robert's principal supporter in the midlands in his rebellion against Henry II in 1173–74, where his achievements as a thorn in the government's flesh put those of Sir Thomas of Newbold Revel in the shade. Although his lord was in France, Anschetil not only successfully defended Leicester Castle but with the King of Scotland's brother led destructive raids against the towns of Nottingham and Northampton. However, when King Henry captured Earl Robert and threatened to starve him to death, Anschetil had to surrender the castle and his own lands were sequestered.[43] They are not named, but from his sons' holdings they presumably included Walton and Tachbrook. He died in 1185 owing a large debt that the exchequer transferred to his son Robert: after a total of 31 years, with half the fine paid off, the rest was cancelled.[44] Robert's brother Henry, who held land at Walton and Tachbrook, acquired a fine of his own for supporting Earl John against King Richard in 1194 (and in some years also helped pay off Robert's).[45] In 1208, when Robert died and Henry succeeded to the rest of the family lands, John pardoned him a second and almost unbelievable fine of £1216 allegedly owed by his father and brother.[46] Henry was called a knight in a lawsuit in 1200 and was summoned to war in Poitou as a feudal tenant of the Honour of Leicester in 1214.[47]

He was dead by 1222, when an incumbent was presented to Walton church by the guardian of Gilbert his son and heir.[48] Gilbert was alive in

---

41 *Feet of Fines (Warwicks.)*, ed. Ethel Stokes et al., 3 vols, Dugdale Soc. Pubs 11, 15, 18 (1932–43), ii, no. 1171.

42 *Documents of the Danelaw*, ed. Stenton, pp. 346–7, 249–50.

43 *V.C.H., Leics.*, i 51, 82–3.

44 *Pipe Roll 1185–6*, p. 126; *1207*, p. 191, and passim.

45 *Pipe Roll 1194*, p. 14; *Feet of Fines (Warwicks.)*, i 82, 120; *1196*, p. 270; *1197*, p. 170, and passim; cf. *V.C.H., Warwicks.*, v 162.

46 Farnham, *Notes*, iii 147–50.

47 *Curia Regis Rolls*, i (Richard I – 2 John) 233n, *Pipe Roll 1215*, p. 103.

48 *Rolls of Hugh of Wells, Bishop of Lincoln 1206–35*, Canterbury and York Society Publications 1–2 (1906–7) ii 283; Farnham, *Pedigrees*, pp. 134–5; idem, *Notes*, iii 150–1.

1236, but in 1243 his widow Cecily de Segrave was suing for dower; his heir was his son John, who also succeeded as a minor, and was still a minor in 1247.[49] Like many in the midlands he followed Simon de Montfort against the king in 1265, and for that temporarily lost Walton; he was a knight when he witnessed a grant by his mother in 1281, and was still alive in 1284.[50] He was succeeded by his son John, who undertook military service for John de Segrave in 1277, and was in trouble with the law for concealing a murder in 1284 and for committing one in 1289.[51] This John was involved in legal processes about Walton and Tachbrook with Reginald his son and heir from 1291 to 1315.[52]

Reginald was a knight in 1320, was expecting to go abroad with John de Segrave in 1322, and was collector of scutage for Leicestershire in 1320 and 1325, for which he 'or his heirs' still owed money in 1327.[53] He was succeeded by his son John, who was already lord of Botley in 1323, and dealt in land in Tachbrook in 1332–4.[54] John was granted free warren of his lands in Botley, Tachbrook, and Walton in 1335, and as a king's yeoman, was licensed to found a chantry in 1336.[55] He engaged to serve against the Scots and arrayed Warwickshire men-at-arms for France in 1346.[56] In the same year he and his wife bought an estate for their son John Malory,[57] who must have succeeded his father at some time after that: we cannot now accurately divide the records between them.

A John Malory who may or may not be the younger one investigated a killing at Burton-on-the-Wolds in 1347, was taker of the king's victuals in Warwickshire in 1351, collector of subsidy in Leicestershire in 1352, 1353, and 1354, and was raising archers in that county in 1359.[58] He was a 'guardian' of Garendon Abbey in 1360, was involved in a lawsuit with his sons John and Walter (perhaps his younger sons) in 1366, was dealing in

---

[49] *Curia Regis Rolls XV* (17–21 Henry III) p. 428; Farnham, locc. citt.

[50] *Close Rolls (Supplementary) of the Reign of Henry III* (1975) p. 43; Stratford-upon-Avon, Shakespeare's Birthplace Trust MS DR37/Box 50/2909; Farnham, *Quorndon Records*, 2 vols (London 1912) i 58.

[51] *Parliamentary Writs*, I 722; Farnham, *Quorndon Records*, loc. cit; *C.P.R.* (1281–92) p. 328.

[52] *Feet of Fines (Warwicks.)*, ii no. 1171; Farnham, *Pedigrees*, p. 136.

[53] *Ancient Deeds*, iv 119, *C.P.R.* (1321–24) p. 188, *C.F.R.* (1319–27) p. 27; *Parliamentary Writs*; II 1136, *Calendar of Memoranda Rolls (Exchequer)* (London 1968) p. 243.

[54] Shakespeare's Birthplace Trust MS DR37/Box 50/2927; *Feet of Fines (Warwicks.)*, ii no. 1743.

[55] *Cal. Ch. Rolls*, iv 350; *C.P.R.* (1334–38) p. 251.

[56] *Foedera*, ed. T. Rymer, 3 vols (London 1816–69) iii 69; G. Wrottesley, *Crecy and Calais from the Public Records*, William Salt Soc. Pubs 18(ii) (1897) 66.

[57] Farnham, *Pedigrees*, p. 136.

[58] *C.P.R.* (1345–48) p. 456; *C.F.R.* (1346–56) 276, 334, 376, 415, *Foedera*, iii 416.

land in Tachbrook in 1369, and was called John Malory senior of Walton in 1375.[59]

By 1377, John had been succeeded by William Malory, relationship unknown, who was a tax collector in 1384, conveyed his manors of Walton, Tachbrook, and Botley to Sir Anketil Malory II of Kirkby and others in 1389, took out a general pardon in 1388, and was last recorded in 1394/5.[60] His successor, also called William, who was over forty in 1406, held Botley in 1416, acquired Saddington in Leicestershire with the help of John Malory of Newbold Revel in 1416–19, was M.P. for Leicestershire in 1419, held property in Walton in 1428, and as of Saddington was a tax-collector in Leicestershire in 1437.[61] His successor John, grandson of the first William, held property in Harbury in Warwickshire in 1428, as of Walton acquired Botley from his mother in 1434, with Anketil his son and heir sold it in 1443 (with Sir Thomas of Newbold Revel as a witness), held property in Tachbrook in 1465, and died in 1469, when his heir was John Malory junior, aged twenty-six, son of 'Anthony' his son.[62] John junior was dealing in land at South Croxton, Leicestershire, and elsewhere with his mother, stepfather, and father-in-law in 1483 and 1484, and died in 1489, when his heir was his son John, aged twenty-two.[63] This John, the last Malory of Tachbrook and Walton, sold Tachbrook in 1496, was in the retinue of Thomas Marquis of Dorset for the French war in 1511, and was killed at Tournai or Therouanne in 1512, leaving his estate, including the manors of Walton and South Croxton, to his coheirs, his five daughters.[64]

Mowthorpe

The short Mowthorpe branch begins in 1229 with another Anketil Malory. The only clues to his origins are his first name and the fact that he was a ward of Stephen de Segrave; both would suggest an origin in Tachbrook

59 *C.P.R.* (1358–61) p. 358; Farnham, *Pedigrees*, p. 136; Warwickshire C.R.O., MS. CR 1908/78; Farnham, loc. cit.

60 Farnham, *Notes*, iv 396; *C.F.R.* (1383–91) p. 72; Nichols, iii 497–8; P.R.O. 'Index to Pardon Rolls 1377–99', p. 183; H.M.C. Reports, vol. 55 (1914) (= 15th rpt, Appx, Various Collections VII) p. 379.

61 K.S.S. Train, *Abstracts of Inquisitions Post Mortem relating to Nottinghamshire 1350–1436*, Thoroton Soc. Record Series 12 (1952) 145–6; Shakespeare's Birthplace Trust MS. DR37/Box 50/2933; Leics. C.R.O. DE 2242/6/61–7, Nichols, iii 477–8 (where 'Mowbray' should be 'Malory'); *Return of Members; Feudal Aids*, iii 121; *C.F.R.* (1430–37) p. 538.

62 Dugdale, *Warwickshire*, p. 365 ('1346', which has the same man dealing in land for 137 years, must be wrong: read '1480' (20 Edw. IIII for 20 Edw. III); *Feudal Aids*, v 194; Shakespeare's Birthplace Trust MS DR37/Box 50/2937–42, Dugdale, p. 820; *V.C.H., Warwicks.*, v 162; P.R.O. C140/31/17.

63 Leicester C.R.O., Stapleford MSS. 180–4; *Cal. I.P.M., Henry VII*, ii 194–5.

64 *Feet of Fines (Warwicks.)*, iii no. 2754; Farnham, *Notes*, iv 397; Nichols, iii 498.

Mallory.[65] If he came from there, however, he moved his domicile decisively to Yorkshire. In 1229 the king granted to Anketil Malory the marriage of an heiress, Sarah de Mowthorpe, who brought him land in Mowthorpe, Wigganthorpe, Terrington, and North Dalton, in Yorkshire,[66] and he also held property at Sutton-on-Derwent in 1230, Oakton (as the king's 'valettus') in 1231, and Pocklington in 1232, all in the same county.[67] As might be expected of a Segrave adherent, he opposed Hubert de Burgh, the powerful Earl of Kent, who held him responsible for his imprisonment in 1232; he obtained Hubert's manor of Upper Arley in Staffordshire (now in Worcestershire) in 1233, but Hubert won it back in 1235.[68] He was also granted South Fawley, Berkshire, in 1239–40, and held land in Huntington, Clifford, Bramham, and Thouless, in Yorkshire, in 1242/3.[69] He was a knight when he witnessed a Segrave charter in 1241, and king's marshal to Henry III in 1245.[70] In 1247 he witnessed a charter with Sir Robert Malory of Welton.[71] Anketil served the king in arms at home and abroad, witnessed his charters and treaties, tallaged his counties, ran the temporalities of a vacant diocese, and went to Scotland to look after King Henry's daughter when she became queen of that country.[72] The king in return gave him not only a wife but oaks for building, bream from his fishponds, deer from his forests, and wine from his cellars, cancelled his debts to the Jews, and exempted him from assizes and jury service for life.[73] He seems to have been indispensable: the last known record, in 1253, is an order to send someone else to Scotland so that Anketil could return to King Henry's service; but the silence that follows suggests that Anketil had received a summons that overrides even that of kings.

He was succeeded by his son Anketil, who also became a knight, who was a juror in York in 1267.[74] The younger Anketil died childless and was

65 *Early Yorkshire Charters*, i 506. If the Tachbrook Malorys in this generation observed the custom of calling a son after his father's father, he might be a son of Henry son of Anschetil Malory the constable of Leicester Castle.

66 C.C.R. (1227–31) p. 257; *V.C.H., Yorks. N.R.*, ii 202–5, and cf. *Early Yorkshire Charters*, x 102.

67 C.C.R. (1227–31) p. 370–1; *Book of Fees*, 3 vols (London 1920–31) iii 1354; *Feet of Fines, Yorks.*, Y.A.T.A.R.S. 62 (1921) 137–8; C.C.R. (1231–34) p. 42.

68 Matthew Paris, *Chronica majora*, ed. H.R. Luard, R.S., 7 vols (London 1872–83) vi 73, and cf. iii 233; *Cal. Ch. Rolls*, i 182; Henry Bracton, *Notebook*, ed. F.W. Maitland, 3 vols (Cambridge 1887) iii 156–7, 246–7.

69 C.C.R. (1237–42) pp. 158, 192; *Book of Fees*, iii 1098–9.

70 *Descriptive Catalogue of the Charters at Berkeley Castle*, ed. Isaac Jeayes (Bristol 1892) no. 266; *Cal. Lib. Rolls* ii 314.

71 Farnham, v 417.

72 C.P.R. (1225–32) p. 359, and cf. Rymer, *Foedera* (1816–19) i 212; C.D.I., i 399, 436; C.C.R. (1247–51) p. 216; C.P.R. (1232–47) p. 460; C.P.R. (1247 58) pp. 152, 237.

73 C.C.R. (1231–4) p. 405; (1242–7) p. 162, 198 (1247–51) p. 92; (1227–31) pp. 434, 485; C.P.R. (1232–47) p. 42.

74 *Yorkshire Inquisitions*, Y.A.T.A.R.S. 12 (1892) 104.

succeeded by his brother Nicholas, who died in 1275, a minor, also child-less, and apparently overseas, leaving his estate to be divided between his heirs, his four sisters.[75]

Welton

The Malorys of Welton in Northamptonshire look like a second branch separating itself out from Kirkby Mallory. As we have seen, Richard son of Robert Malory of Kirkby apparently held land in Welton in the twelfth century, and in 1361 the Malorys of Welton held Welton of Kirkby Malory.[76] The simplest explanation of the known facts is that Sir Simon Malory, the first known Malory of Welton, was a younger son of Richard son of Robert Malory, but no contemporary evidence of relationship is known.

Sir Simon held land in Welton and in Holwell in Bedfordshire between 1174 and 1198.[77] As a knight, he was on the grand assize in Northampton-shire, Bedfordshire, and Leicestershire 1200–8, and he was a juror in a Leicestershire case in 1209.[78] He was succeeded by his son Bertram, who was involved in a Northamptonshire land case in 1208 and is named as the husband of Egelina Malory in 1227.[79] Egelina survived Bertram and, with the consent of Robert her son, freed a serf at Welton at an unknown date; that Robert is no doubt the Robert Malory who was seeking the advowson of Holwell in 1231, who held Holwell in 1241 and half a fee in Welton of the Honour of Leicester about 1242, who witnessed a charter with Sir Anketil Malory of Mowthorpe in 1247, and who was one of the knights of the Hundred of Fawsley in 1255.[80] This Sir Robert Malory was succeeded by another of the same name.[81] It was probably the second man who, like his cousin at Tachbrook, followed Simon de Montfort: he was captured with

---

[75] C.F.R. (1272–1307) 53, 62; Coucher Book of Kirkstall Abbey, Thoresby Soc. Pubs 8 (1904) 138; Year Books of Edward II, XIII, Selden Soc. Pubs 34 (1917) 85–91.

[76] Cf. Baker, Northants., p. 458.

[77] Pipe Roll for 1174–5, p. 54; 1182–3, p. 122; 1198–9, pp. 126–7; Curia Regis Rolls, i (Richard I – 2 John) 17, ii (3–5 John) 80, 82; Placitorum in domo capitulari Westmonasteriensi abbreviatio (London 1811) p. 81; T. Madox, The History and Antiquities of the Exchequer, 2 vols (London 1769) ii 43–4.

[78] Curia Regis Rolls, i (Richard I – 2 John) 341, 402, 506, ii (3–5 John) 28, 72, 157, 214, iii (5–7 John) 189, v (8–10 John) 41, 139, 159, 176, 232; Farnham, iii 74–5.

[79] Pleas before the King and His Justices 1198–1212, IV, Selden Soc. Pubs 84 (1967) 56; V.C.H., Bucks., iv 352n.

[80] Ancient Deeds, iv 456; Curia Regis Rolls, xiv (14–17 Hen. III) 406; V.C.H., Beds., ii 286; Baker, p. 458; Farnham, v 417; Book of Fees, ii 1279, 1289.

[81] The length of time during which the head of the Welton Malorys is a Sir Robert would suggest this strongly on its own: taken with the evidence that Bertram was the 'fifth ancestor' of the Sir John who was head of the branch in 1330, it amounts to proof.

Simon de Montfort the Younger at Northampton and imprisoned in 1264.[82] His lands were confiscated but he eventually got the Northamptonshire ones back; he was still alive in 1282.[83]

The second Sir Robert at an unknown date bought land in Welton for John his second son, the deed witnessed by a Sir William Malory who may have been the elder son.[84] The elder son, whatever his name, must have been dead by 1275, when an incumbent was presented to Holwell in the right of John son and heir of Robert Malory.[85] John appears to have spent some time in Ireland about 1282, but other evidence shows he was in England both earlier and later in this decade.[86] In 1291 he was accused of having been party to an illicit burial in Welton chapel, but when the case came to court in 1294, he was dead.[87] He was succeeded by a second John Malory, who paid a lay subsidy in Holwell in 1309, was lord of Welton and Holwell in 1316, as an esquire was summoned for military service in 1322 and to the great council at Westminster in 1324, and was a knight in 1324.[88]

The second John Malory was succeeded by a third, who was lord of Welton in 1329, when he was not a knight, but who had been knighted by the following year.[89] This Sir John proved that he held Holwell 'by hereditary descent from Bertram Malory his fifth ancestor'.[90] He was M.P. for Hertfordshire in 1337 and 1341, having established a connection with that county by marriage; he was still alive in 1348, but was dead by February 1350, when he was succeeded by a fourth John Malory.[91] The fourth John Malory of Welton was accused with his parents of riotous assembly, assault, vandalism, and theft in 1336; he made a Welton land-grant as son and heir of John Malory knight in 1349, and was himself often recorded as a knight in Welton 1350–79.[92] He held Holwell in 1357–8; in the latter year he was dragged out of Welton church during Mass by armed men and

---

82 *The Miracles of Simon de Montfort*, ed. J.O. Halliwell, Camden Soc. Pubs, First Series, xv (1840) 124–25n.

83 *Rotuli selecti ad res Anglicas et Hibernicas spectantes*, ed. Joseph Hunter (London 1834) pp. 171, 255; *Ancient Deeds*, iv 34.

84 *Ancient Deeds*, iii 224.

85 *Rolls of Richard Gravesend, Bishop of Lincoln 1258–79*, Canterbury and York Soc. Pubs 31 (1925) 203.

86 *C.P.R.* (1281–92) p. 43; *Ancient Deeds*, v 151, iv 268, 274.

87 *Cartulary of the Medieval Archives of Christ Church*, ed. N. Denholm-Young, Oxford Historical Soc. 92 (1931) 116–18.

88 *Two Bedfordshire Subsidy Lists*, Suffolk Green Books 18 (1925) 7; *Parliamentary Writs*, II(3) 1136; *Ancient Deeds*, v 104.

89 P.R.O. E40/15856, 15854.

90 *Placita de Quo Warranto temporibus Edw. I II III in Curia Receptae Scacarii Westm. asservata* (London 1818) pp. 61–2.

91 *Return of Members*; V.C.H., Herts., iii 178, 245; *Ancient Deeds*, iv 265, 259, 395.

92 *C.P.R.* (1334–8) p. 360; *Ancient Deeds*, iv 259, 443 and passim; *Cartulary of Christ Church*, p. 122.

beaten up.[93] In 1361, he held Welton of Sir Anketil Malory II of Kirkby, and in 1373, granted his goods in Welton to his sons John and Thomas.[94] The records end in 1379, and in 1383 his widow was dealing in land at Welton, along with his son and heir John.[95]

The fifth and last John Malory of Welton was first recorded, with his brother Thomas, as recipients of his father's grant in 1373; the two of them also received a legacy in 1381.[96] Something has been said of Thomas in Chapter IV. John is called 'lord of Welton' in 1408 and 1415, and held property in Holwell in 1412.[97] In April 1429 he and Elizabeth his wife granted the reversion of Welton to his daughter Ellen, but in March 1430 Elizabeth was dealing in land at Welton as his widow.[98] The settlement of Welton was a comprehensive one apparently designed to exclude Thomas and his heirs from Welton for as long as Ellen or her heirs survived, in which it was successful. Ellen's first husband John Swinnerton had died in 1408, leaving her with a son named after him (or his father) who died in 1430; Ellen remarried Sir John Bernard of Isleham, Cambridgeshire, died in 1440, and was buried at Isleham; her epitaph said that her father had been a knight, but more authoritative posthumous evidence, including the documents by which Elizabeth conveyed her rights in the manor to Ellen and her husband, call him esquire.[99] Ellen bore Sir John a daughter Margaret, who married Thomas Peyton of Melford, Suffolk, whose grandson, namesake, and heir exchanged Welton for property in Kent in 1485.[100]

[93] *V.C.H., Beds.*, ii 286; *Cal. I.P.M.*, 10 (1921) 348.

[94] Nichols, iv 762 col. 1, P.R.O. E40/15855.

[95] *Ancient Deeds*, v 72, cf. iv 184.

[96] Alfred Gibbons, *Early Lincoln Wills* (Lincoln 1888) p. 49.

[97] *Ancient Deeds*, iv 283, 296; *Feudal Aids*, vi 395.

[98] *Ancient Deeds*, iv 192 (and cf. 299), 446, 467.

[99] *Ancient Deeds*, iv 59, 299, *An Account of the Family of Swynnerton*, William Salt Soc. Pubs 7(ii) passim; Robert E. Waters, *Genealogical Memoirs of the Extinct Family of Chester of Chicheley*, 2 vols (London 1878) i 202–3. Ellen's epitaph appeared on a monumental brass (that appropriately named medium), reproduced in Mallory Smith p. 79; its error is repeated by Baker, p. 458, from 'Spencer evidences'. Contrast *Ancient Deeds*, iv 446, 467, and P.R.O. E42/287.

[100] Waters, loc. cit.; *C.C.R.* (1476–85) 404–6, *Ancient Deeds*, iii 104, iv 302. A curious intrusion into the Peytons' other Malory-of-Welton manor, Holwell, about 1490 by a William Malory might possibly be another attempted come-back by the descendants of Thomas Malory of Welton: see P.R.O. C1/106/7.

Draughton and Newbold Revel

Given that the author of the *Morte Darthur* was a Malory of Newbold Revel in Warwickshire, it is a pity that there is some uncertainty about the exact beginnings of the Newbold Revel branch of the family. It must be traced from Segwyn, a younger son of Sir Simon Malory of Welton, who was involved in an Northamptonshire land case in 1208, and represented his widowed mother in two lawsuits over Holwell in 1227.[101] Segwyn's son and heir Simon Malory of Holwell sold land in Welton at an unknown date and a Simon Malory, with his wife Isobel, bought land in Catthorpe, Leicestershire, in 1232.[102] The Simon who bought in Catthorpe may not have been the one who sold in Holwell: there were two other Simon Malorys about at the time, a first cousin, and a first cousin once removed.[103] Simon of Holwell's is perhaps a neater claim than the others, but whichever Simon bought into Catthorpe will have been a Malory of Welton and will also be the founder of the branch of the family that became the Malorys of Newbold Revel.

That purchase was the beginning of a sustained Malory interest in the little hamlets in the extreme south of Leicestershire, where Sir Thomas of Newbold Revel's great-granddaughters still held land in the early sixteenth century. Simon Malory of Catthorpe was succeeded there by a Richard Malory who witnessed a deed about land at Shawell, Leicestershire, about 1235, who as a knight and lord of Stormsworth (modern Starmore, north-east of Swinford) witnessed four Stormsworth charters in 1254/63 or 1269/80, who also held half a knight's fee in Hoton and Avereton (Cole Orton) of the Honour of Winchester in 1264, and witnessed a Kilworth charter about the time of Edward I.[104] He and his son Simon also witnessed an undated grant by Stephen de Blukevile of livestock in Winwick to the monks of Pipewell.[105]

Simon held half a knight's fee in Houton and Swinford of the Honour of Winchester in 1264, and in 1267/8 was mainpernor for a supporter of

---

101 *Pleas before the King and His Justices*, p. 56; *Bedfordshire Historical Record Soc.* 3 (1916) 10, 44, 77.

102 *Ancient Deeds*, v 473, cf. iv 190; Farnham, *Notes*, vi 279.

103 The first cousin, Simon Malory of Daventry, witnessed a Daventry Priory charter c.1228, and was called brother of Robert Malory of Welton in a Welton land case in 1240: *Daventry Priory Charters*, ed. M.J. Franklin, Northamptonshire Record Soc. Pubs 35 (1986–7) p. 124; *Bedfordshire Historical Record Soc.* 9 (1925) 80. The first cousin once removed was Simon son of Robert brother of Sir Simon Malory of Welton, to whom Sir Simon granted land in Holwell during the reign of King John: *V.C.H., Beds.*, ii 286.

104 Farnham, *Pedigrees*, p. 86; *Coucher Book of Selby*, pp. 263, 265–6, 270; *The Manuscripts of R.R. Hastings* i, H.M.C. Reports 78 (1925) 323–32; B.L. Add. Ch. 21280.

105 P.R.O. E315/53/170.

Simon de Montfort.[106] He held Houghton-and-Hathern in Leicestershire in 1271, and held land in Houghton and was lord of Draughton in Northamptonshire in 1277.[107] He also witnessed a Stormsworth charter and fifteen Draughton charters, all undated.[108] His interests in Draughton and in Winwick, Northamptonshire, came by marriage to Beatrice de Blukevill alias Bokervile, who was his widow in 1285/6 and 1295/6.[109]

Simon was succeeded by his son Roger, born by 1250, who held land in Swinford and Catthorpe in 1279, acquired land in Houghton-on-the-Hill from Nicholas his brother in 1283, held Swinford-with-Houghton, Catthorpe, and West Haddon in Northamptonshire in 1284/5, was lord of Draughton in 1293 and of Swinford-with-Houghton in 1296, was heir to Sir Peter his brother in 1311, and is named in eleven Draughton charters, mostly undated.[110]

Sir Peter, although not head of his branch of the family, should be mentioned here because later members of the branch thought him important enough to reproduce his coat of arms. He took to the law and made a success of it, which made him the best-recorded mediaeval Malory. He is first known as attorney to Elias de Rabayn and Matilda his wife, coheiress of the barony of Bayeux.[111] Peter Malory held half a fee in Winwick of them, and after Elias died, he married Matilda, a marriage that made him technically a baron.[112] He spent a good deal of time attempting to defend his wife's rights in her barony, with very little success, perhaps because his principal opponent was the king. He was a knight by July 1291, and was appointed Justice of the Common Pleas in 1292 and Justice of the King's Bench in June 1305: two months after his appointment he presided over the trial of William Wallace.[113] His guiding principle in that may well have been less the law than the conspicuous loyalty to the king of England proclaimed by his coat of arms: *or 3 lions passant guardant sable*, the king's

---

106 *The Manuscripts of R.R. Hastings*, loc. cit.; *Rotuli selecti*, p. 176.

107 *Cal. I.P.M.* 1 (1904) 257; Nichols, iii 372, iv 364.

108 *Coucher Book of Selby*, p. 265; B.L. Add. Ch. 21708–10, 21712, 21752, 22112, 22115, 22118, 22121, 22124–5, 22127, 22129, 22131, 22134; he was a party to Add. Ch. 21705.

109 Bridges and Whalley, ii 28–9, i 603–4, cf. *Cal. I.P.M.*, 5 (1908) 131.

110 B.L. Add. Ch. 22127, *Cal. I.P.M.*, loc. cit.; Nichols, iv 360–9, ii 612; *Feudal Aids*, iii 97, 99, iv 442; B.L. Add. Ch. 21728; Nichols, iv 361–9; B.L. Add. Ch. party 21706, 21713, 21715, 21722, 21734 (dated 1310), witness 21718–9, 21729 (dated 1298), 22116, 22127, 22407.

111 *C.P.R.* (1272–81) p. 147; *Select Cases in the Court of the King's Bench under Edward I*, ed. G.O. Sayles, vol. II, Selden Soc. Pubs 57 (1938) pp. cxxvi–cxxvii, vol. III, ibid. 76 (1957) p. xc; J.W.F. Hill, 'The Manor of Hungate', *Associated Architectural Societies Reports & Papers* 38 (1926–7) 175–9; I.J. Sanders, *English Baronies* (Oxford 1960) pp. 88–9.

112 *Cal I.P.M.* 2 (1906) 426; *C.C.R.* (1822–96) p. 150; Sanders, introduction.

113 P.R.O. E326/6311; Edward Foss, *The Judges of England*, 4 vols (London 1848–51), iii 278–9; *C.P.R.* (1301–7) p. 400; *Calendar of Documents relating to Scotland*, ii 454; *D.N.B.*; G.W.S. Barrow, *Robert Bruce* (London 1965) pp. 193–4.

own coat of arms with the tinctures varied.[114] Though reappointed on the accession of Edward II, he was apparently removed from office in 1309, but summoned to parliament as assistant to the council in 1310.[115] He died in 1311 holding three-quarters of a fee in Winwick, and Roger, his eldest brother, was his heir.[116] Roger's inheritance included of course Sir Peter's coat of arms, since armorial bearings are real property.[117]

Roger was succeeded by his son Simon, who is recorded from 1312, held two quarter-fees in Draughton in 1313–14, and was a supervisor of the commission of the peace in Northamptonshire in 1314/16.[118] He paid Matilda's jointure out of Winwick in 1317, headed the Swinford lay subsidy in 1327, and with Margaret his wife sold land in Teversham, Cambridgeshire, in 1328/9.[119] He was the guardian of Peter Malory of Litchborough in 1329/30, headed the Swinford lay subsidy again in 1332, and as lord of Winwick granted Draughton to Stephen his son and Stephen's wife Margaret Revell in 1332, presumably on Stephen's marriage.[120] He and Stephen witnessed a Draughton deed in 1334.[121]

Stephen was a knight by 1343, held Winwick and Swinford in 1346, was replaced on a Northamptonshire parliamentary commission in 1349, leased out land in Draughton in 1357, and was mustering Northamptonshire soldiers in 1359 and 1360.[122] He married Margaret Revell of Newbold Revel, who is said to have survived him and to have remarried to Robert Langham of Gopsal.[123]

He was succeeded by his son John, who sealed a charter as son and heir of Stephen Malory lord of Winwick in 1362; John was himself called lord of Winwick in 1365.[124] He was a knight in March 1366 when he and Sir Peter Malory of Litchborough witnessed a Welton deed; later that year Sir Peter witnessed his sale of Draughton.[125] Sir Peter granted all his lands in Litchborough to Sir John and Sir John's wife Agnes and son Nicholas in

114 *Parliamentary Writs*, i 417.

115 Foss, loc. cit.

116 *Cal I.P.M.* 5 (1908) 131. Bridges (i 526–8) says Sir Peter had a daughter who married Sir Robert Holdenby of Holdenby: if so she must have died *v.p.* and *s.p.*

117 Antony R. Wagner, *Historic Heraldry* (London 1939) p. 20.

118 B.L. Add. Ch. 21735; *Cal I.P.M.* 5 (1908) 235, 345; *Rolls of the Northamptonshire Sessions of the Peace*, ed. M. Gollancz, Northamptonshire Record Soc. 11 (1940) 2.

119 B.L. Cotton Ch. xxix 2; Sir Christopher Hatton, *Book of Seals*, ed. L.C. Loyd (Oxford 1950) p. 187; Farnham, *Notes*, iv 208; *Pedes finium, or Fines relating to the County of Cambridge*, ed. Walter Rye (Cambridge 1891) p. 95 (and cf. *C.C.R.* (1327–30) p. 381).

120 Bridges, i 75–6; Farnham, *Notes*, iv 209 (I discount the Master of the Hospital [of St John of Jerusalem] whose name precedes Simon's in this case); B.L. Add. Ch. 21753.

121 B.L. Add. Ch. 21754.

122 B.L. Add. Ch. 21763; *Feudal Aids*, iv 445, Nichols, iv 361; Add. Ch. 21771; *Foedera* (1816–69) iii 457, *C.P.R.* (1358–61) p. 349.

123 Nichols, iv 364.

124 B.L. Add. Ch. 22549; *Cal. Inq. Misc.*, iii 580.

125 B.L. Add. Ch. 21552, 21860, 21777, 21779.

1367 in return for an annuity of £10 a year for life.[126] In 1376, Sir John was in the Fleet Prison in London for debt.[127] He was called lord of Stormsworth in 1377, and in the same year put Winwick into the hands of feoffees; he was a tax-collector for Northamptonshire in 1379.[128] In 1383, his mother's family having failed in the male line, the Revell estates were divided between heiresses' representatives, and Sir John got the manors of Newbold Revell and Swinford.[129] He was granted a licence for private oratories in 1384.[130] He seems to have moved his domicile to Warwickshire, since he witnessed a deed in 1386 as of Fenny Newbold (i.e. Newbold Revel).[131] He seems to have caught the government's eye about this time, being associated in military recruitment with the king's friend Robert de Vere Earl of Oxford in 1386, and being appointed a justice of the peace for Warwickshire and a commissioner to enquire into the lands of the alien priory of Monks Kirby in 1389–90, and sheriff of Warwickshire and Leicestershire in 1391–2 and Northamptonshire in 1392–3.[132] In 1393, he made a new disposal of a part of his inheritance, settling Newbold Revel and some associated lands on himself and Alice his wife in tail.[133]

Sir John was succeeded in his estates by John Malory, father of Sir Thomas Malory of Newbold Revel. John is discussed in Chapter III above, Sir Thomas is the principal subject of this book, and Robert Malory, Sir Thomas's son and heir, is discussed in Chapter VIII. Robert succeeded to very little on his father's death, since his mother apparently held all Sir Thomas's lands in jointure for life.[134] When she died in 1479, her heir was Robert's son Nicholas, aged 13, whose upbringing and marriage are discussed in Chapter VII.

Nicholas was sheriff of Warwickshire and Leicestershire in 1502–3, and a justice of the peace and justice of gaol delivery in 1502 and 1507, and justice of the peace again from 1509 until his death.[135] (It is one of the ironies of history that his second commission of gaol delivery was headed by the then Duke of Buckingham, whose grandfather his grandfather had allegedly tried to murder.) He seems to have been in demand as a feoffee,

---

126 Baker, pp. 406–7.

127 C.P.R. (1374–77) p. 281.

128 Nichols, iv 368; Bridges, i 603–4, C.F.R. (1377–83) p. 142.

129 Nichols, iv 361.

130 Register of Robert de Stretton, Bishop of Coventry and Lichfield, ed. Rowland Wilson, William Salt Soc. Pubs, n.s. 8 (1905) 87.

131 P.R.O. E326/10777.

132 J.S. Roskell, 'Two Medieval Westmoreland Speakers', Cumberland and Westmoreland Archaeol. Soc. Trans. n.s. 62 (1962) 113–144, at p. 118; C.P.R. (1385–89) pp. 136, 139, 208, 343; List of Sheriffs.

133 Feet of Fines (Warwicks.), iii no. 2330.

134 P.R.O. C140/75/46, translated in Hicks, pp. 108–9.

135 List of Sheriffs; C.P.R. (1494–1509) pp. 295, 560, 663; Letters and Papers, Foreign and Domestic, Henry VIII, i 1546.

serving in that capacity for his father-in-law Thomas Kingston, and for his neighbours Sir Thomas Pulteney and John Seyton of Maidwell: he was also Kingston's executor.[136] He died in January 1513, leaving as his heirs two daughters, the last Malorys of Newbold Revel. They were Dorothy, born 1491/2, who married first Edward Cave and second George Ashby and who inherited Winwick and Swinford; and Margery, born 1503, who married first Clement Cave and second Sir John Cope and who inherited Newbold Revel.[137] Sir John and Margery Cope sold Newbold Revel in 1537.[138]

Litchborough

The Malorys of Litchborough in Northamptonshire, are a junior branch of the Malorys of Draughton and Newbold Revel. The first of them seems to be a William Malory who witnessed two Litchborough deeds in 1280, who may be the William Malory who in 1325 held one of the quarter fees in Draughton earlier held by Simon Malory of Draughton.[139] In 1316, however, Richard Malory was lord of Litchborough; as an esquire he was summoned for military service in 1322, he was a juror in Northampton in 1323, and died in 1329/30 holding land in Winwick of Simon Malory and in Litchborough of Geoffrey de Cornwall.[140] His widow Margaret was raped about 1332.[141]

Because the Winwick tenure was the older, Simon Malory of Winwick became the guardian of Richard's under-age son Peter, who was to go abroad with the Earl of Salisbury in 1338, and later was on the Crecy campaign in 1346–7 under the Black Prince, by which time he was a knight.[142] He was escheator, sheriff, and M.P. for Northamptonshire in 1350–1 and escheator again 1351–2.[143] When his mother's brother died in 1352, he inherited a share of his estate in Weedon and Weston, Northamptonshire.[144] He was in the Fleet Prison for debt in 1353, but he was

---

136 C.P.R. (1494–1509) p. 132; Cal. I.P.M., Hen. VII, iii 128–30, 168; B.L. Add. Ch. 22304; P.R.O. Prob 11/15, fol. 19.
137 P.R.O. C142/27/115–16, 142/28/41, 142/30/85; Dugdale, Warwickshire, pp. 81–3; and cf. W. Berry, County Genealogies (London 1883) p. 302.
138 Dugdale, loc. cit.
139 Ancient Deeds, i 246; Cal. I.P.M., 6 (1910) 391.
140 Feudal Aids, iv 30; C.H. Hartshorn, Historical Memorials of Northampton (Northampton 1848) p. 145; Bridges, i 75–6.
141 C.P.R. (1330–34) p. 239.
142 Bridges, loc. cit.; Treaty Rolls, ii 145; C.P.R. (1345–8) p. 494; Crecy and Calais from the Public Records, pp. 31, 93, 175, 239.
143 List of Sheriffs; List of Escheators, P.R.O. Lists and Indexes no. 72; Return of Members.
144 Cal. I.P.M., 10 (1921) 5.

appointed a justice of oyer and terminer in Northamptonshire in 1355, and went to Ireland in the king's service in 1357; as an Irish landowner, he had to answer to the king's council over measures to pacify Ireland in 1361.[145] He held the advowson of Maidford, Northamptonshire, in 1361.[146] With his son Giles he assaulted the Lord Chief Justice in 1363, for which they were sent to prison and fined £300, but he was pardoned at the request of King David II of Scotland.[147] In 1366–7, he and Sir John Malory of Winwick witnessed a Welton deed, he witnessed Sir John's sale of Draughton, and later he granted his Litchborough lands to Sir John and his family for a £10 life annuity.[148] He was still alive in 1379.[149]

He was succeeded by Giles, who was due to go abroad with the Earl of Kent in 1374, and married Joan widow of Sir Richard Baskerville by 1375.[150] He was knighted between July 1379 and March 1380, and was M.P. for Northamptonshire six times 1382–1402.[151] He was granted land by Ralph Lord Basset of Drayton in 1386, was an officer of the Earl of Derby (the future King Henry IV) in 1386/7, was due to go abroad with the Earl of Huntingdon as Captain of Brest in 1394/5, and was chief steward to the Earl of Warwick, and then as a commissioner and as escheator for Bedfordshire, expropriated his midland lands in 1397.[152] He was 'of Litchborough' in 1399; in the same year he was a commissioner of array, in 1401 a commissioner of oyer and terminer, and in 1402 was granted the Hundred of Fawsley in Northamptonshire for life in 1402.[153] He was sheriff of Northamptonshire for 1402–3, but died 15 August/24 September 1403, when his widow Marina rendered his shrieval accounts.[154]

At this point, the Litchborough Malorys without warning disappear into the deepest obscurity of any of the eight mediaeval branches of the family. They are next heard of two generations later, in 1467/73, when John Middleton and Amice alias Anne his wife, widow of John Malory esquire of Litchborough, sued in Chancery for the restitution of a variety of documents that they alleged Malory's feoffees had improperly given to one Robert Malory, which impede them in their possession of the manor, and also for a piece of silverware that John Malory pawned, whose holder was

[145] *C.P.R.* (1350–4) p. 526; *C.P.R.* (1354–8) pp. 237, 626; *Foedera* (1816–69) iii 610.
[146] Bridges, i 249.
[147] *C.C.R.* (1360–4) p. 562, *C.P.R.* (1361–4) p. 435.
[148] B.L. Add. Ch. 21552, 21777, 21779; Baker, pp. 406–7.
[149] *C.C.R.* (1377–81) pp. 108, 248.
[150] *Foedera*, iii 1013; *C.P.R.* (1374–77) p. 281, and cf. *Cal. I.P.M.*, 15 (1970) 7.
[151] *C.P.R.* (1377–81) pp. 416, 470; *Return of Members*.
[152] *C.P.R.* (1385–9) p. 225; G. Wrottesley, *Extracts from the Plea Rolls*, William Salt Soc. Pubs 15 (1894) 56; *Catalogue des rolles gascons*, ii 70; *C.P.R.* (1396–99) pp. 308, 420, 466; *C.C.R.* (1396–99) pp. 160, 162, 164; *Cal. Inq. Misc.*, vi 155–9, 162–4, 169.
[153] *C.P.R.* (1396–99) p. 396; *C.P.R.* (1399–1401) pp. 212, 551 (1401–05) p. 110.
[154] *List of Sheriffs*; *Ancient Deeds*, ii 427.

allegedly demanding excessive payment.[155] There is presumably a missing generation between Giles and John of which nothing at all is known.

A Robert Malory, probably the man named in Chancery, succeeded to Litchborough, which he held in 1471/2; he was called a gentleman in a small Northamptonshire land deal in 1477 and when he died in May 1487, leaving as his heir his son John Malory of Greensnorton, Northamptonshire, gentleman, who, like most of his family, was attainted for fighting against the king at the battle of Stoke-by-Newark on 16 January 1487.[156] John's lands were immediately granted to someone else, and although he was pardoned with restitution of goods by letter patent in 1488, it was not until after his death in 1522 that Litchborough was restored to his son and heir Thomas.[157] Thomas restored the standing of the family in the locality sufficiently to buy some of the Litchborough lands of the suppressed monastic houses, and to earn by the time he died in 1552, the rank of esquire.[158]

Hutton Conyers and Studley

The third branch to derive from Kirkby Mallory is that of Hutton Conyers and Studley in Yorkshire. The first known Malory of that branch is Sir Christopher, who served (with a la Zouch) under the Earl of Lancaster for the post-Crecy war in 1347, and who granted land in Linton Conyers, Yorkshire, to Fountains Abbey in the same year.[159] He was a collector of a North Riding subsidy in 1354, an executor of Archbishop la Zouch of York in 1359, and is last recorded in 1374.[160] The la Zouch connection makes it most likely that he was a brother of Sir Anketil II of Kirkby Mallory; Walbran's statement that his *father* was a Sir Thomas Malory probably derives from a confused memory of one of the two earlier heads of the Kirkby Malorys of that name.[161]

Sir Christopher was succeeded by his son William, born in 1351, who dealt in land at Hutton Conyers in 1372, and was a knight when, as a witness in the Scrope-Grosvenor case, he reported that he had fought in the

---

155 P.R.O. C1/38/254, C1/72/100.
156 Baker, pp. 406–7; P.R.O. E210/2741; *Cal. I.P.M.*, *Hen. VII*, iii 507.
157 *Materials for a History of the Reign of Henry VII*, ed. William Campbell, R.S., 2 vols (London 1873–7) ii 187, 251; Baker, loc. cit.; Martin, p. 182.
158 Baker, loc. cit.
159 *Crecy and Calais*, p. 123; Leeds Archives Department, Vyner Papers, MS. olim 51/51.
160 *C.F.R.* (1347–56) p. 415; *Testamenta Eboracensia*, pp. 55–6; Vyner Papers, MS. VR 1662, olim 304/4.
161 J.R. Walbran, 'A Genealogical and Biographical Memoir of the Lords of Studley in Yorkshire' in *Memorials of the Abbey of St Mary of Fountains, II*, Surtees Soc. Pubs 67 (1878) 311 ff., at p. 315.

wars in France and Scotland: his will was made in 1411 and proved in 1412.[162] He was succeeded by his son William, who was dealing in land at Nunwick in 1405, was left money by Archdeacon Scrope in 1418, and was dead by 1422.[163]

The younger William's son, also called William, succeeded to the estates, perhaps when very young indeed. This William, his wife Denise, and their children have been discussed in Chapter I, but as the putative father of one of the claimants to authorship of the *Morte Darthur* this William deserves fuller treatment than he would otherwise. Isobel Vincent quitclaimed land in Hutton to him in 1438, and he witnessed (as an esquire) a Ripon deed in 1444, and is named in a Hutton manor court roll in the same year.[164] Also as an esquire, he served as a juror investigating a Norton chantry in 1446.[165] His wife Denise inherited the manor of Sand Hutton in Bossall and other property probably by that year, and the second half of the Tempest lands when her nephew died in 1451; she and William settled property on a Tempest in 1452, and sold Sand Hutton in 1463.[166] William witnessed Ripon church accounts 1453/7, and paid off a small sum owed to Fountains Abbey in 1456/7[167] In 1456, he and his son John made an agreement about the Tempest lands, and he dealt in land at Studley and Linton, and in 1457 he and Denise made an agreement with John and, he, as William Malory senior, dealt in land at Hutton.[168] He and Denise were granted a licence for an oratory in 1458, a licence that was renewed in 1467.[169] It was presumably under this licence that he founded the chantry of St John the Baptist in Hutton, to which he presented a priest in 1463.[170] In 1468, he and Denise presented a priest to Linton-in-Craven, and he was assessed for tithes in Studley and elsewhere.[171] His will, made in 1472 and proved in 1475, said

---

162 *De controversia in curia militari inter Ricardum le Scrope et Robertum Grosvenor* [ed. N.H. Nicolas (London 1832)] pp. 123–4; Vyner Papers, MS. VR 1660, olim T/50; 5822, olim T/60.

163 *C.F.R.* (1405–13) p. 21; *Testamenta Eboracensia*, p. 388; Vyner Papers, MS. VR 1672, olim 53/2.

164 *V.C.H., Yorks. N.R.*, i 403–4; *Yorkshire Deeds V*, Y.A.T.A.R.S. 69 (1926) 116; Vyner Papers, MS. VR 5278, olim 51/39.

165 *Registers of the Archdeaconry of Richmond*, ed. A.H. Thompson, Y.A.T.J. 30 (1931–33) 93.

166 *V.C.H., Yorks. N.R.*, ii 94, i 79, cf. F. Ragg, 'Appendix to "The Feoffees of the Cliffords" ', *Cumberland and Westmoreland Archaeological Society Transactions* n.s. 22 (1922) 340–1; Vyner Papers, MS. VR 5157, olim T/69.

167 *Memorials of the Church of SS. Peter and Wilfrid, Ripon, I*, Surtees Soc. Pubs 74 (1881) 164; *Memorials of the Abbey of St Mary of Fountains III*, Surtees Soc. Pubs 130 (1918) 34.

168 Vyner Papers, MSS. VR 4410, olim 304/22; 4412, olim 304/23; 4413, olim 51/37; 1676, olim 51/58.

169 Walbran, p. 316.

170 *Acts of Chapter of the Collegiate Church of SS. Peter and Wilfrid, Ripon*, Surtees Soc. Pubs 64 (1874) 110.

171 *Fasti Parochiales IV*, Y.A.T.A.R.S. 133 (1970) 94, cf. 87; Bodl. MS. Dodsworth 50, fol. 63ᵛ.

that Denise was lately dead.[172] After his death, the authorities made several attempts to have an inquisition post mortem held on him, apparently without success.[173]

William's son Sir John having died before him, he was succeeded by Sir John's son William, who was admitted to the Corpus Christi Guild at York in 1470.[174] As William Malory esquire of Studley, son and heir of Sir John Malory and heir of William Malory, he did homage for land in Hutton to Ripon Chapter in 1475,[175] probably on coming of age. He was knighted in 1482, and died in 1498, holding Hutton and Studley, when his heir was his son John aged 26.[176] We can leave the Malory family here, although this branch held their Yorkshire estates until the later seventeenth century and their descendants can be traced to the present day.[177]

[172] York, Borthwick Institute, MS. Prob. Reg. 4A, fol. 125ᵛ.

[173] C.C.R. ((1476–85) p. 5, C.F.R. (1471–85) pp. 100, 119, 126.

[174] Register of the Guild of Corpus Christi, York, Surtees Soc. Pubs 57 (1871) 75.

[175] Acts of Chapter, pp. 246–7.

[176] Shaw, Knights of England, ii 20; Cal. I.P.M., Hen. VII, ii 199.

[177] See Walbran, p. 318 ff.; and anon. 'The Mallory Family', The Virginia Magazine of History and Biography, 13–15 (1906–08) passim; and Mallory Smith, pp. 96–110, 141–6.

APPENDIX II

Edward IV's Knight-Companions, November 1462

The 1462 chronicle entry is of unusual interest to Malory's biographer. It is one of only a handful of documents naming a Sir Thomas Malory from the decade in which *Le Morte Darthur* was written, and the only known fifteenth-century document recording a Sir Thomas Malory as taking part in the knightly warfare that was to be transformed and immortalised in the *Morte*.

To identify King Edward's and Malory's supposed companions, one needs a 1462 census of the adult male gentry, plus sufficient evidence to distinguish different men of the same name. Something not impossibly far from such a census can be adumbrated from the calendared public records. For most of the names revealed there, however, the only further evidence of presence is the pattern as a whole, and, once carelessness or fraud is suspected, both hypothesis and verification become difficult. Even groups of fraudulent cases may provide confirmation-patterns of a sort, but the smaller the group the weaker the pattern, and the more the investigator is at the mercy of chance, circularity of argument, and *parti pris*.

Professor Matthews was energetic, intelligent and subtle, but not as careful or thorough as the job required. For instance, Norris did not support the readeption, Saville did not come from 'Bewbiggin' (there is no such place; cf. Brinklow for Drakelow with Gresley, and Warmington for Warrington with Butler), John Stanley was on the Lancastrian not the Yorkist side at Blore Heath, Henry VI did not go to Nottingham during the readeption, there was no Lord Conyers until 1509, Scott may not have been M.P. for Kent in 1461–62, Docket and William a Legh were not attainted by Parliament until November 1461, and Margaret Malory did not marry John Constable junior until after 1475. Error affects still more seriously his assessment of how many men on the list came from the north, and particularly from Yorkshire. Of the fifty-nine names in his original, he left two out of his Appendix, both southerners, and five more out of the analysis in the body of his book, four of them southerners.[1] The distortion this produced was reinforced by not looking beyond the north for evidence. That

---

1 (a) My nos. 2 and 32; (b) Matthews's one from Durham, three from Suffolk, and one of his two from Staffordshire. He also gives an Oxford man to Cambridge.

apparently explains why, without justification, he identifies the Colville of the list with a Yorkshire esquire rather than with the Cambridgeshire knight.

In other cases, however, he found evidence and ignored it. Colonel Wedgwood is his principal source, supplying for instance seventeen of his eighteen birth-and-death dates. Wedgwood makes it plain that Gresley was uncrowned king of Derbyshire, and that Fogge's family roots in Kent went back beyond living memory. Professor Matthews used both biographies, but turned both subjects and others too to one degree or another into Yorkshiremen. Ten of Wedgwood's subjects disappear without trace, and nine of them are southerners.[2] Matthews filled out the insubstantial Roger Danby of the list by conflating the only Danby in Wedgwood, Thomas (who had died in 1458) with the Hutton Malorys' feoffee Robert Danby. His Crackenthorpe apparently combines a dead man and two living ones, though in this case all three had the same name. Wedgwood shows William a Legh had died before the northern expedition: Professor Matthews resurrects him. He does the same, at a later date, with Strangways. In calculating ages (p. 129) he used Strangways's birthdate along with the 18 he prints in his Appendix.[3] He therefore knew Strangways's birth-and-death dates, but he did not print them with the other 18. That allowed him, despite an intervening writ of *diem clausit extremum* and a warning footnote in Wedgwood, to have the 1462 Strangways appear in a 1487 list with a Malory of Hutton. In fact, the later Strangways was grandson to the earlier one. All in all, it is not surprising that Professor Matthews concluded that the list had a northern bias, but the bias was not in the list.

As a consequence of all this, Professor Matthews was only able to give a plausible place, rank, and name for 25 out of 59 men.[4] What follows is an attempt to do better.

1. Sir John Ashton of Ashton, Lancs., d.1484.
    Kt 1460. J. Wedgwood, *History of Parliament: Biographies* (1936) *s.n.*; P.R.O. C67/46 m. 8.
2. Thomas Acton ('Acheton') of Longnor, Salop, Lancastrian, d.1480.
    Wedgwood, *s.n.*
3. Roger ('John') Appleton esq. of Horton-by-Farningham, Kent, Yorkist, d.1488/91.
    Preferable to the obscure John Appleton gent. of Suffolk who fl. 1461. Wedgwood, *s.n.*; *Ancient Deeds*, v 283.

---

[2] My nos. 1 (a northerner), 2, 3, 9, 16, 24, 32, 41, and 58.
[3] He does not notice that Wedgwood printed most of these in italics as a warning that they were only estimates.
[4] My nos. 5, 6, 7, 12, 13, 15, 19, 20, 23, 25, 26, 27, 30, 36, 37, 38, 42, 44, 45, 46, 47, 52, 53, 55, and 59.

4. Sir John Astley ('Aschley') K.G. of Patshull, Staffs., Yorkist, d.1486/7.
    Kt by July 1462, present at the siege. *C.P.R.* (1461–7) p. 190, (1485–94) pp.
    114, 169; Dugdale, *Warwickshire* (1656) pp. 74–8.
5. Maurice Berkeley esq. of Beverstone, Glos., Yorkist, d.1474.
    Kt 1471, but much more in politics than namesakes who were kts earlier.
    Wedgwood, *s.n.*; *C.P.R.* (1461–7) p. 117, *C.F.R.* (1461–71) p. 127.
6. Sir Edward Beetham ('Ewrard of Bedoun') of Beetham, Westmorland,
    Yorkist, d.1472.
    Fauconberg's son-in-law. Wedgwood, *s.n.*
7. Sir Henry Bold of Bold, Lancs., d.1466/8.
    Kt by 1461, Master Forester of Snowdon and Captain of Conway. *C.F.R.*
    (1461–71) p. 144, *C.C.R.* (1461–8) p. 376, *C.P.R.* (1467–77) pp. 54, 113.
8. Sir William Booth of Dunham Massey, Cheshire, d.1476.
    Kt by Feb. 1462. P.R.O. C67/45 m. 47; G. Ormerod, *History of Cheshire*
    (1882) i 524.
9. John Butler of Badminton, Glos., d.1477.
    Kt by 1465, but even as esq. preferable to the much more Lancastrian Sir
    John Butler of Warrington, Lancs. Wedgwood, *s.nn.*
10. Sir Robert ('Piers') Clifton of Clifton, Notts., d.1478.
    Preferable to his deeply Lancastrian half-brother Sir Gervase. Wedgwood,
    s.n.; Payling, *Political Society in Lancastrian England*, p. 233 and passim.
11. Sir John Colville of Newton, Cambs., d. 1469.
    Kt by 1456. *C.C.R.* (1454–61) p. 156, *C.P.R.* (1461–71) p. 304, *C.C.R.* (1461–8)
    p. 331, *V.C.H., Cambs.*, iv 202.
12. Sir John Constable of Halsham, Yorks., d. by 1472.
    Kt by 1461; his heir married Margaret Malory of Hutton after 1475. *C.P.R.*
    1461–7) p. 576; *Genealogist* n.s. 20 (1904) p. 177; J. Walbran, *A Genealogical
    Memoir of the Lords of Studley* (Ripon 1841) p. 316.
13. Sir Robert Constable of Flamborough, Yorks., d.1488.
    Wedgwood *s.n.*.
14. Sir Christopher Conyers of Sockburn, Yorks, d.1487.
    Kt by March 1463, perhaps on this expedition. *C.P.R.*, p. 537; *Yorkshire
    Deeds*, Yorks. Archaeol. Soc. Record Series 63 (1922) 59; *C.F.R.* (1485–1509)
    p. 49.
15. Sir John Conyers of Hornby, Yorks., Yorkist, d.1490.
    Kt by 1461, probably 'Robin of Redesdale' in 1469. C. Scofield, *Life of
    Edward IV* (1923) i 33, 38, 488–97, 517; *C.F.R.* (1485–1509) p. 118.
16. Sir Robert ('Roger') Conyers of Great Elingham, Norfolk, Yorkist, d.1466.
    Wedgwood *s.n.*; F. Blomefield, *An Essay towards a History of Norfolk* (1805–
    10) i 483, viii 345.
17. Sir John Crackenthorpe of Newbiggin, Westmorland, Lancastrian, d.1461.
    Absent. The only kt among 4 men of this name died at Towton in 1461.
    Wedgwood *s.n.*; 'Brief Notes', p. 161 *bis*.
18. Sir Ralph ('Piers') Crathorne of Crathorne, Yorks., d.1490.
    Kt by 1460, son-in-law of Montfort infra. Wedgwood, sub Montfort; *C.P.R.*
    (1461–7) p. 348; *Cal. I.P.M, Hen. VII*, i 275.

19. Christopher Curwen esq. of Cumberland, d. after 1481.
    Knighted 1482. *C.F.R.* (1452–61) p. 222; W. Shaw, *The Knights of England* (1906) ii 21.

20. Sir Thomas Curwen of Workington, Cumb., Lancastrian, d.1486/7.
    Wedgwood, *s.n.*

21. Sir Robert ('Roger') Danby of Thorpe Perrow, Yorks., Lord Chief Justice, Yorkist, d. after 1472.
    Feoffee of Malorys of Hutton 1452, knighted 1461. E. Foss, *The Judges of England* (1848–51) iv 426; Walbran, p. 314; *Yorks. Deeds*, x YASRS 120 (1955) p. 127; *C.F.R.* (1485–1509) p. 112; *V.C.H., Yorks. N.R.*, i 351; P.R.O. C67/46 m. 7.

22. Richard Docket of Kendal, Westmorland, d. after 1467.
    Kt by 1468. P.R.O. C67/46 m. 7; *Cumb. & Westmorland Antiq. & Arch. Soc. Tr.*, n.s. 8 (1908) 329; 28 (1928) 194–255.

23. Sir William Everingham of Birkin, Yorks., Lancastrian, perhaps d. by 1468.
    Kt by Jan 1462. P.R.O. C67/45 m. 35; cf. Wedgwood, *s.n.* Henry Everingham, and Nichols, *Leicestershire*, iv 368.

24. Sir Thomas Ferrers of Tamworth, Leics., Yorkist, d.1498.
    Knighted 1461, brother-in-law of Lord Hastings. *C.F.R.* (1461–71) pp. 10, 71; Wedgwood, *s.n.* Sir John Ferrers.

25. Sir Thomas Findern of Carlton, Cambs., Lancastrian, d.1464.
    Absent: commanding one of the castles the king was on his way to besiege. Wedgwood, *s.n.*

26. Sir John Fogge of Ashford, Kent, Yorkist, d.1490.
    Controller of the Household. Wedgwood, *s.n.*

27. Sir Geoffrey Gate of High Easter, Essex, Yorkist, d.1471/7.
    Knighted March 1462/February 1463, perhaps on this expedition. *C.P.R.* (1461–7) pp. 203, 230, (1467–7) p. 290; *C.F.R.* (1471–85) p. 122.

28. Thomas Gerard of Brayn, Cheshire, d. after 1477.
    Kt by 1468. *C.P.R.* (1467–77) pp. 103, 426, 575; *C.C.R.* (1476–85) p. 177.

29. Sir John Gresley of Drakelow, Derbys., Yorkist, d.1487.
    Wedgwood, *s.n.*

30. Sir Ralph Grey of Heaton, Northumb., d.1464.
    Present. Wedgwood *s.n.*; *Paston Letters*, ed. N. Davis (Oxford 1971–) i 523.

31. Sir John Griffith ('Griffon') of Alrewas, Staffs., d.1470.
    Kt by 1458. *C.P.R.* (1452–61) p. 422; *C.F.R.* p. 100, (1471–85) pp. 34, 213; *C.I.P.M.* iv 406; *Miscellanea genealogica et heraldica*, i 64; *V.C.H., Yorks. E.R.*, ii 108, 117.

32. Sir Robert Harcourt of Stanton Harcourt, Oxon., Yorkist, d.1470.
    Present: pensioned for it. Wedgwood, *s.n.*

33. William Harington esq. of West Leigh, Lancs., d.1488.
    Knighted 1473/7. Wedgwood, *s.n.*

34. Sir Leonard Hastings of Kirby, Leics., d.1455.
    Absent: dead. Wedgwood, *s.n.*

35. Sir William Hastings of Kirby, Leics., Yorkist, d.1483.
    King's chamberlain; already Lord Hastings and listed as such among the barons. 'Brief Notes', p. 157; *Complete Peerage, s.n.*

36. Sir John Heveningham of Heveningham, Suffolk, d.1499.
    Kt by 1454. *C.P.R.* (1452–61) pp. 677–78, (1494–1509) p. 659; *Cal. I.P.M, Hen. VII*, ii 290; *Paston Letters*, ii 350–1; W.A. Copinger, *The Manors of Suffolk* (Manchester 1905–11) vii 342.
37. Sir John Howard of Stoke-by-Neyland, Suffolk, Yorkist, d.1485.
    Present. Wedgwood, *s.n.*; *Paston Letters*, i 523.
38. Sir John Huddleston ('Hodyliston') of Millom, Cumb., Yorkist, d.1492.
    Wedgwood, *s.n.*
39. Thomas Kingston ('Nocston') of Childrey, Berks., d.1506.
    Summoned to be knighted at the coronation of Edward V. *C.F.R.* (1437–45) p. 53; *C.C.R.* (1454–61) p. 157; *V.C.H., Berks.*, iv 350; *C.F.R.* (1485–1509) p. 371; *Grants from the Crown during the Reign of Edward V*, Camden Soc. 60 (1854) 69–71; P.R.O. C67/45 m. 15.
40. Sir Thomas Lamplugh of Lamplugh, Cumb., d.1474/5.
    Kt by 1461. *C.F.R.* (1461–71) p. 44; *C.P.R.* (1467–77) p. 610; *C.C.R.* (1468–76) p. 365.
41. Sir Piers a Legh ('Ale') of Lyme, Cheshire, Yorkist, d.1478.
    Wedgwood, *s.n.* (grandson); *The Visitation of Cheshire*, ed. G. Armitage, Harl. Soc. (1909) p. 141.
42. Sir William a Legh ('Ale') of Isel, Cumb., d. March 1462.
    Absent: dead. Wedgwood, *s.n.*; and cf. *C.C.R.* (1461–8) p. 361.
43. Sir Thomas Malory of Newbold Revel, Warwicks., Yorkist, d.1471.
    Wedgwood, *s.n.* and see Chapters I–II supra.
44. Sir William Martindale ('Marcham Dale') of Newton-in-Alderdale, Cumb., d. after 1465.
    Wedgwood, *s.n.*
45. Sir Thomas Montfort of Hackforth, Yorks., Yorkist, d.1463/5.
    Wedgwood, *s.n.*
46. Sir Thomas Montgomery ('Mongorye') of Faulkborne, Essex, Yorkist, d.1495.
    King's Carver and royal favourite. Wedgwood, *s.n.*
47. Sir William Norris of Yattendon, Berks., d.1506.
    Wedgwood, *s.n.*
48. Piers Padolyse.
    Not identified. Christian name unreliable (cf. 10 and 18 supra). John Paddesle was alderman and goldsmith of London 1429–50 and Lord Mayor 1440–41. *Ancient Deeds*, ii 249; *Cal. of Letter-Books of the City of London*, ed. R. Sharpe (1899–1912) I 268, 285; K passim; *Historical Collections of a London Citizen*, ed. J. Gairdner, Camden Soc. (1876) p. 257.
49. Ralph Piggott of Clotherholme, Yorks., d. about 1466.
    Feoffee of Hutton Malorys 1452, '62. Walbran, p. 314; Matthews, p. 164; *Testamenta Eboracensia*, Surtees Soc. iii 156; *V.C.H., Yorks. N.R.*, i 222.
50. William Rayner of Norwich, d.1467.
    Sheriff of Norwich 1458. Blomefield, iii 165, iv 389; *C.F.R.* (1461–71) p. 107.
51. Sir William ('George') St George of Hadley St George, Cambs., d.1472.
    Kt by 1461. *C.P.R.* (1461–7) p. 132; *V.C.H., Cambs.*, v 8, 72, 107–8, 254.

52. Sir John Saville ('Savey') of Thornhill-by-Dewsbury, Yorks., Yorkist, d.1482.
    Wedgwood, *s.n.*
53. Sir John Scott of Smeeth, Kent, d.1485.
    Controller of the Household. Wedgwood, *s.n.*
54. Henry del See ('of Osey').
    The family, from Barneston-in-Holderness, Yorks., is well attested, but with a gap between Brian (fl.1417) and Sir Martin (fl.1466–84): *C.I.P.M.*, iv 438; *V.C.H., Yorks. E.R.*, ii 91, 105, 314–16; Shaw, ii 19; *C.P.R.* (1467–77) p. 199, (1477–85) p. 579; *Chronicles of the White Rose* (1843) p. 40; G. Poulson, *The History of Holderness* (Hull 1840–1) i 185–227, 374.
55. Sir John Stanley of Elford, Staffs., Lancastrian, d.1476.
    Wedgwood, *s.n.*; P.R.O. C47/46, m. 1.
56. Sir William Stanley of Ridley, Cheshire, d.1495.
    Kt by September 1462. *C.P.R.* (1461–7) p. 198; *D.N.B.*, *s.n.*
57. Sir James Strangways ('Stannyewyssche') of Harlsey, Yorks., Yorkist, d.1480.
    Wedgwood, *s.n.*.
58. John Swan of Sandwich, Kent, d. after 1482.
    Wedgwood, *s.n.*
59. Sir John Wingfield of Letheringham, Suffolk, Yorkist, d. by 1481.
    Wedgwood, *s.n.*; P.R.O. C/67/51 m. 12.

Analysis

(a) Ignoring corrupt spelling (e.g. 6, 44, 57) but not wrong names, and giving the benefit of the doubt to 14 and 27, a knight of the right name was alive at the right time in these cases: 1, 5, 6, 7, 8, 9, 11, 12, 13, 14, 15, 20, 23, 24, 25, 26, 27, 29, 30, 32, 36, 37, 38, 40, 41, 43, 44, 45, 46, 47, 52, 53, 55, 56, 57, 59.

	Total:	36	36

One man who was not a knight and one who may not have been seem more plausible than namesakes who were: 5, 9. One enemy captain certainly absent: 25.

	Less:		3
Correctly named knights present:		33	

(b) This leaves 26 names unexplained. Knights given wrong Christian name: 10, 16, 18, 21, 51. Ditto wrong surname: 4, 31.

	Add:	7	
Knights present:		40	40

(c) 19 names unexplained. Men who were not knights: 2, 19, 33, 49, 50, 58. Ditto with wrong Christian name: 3. Ditto with wrong surname: 39.

	Add:	8	

		Plus:	1	
Add from (a) supra: 5.				
Non-knights present:			9	49

(5 and 19 later knighted, 39 summoned for it.)

(d) 10 names unexplained. Men who may or may not have

been knights: 22, 28.		Total:	2	
Add from (a) supra: 9.		Plus:	1	
Possible knights present:			3	52

(All three later knighted.)

(e) 7 names unexplained. One peer listed under his

title: 35. Three dead men: 17, 34, 42.		Total:	4	
Add from (a) supra: 25.		Plus:	1	
Absentees:			5	57

(f) 2 names unexplained: 48, 54.		Total:	2	
Unexplained:			2	59

(g) Certainly present: 4, 30, 32, 37:   4
Certainly absent (see (e) supra):   5
Of the 54 possibly present, 22 were from the 6 northern
counties, 11 of them from Yorkshire: 40.1% and 20.0%
respectively.

(h) Yorkists: 3, 4, 5, 6, 13, 15, 16, 21, 24, 26, 27, 29, 32, 35, 37, 38,

41, 43, 45, 46, 52, 53, 57, 59.		Total:	24
(j) Lancastrians: 2, 20, 23, 55.		Total:	4

APPENDIX III

The Manor of Newbold Revel, 1180–1480

The fact that Sir Thomas Malory's widow held Newbold Revel of the heir of the Duke of Norfolk when she died has been the basis of some misunderstanding. It has even been possible for a historian to believe that the Malorys held the manor of the dukes of Norfolk for the whole of the fifteenth century, and largely on the strength of this to say that Sir Thomas's father John Malory of Newbold Revel was a member of the Norfolk affinity (Carpenter, 'Warwickshire', Appx 108). Such errors make the complicated descent of the manor worth tracing.

In Domesday Book, Geoffrey de Wirce's extensive lands in Warwickshire included by name Fenny Newbold, which descended to the Stutevilles, but Robert de Stuteville having picked the wrong side at the Battle of Tinchbrai in 1106, the king granted his lands to another de Wirce descendant, Nigel Mowbray I (*V.C.H.*, *Warwicks.*, vi 174–5, *Complete Peerage*, ix 367, 373–4). In 1200, however, William de Stuteville, great-grandson and heir of Robert, sued for these lands, and in the resulting settlement was granted 12 librates of land in Brinklow and the service of 9 knights. Fenny Newbold descended from William de Stuteville to the Wake family, and when Thomas second Lord Wake died *s.p.* in 1350, he held *inter alia* 2 knights' fees in Wappenbury and Fenny Newbold, which were held of him by Roger de Wappenbury, Lora widow of Richard de Beyville, and John Revell (*Cal. I.P.M.*, ix 208). Wake's sister Margaret having had children only by her second husband, Edmund of Woodstock, Earl of Kent, sixth son of Edward I, Fenny Newbold descended to her eldest surviving son by him, John Earl of Kent, who died *s.p.* in 1352 (*Cal. I.P.M.*, x 51). The manor was then assigned in dower to his widow, Elizabeth of Juliers, who held it when she died in 1411 (*C.I.P.M.*, iii 333). It was she therefore who held in during John Malory's childhood.

The reversion of the manor had meanwhile passed to the late earl's sister, Joan of Kent (d.1385), then to Thomas Earl of Kent (d.1397), her son by her first husband, then to his son and successor, Earl Thomas (o.s.p. 1400), then to his brother and successor Earl Edmund (o.s.p. 1408), and finally to Edmund's six sisters and heiresses or their descendants. In the division of Earl Edmund's estate, Fenny Newbold was allocated to his second sister, Joan, who married successively Edmund of Langley, Duke of York (d.1402), William Lord Willoughby (d.1409), Henry Lord Scope of Masham (d.1415), and Sir Henry Bromfleet, later Lord Vessy (d.1469). The Duchess Joan's *inquisitio post mortem* said that she died on 12 April 1434, holding *inter alia* of the king in chief a knight's fee worth £10 a year in Wappenbury and Fenny Newbold that Roger de Wappenbury and the heirs of Richard Boyville and John Beuvyllys had once held (P.R.O. C139/66/43). For the remainder of John Malory's life, with the possible exception of the last few weeks, he will have held Newbold Revel of the Duchess Joan. In the last few weeks of his life, he may have held it of her heirs.

The inquisition said that Joan having died *s.p.*, her heirs were her sister Margaret Duchess of Clarence, her nieces Alice Countess of Salisbury and Joyce Lady Tiptoft, her nephew Ralph Earl of Westmorland, and her great-nephews Richard Duke of York and Henry Grey of Tankarville. The heirs had already established their claims in law when they had petitioned parliament in 1430–31 to resist the claims of an imposter (*Rot. Parl.*, iv 375).

None of them is ever recorded as holding Fenny Newbold: it next appears among the lands of John (Mowbray) Duke of Norfolk (d.1461) from which dower is to be assigned to his widow Eleanor Bourchier (d.1474) (*C.I.P.M.*, iv 316). It seems likely that he picked it up from the Duchess Joan's heirs because it conveniently rounded out his lands in the area: his grandfather Duke Thomas (d.1399) had died holding land in Brinklow (*C.I.P.M.*, iii 256). With it he will have acquired Philippa Malory or her son Thomas as his undertenant. The mesne tenancy will then have descended to the next duke of Norfolk, John (d.1476), and from him to his daughter and heiress Anne Duchess of Norfolk, who was born in 1472, married Richard Duke of York in 1478, and died in 1481. Because Anne was a minor in the wardship of the king when Lady Malory died in 1479, the Malory tenure of Newbold Revel counted as tenure of the king in chief. Although the wardship of Lady Malory's under-age grandson and heir would presumably have fallen to the Prior of Coventry, of whom the Malorys had held Winwick for longer than they had held Newbold Revel of their succession of mesne lords, the king's rights overrode those of all other lords, and Nicholas Malory's wardship and marriage therefore fell to the king.

APPENDIX IV

Constables of the Tower of London, 1387–1513

Thomas Holland 7 Earl of Kent made Constable for life 9 May 1387, died 25 April 1397.[1]

Ralph Neville of Raby, later 1 Earl of Westmorland, made Constable during pleasure 21 September 1397.[2]

Edward Duke of Albemarle 'the king's brother', later 2 Duke of York, made Constable for life 30 October 1397.[3]

Thomas of Rempston, king's knight, made Constable for life on surrender of patent by Edward Duke of Albemarle 31 August 1399.[4]

Accession of Henry IV, 30 September 1399

Thomas of Rempston, king's knight, granted constableship for life 1 October 1399 as Thomas Earl of Kent had had it; Rempston drowned 31 October 1406.[5]

Edward 2 Duke of York made Constable for life 1 November 1406; killed at Agincourt 25 October 1415.[6]

William Bourchier king's knight made Constable for life 26 November 1415; dead by 1 July 1420.[7]

Roger Aston king's knight made Constable during pleasure 26 June 1420.[8]

John Holland 14 Earl of Huntingdon, later 3 Duke of Exeter, made Constable for life 20 August 1423.[9]

John Holland 3 Duke of Exeter and Henry his son made Constables for life in survivorship 28 February 1447; Exeter dies 5 August 1447.[10]

1 *Complete Peerage, s.v.*
2 C.P.R. (1396–99) p. 194.
3 Ibid., p. 250.
4 Ibid., p. 593.
5 C.P.R. (1399–1401) p. 264; J.H. Wylie, *The History of England under Henry IV* (London 1884–8) ii 480–1.
6 C.P.R. (1405–08) p. 281; *Complete Peerage, s.v.*
7 C.P.R. (1413–16) p. 375; C.F.R. (1413–22) p. 332.
8 C.P.R. (1416–22) p. 294.
9 C.P.R. (1422–29) p. 41.
10 C.P.R. (1446–52) p. 32; *Complete Peerage, s.v.*

James Fiennes Lord Saye and Sele made Constable during the minority of
Henry 4 Duke of Exeter 7 August 1447; Saye killed 4 July 1450.[11]
Henry Holland 4 Duke of Exeter licenced to enter his lands (and presumably
this office) without proof of age 23 July 1450; attainted by parliament 21
December 1461.[12]

Accession of Edward IV, 4 March 1461

John Tiptoft Earl of Worcester made Constable for life 2 December 1461.[13]
Worcester having surrendered his patent, he and John Sutton 1 Lord Dudley
made Joint Constables for life 18 February 1468.[14]

Readeption of Henry VI, c.9 October 1470

Constableship reverts to Exeter.
Worcester executed 18 October 1470.[15]

Restoration of Edward IV, 11 April 1471

Constableship reverts to Dudley (who dies 30 September 1487).[16]
Richard Fiennes Lord Dacre granted reversion of Constableship 29 November
1473; but dies 25 November 1483, before Dudley.[17]
John Howard 1 Lord Howard, later 6 Duke of Norfolk, granted next reversion
after Dacre 10 February 1479; killed at Bosworth 22 August 1485, before
Dudley.[18]
Dudley appoints Anthony Earl Rivers his deputy with right to appoint officers
for £200 per annum, 1 February 1480.[19]
Rivers transfers the office of Deputy Constable to Thomas Grey 4 Marquis of
Dorset c.8 March 1483.[20]

[11] Ibid., p. 84; Scofield, i 220, 227; *Complete Peerage, s.v.*
[12] *Complete Peerage, s.v.*
[13] *C.P.R.* (1461–67) p. 61.
[14] *C.P.R.* (1467–77) p. 45.
[15] *Complete Peerage, s.v.*
[16] P.R.O. E403/844 (payment as Constable 29 May 1471); *Complete Peerage, s.v.*
[17] *C.P.R.* (1467–77) p. 412; *Complete Peerage, s.v.*
[18] *C.P.R.* (1476–85) p. 137; *Complete Peerage, s.v.*
[19] *C.C.R.* (1476–85) p. 174.
[20] I regret that I have lost my reference for this.

Accession of Richard III, 26 June 1483

Robert Brackenbury esquire made Constable for life 17 July 1483, reappointed with fuller terms 9 March 1484, knighted 15 December 1484/26 January 1485, killed at Bosworth 22 August 1485.[21]

Accession of Henry VII, 22 August 1485

John de Vere 13 Earl of Oxford made Constable for life 22 September 1485, reappointed because first grant invalid 29 June 1487, died 10 March 1513.[22]

[21] *C.P.R.* (1476–85) pp. 364, 418, 505, 521.
[22] *C.P.R.* (1485–94) pp. 23, 177; *Complete Peerage, s.v.*

Index

ARTHURIAN STUDIES